The Postmodern Humanism
of Philip K. Dick

Jason P. Vest

THE SCARECROW PRESS, INC.
Lanham, Maryland • Toronto • Plymouth, UK
2009

SCARECROW PRESS, INC.

Published in the United States of America
by Scarecrow Press, Inc.
A wholly owned subsidary of
The Rowman & Littlefield Publishing Group, Inc.
4501 Forbes Boulevard, Suite 200, Lanham, Maryland 20706
www.scarecrowpress.com

Estover Road
Plymouth PL6 7PY
United Kingdom

British Library Cataloguing in Publication Information Available

Library of Congress Cataloging-in-Publication Data

Vest, Jason P., 1972–
   The postmodern humanism of Philip K. Dick / Jason P. Vest.
      p. cm.
   Includes bibliographical references and index.
   ISBN-13: 978-0-8108-6212-8 (pbk. : alk. paper)
   ISBN-10: 0-8108-6212-3 (pbk. : alk. paper)
   ISBN-13: 978-0-8108-6697-3 (ebook)
   ISBN-10: 0-8108-6697-3 (ebook)
   1. Dick, Philip K.–Criticism and interpretation. 2. Postmodernism (Literature)
3. Humanism in literature.   Title.
PS3554.I3Z917 2009
813.54–dc22   2008040677

∞ ™ The paper used in this publication meets the minimum requirements of
American National Standard for Information Sciences—Permanence of Paper
for Printed Library Materials, ANSI/NISO Z39.48-1992.
Manufactured in the United States of America.

To Patricia,
for listening and loving better than anyone else

Contents

Acknowledgments

This book would not exist without the unflagging support of my editor, Stephen Ryan. His suggestions, comments, and advice have improved this project's scholarship and its prose. Stephen's intelligence and professionalism are much appreciated.

Meghann French and Jessica McCleary have provided expert advice in matters of style, grammar, and mechanics. Their assistance has been invaluable.

This study compares Philip K. Dick's fiction to the writing of Franz Kafka, Jorge Luis Borges, and Italo Calvino. All four men were significant twentieth-century authors. This project could not succeed without extensively quoting their work.

All citations of Kafka's fiction come from *Franz Kafka: The Complete Stories* by Franz Kafka, edited by Nahum N. Glatzer, copyright 1946, 1947, 1948, 1949, 1954, 1958, 1971 by Schocken Books. Used by permission of Schocken Books, a division of Random House, Inc.

All citations of Borges's fiction are by Jorge Luis Borges, translated by James E. Irby, from *Labyrinths*, copyright 1962, 1964 by New Directions Publishing Corp. Reprinted by permission of New Directions Publishing Corp.

All citations of Calvino's fiction are from *Cosmicomics* by Italo Calvino, copyright 1965 by Giulio Einaudi editore s.p.a., Torino. English translation by William Weaver copyright 1968 and renewed 1996 by Houghton Mifflin Harcourt Publishing Company and Jonathan Cape Limited. Reprinted by permission of Houghton Mifflin Publishing Company.

Citing Dick's writing is crucial to this book's success. All quotations of his fiction are reprinted by permission of the Philip K. Dick Trust and its agents, Scovil Chichak Galen Literary Agency, Inc.

This book began as a doctoral dissertation for Washington University in St. Louis's Department of English and American Literature. The members of my dissertation committee offered valuable guidance and invaluable insight about this project's argument. I am grateful to Guinn Batten, Gerald Early, Marina MacKay, and Richard Ruland of Washington University's Department of English and American Literature, and to Howard Brick and Gerald Izenberg of Washington University's Department of History, for their expertise, fellowship, and good cheer. Guinn Batten and Gerald Early deserve special mention for their ongoing mentorship of my professional career.

My colleagues in the University of Guam's Division of English and Applied Linguistics have consistently encouraged my research. I appreciate their support and their collegiality. Dr. Christopher Schreiner's many professional and personal kindnesses have helped me complete this book during a busy academic year.

My family and friends, as always, have been more patient than I deserve. This project would not have succeeded without them.

Thank you all.

INTRODUCTION

~

The World Dick Made: Science Fiction, Humanism, and Postmodern Literature

The fiction of Philip K. Dick confounds simple understanding, naive interpretation, and easy analysis. Dick, one of the twentieth century's most gifted American science-fiction (SF) writers, published bizarre tales of androids, parallel realities, time travel, and planetary colonization from 1952 until his untimely death in March 1982. For much of Dick's literary career, he toiled in what was regarded as the obscure ghetto of one of American popular fiction's most undervalued genres, largely unknown to readers and scholars of mainstream fiction.

Lawrence Sutin expertly summarizes Dick's critical reputation by beginning his seminal 1989 biography, *Divine Invasions: A Life of Philip K. Dick*, with honest simplicity: "Philip K. Dick remains a hidden treasure of American literature because the majority of his works were produced for a genre—science fiction—that almost invariably wards off serious attention."[1] Sutin situates Dick's writing as authentic American literature despite science fiction's reputation as shallow popular entertainment that fails to achieve the artistic sophistication of canonical literature by authors such as Herman Melville, Henry James, William Faulkner, and Thomas Pynchon. One of Sutin's goals in writing *Divine Invasions* is to rehabilitate his subject's critical stature, leading Sutin to make an extraordinary claim: "Phil Dick used the junk props of the SF genre—the tentacled aliens, alternate worlds, and gee-whiz high-tech gimmickry—to fashion the most intensely visionary fiction written by an American in [the twentieth] century."[2]

Sutin's assertion, no matter how surprising it might have seemed in 1989, has become commonplace in popular and academic assessments of Dick's literary significance. Indeed, Dick no longer toils in obscurity, while the research devoted to his fiction, life, and influence has grown exponentially since the 1970s, allowing literary scholar Istvan Csicsery-Ronay Jr. to rightly declare that "readers can hardly come to his fiction without going through the thickets—indeed by now, the forests—of criticism, simulation, and cultural propaganda"[3] that surround Dick's oeuvre. Thanks to the efforts of journalists, academics, and Hollywood filmmakers, Dick has achieved the reputation that his admirers have long believed he deserves.

Dick's newfound critical respect, however, has not transformed him into a canonical American author so much as an indispensable one. Literary critics like Harold Bloom may not agree that Dick's fiction warrants high praise, but Dick has become a writer whose perplexing, upsetting, and ambiguous fiction places him near the forefront of postmodern American literature. This statement does not ignore America's other significant postmodern novelists, whether John Barth, Robert Coover, William Gaddis, Toni Morrison, Thomas Pynchon, or Kurt Vonnegut Jr. It merely indicates that Dick's contributions to postmodern literature are important enough to merit sustained attention.

Arguing about Dick's place in the pecking order of twentieth-century American novelists, however, is far less interesting than discussing his fiction. Scholars and educators, after all, no longer need to apologize for their interest in Dick's writing or for their belief that science fiction is a valuable genre of contemporary literature. Debates about the artistry, sophistication, and canonicity of SF texts have receded in recent years as science fiction has become a legitimate area of scholarly inquiry. The field has its own academic journals and literary specialists, while numerous SF courses are taught every year in high schools, community colleges, and universities. The number of academic articles and books devoted to science fiction has multiplied each year since 1950, while the 1970s was a watershed decade for SF scholarship. In addition to the numerous critical books and anthologies published during the 1970s, *Science Fiction Studies*, perhaps the field's most important journal, was founded in 1973. To take another measure, the massive number of SF novels, short stories, films, television programs, and popular-press articles published or produced since 1950 far exceeds scholarship about the genre. SF criticism, in other words, has become so common that literary researchers rarely argue about science fiction's validity or significance.

SF scholarship has become an exciting intellectual project that seeks to uncover the lives, work, and art of authors whose fiction has, in many instances, been unjustly ignored. Literary critics and mainstream journalists may have neglected Philip K. Dick for much of his authorial career, but Dick no longer qualifies as an unknown author. He has, in fact, become the object of intense scholarly interest and admiration (as the numerous books, anthologies, and articles devoted to his life and fiction attest). The nine film adaptations of Dick's work (including *Blade Runner*, *Total Recall*, and *Minority Report*) have also introduced millions of viewers to his disturbing, anxious, and pessimistic worldview, tempting many of them to begin reading his fiction. As a result, Dick no longer lives in literary anonymity. His critical and popular reputation now seems secure.

Academic research and mainstream journalism about Dick frequently refer to him as a postmodern author. Some observers, including Csicsery-Ronay and Sutin, discuss Dick as if he is the quintessential postmodern author. These critics imply that Dick's peculiar, fragmentary, and paranoid fiction perfectly expresses the tensions, ambivalences, and dislocations of twentieth-century American life. The postmodern label, therefore, is apt because it describes Dick's writing in much the same sense that M. Keith Booker defines postmodernism in his insightful book *Monsters, Mushroom Clouds, and the Cold War: American Science Fiction and the Roots of Postmodernism, 1946–1964*: "The global hegemony of modern capitalism, by wiping out all vestiges of older social systems and modes of productions, contributes to an overall loss in the ability of postmodern subjects to imagine alternatives to the current system, and thus the diminution of utopian thinking after World War II."[4] Dick's fiction laments how corporate capitalism, political repression, and social inequality not only reinforce one another, but also pervade twentieth-century American life. His short stories and novels typically create future worlds populated by average, working-class characters so oppressed by institutional bureaucracy, political corruption, technological proliferation, and economic stagnation that their lives have become dystopian nightmares. Utopian thinking has not simply diminished in Dick's fiction; it has fully collapsed, becoming the mythical remnant of a better world that his characters can no longer imagine.

Dick's great contribution to American literature, however, is that he dares to rehearse the values of individual autonomy, personal liberty, and political freedom that seem impossible in the fractured pessimism of the postmodern era. These values may be utopian principles, but they more precisely represent the essential humanism of Dick's fiction. This humanism is not a naive faith in the individual's ability to create his or her future no matter what obstacles may arise, but rather a profound compassion for the individual's difficult struggle to overcome these obstacles. Dick's fiction never overlooks the doubt, anxiety, and uncertainty that afflicted people living through the twentieth century, even when it intensifies these complexities to terrifying proportions. Dick, who understands how grim human life can be, never loses sight of his flawed characters' fundamental decency, transforming his fiction into a unique genre: postmodern humanism.

Dick's talent for maintaining humanist values within postmodern contexts brings together two movements that share a tense, even hostile relationship. Humanism's belief that people can not only control but also improve their own lives conflicts with postmodern skepticism about the possibility of progress in an age where the grand narratives and institutions that underlie human advancement no longer function.[5] The collapse of religion, coupled with scientific rationality's inability to liberate humanity from ignorance and poverty, challenges humanism's belief in the universal values of individuality, autonomy, liberty, and reason. Postmodernism, indeed, rejects the concept of universal values to abolish faith in the possibility of progress.

Humanism and postmodernism, moreover, are terms of significant scholarly debate, discussion, and disagreement. This book cannot unify the disparate ideas about these broad intellectual, historical, and cultural movements, nor should it try. Humanism, for the purposes of this argument, comprises the beliefs, theories, texts, principles, and laws that affirm the dignity of human beings regardless of their origin, status, and occupation. Humanist thought, therefore, stresses the autonomy, integrity, and liberty of the individual (who not only determines the course of his or her life, but also actively creates his or her future). Free choice is crucial to humanist philosophy, as is personal responsibility. Although humanism has various historical roots (whether Classical Greece, Renaissance Italy, or Enlightenment Europe), this movement cannot be limited to a single people, place, or time. During the nineteenth and twentieth centuries, humanism became a dominant way (particularly in Europe and America) of thinking about human experience that acknowledges every individual's unique talents (even if the nineteenth and twentieth centuries' litany of state-sanctioned wars, oppression, and neglect treats human beings as worthless). Humanism's individualist bent, it must be noted, also promotes community. Rectitude, responsibility, and respect are important humanist principles that permit civil societies to form around shared values. Underlying humanism's celebration of individual existence is reason. The best path to social, economic, political, and personal progress, humanism asserts, is rationality.

Postmodernism, by contrast, emphasizes the fragmentary, chaotic, and irrational aspects of human life. The ancestry of this twentieth-century social, political, and cultural phenomenon includes Renaissance thought, Enlightenment philosophy, Romantic writing, and modernist aesthetics. Postmodernism, at least in Europe and America, developed in response to modernist approaches to visual art, architecture, music, drama, and literature, as well as to the titanic social, economic, and political changes wrought by World War II. Postmodernism, indeed, became a recognizable movement during the postwar period, as M. Keith Booker, Damien Broderick, Linda Hutcheon, and Brian McHale have argued.[6] McHale, in fact, acknowledges the dilemma faced by all scholars of postmodernism when defining this nebulous subject:

> "Postmodernist?" Nothing about this term is unproblematic, nothing about it is entirely satisfactory. . . . The term does not even make sense. For if "modern" means "pertaining to the present," then "post-modern" can only mean "pertaining to the future," and in that case what could postmodernist fiction be except fiction that has not yet been written? Either the term is a solecism, or this "post" does not mean what the dictionary tells us it ought to mean, but only functions as a kind of intensifier.[7]

Postmodernism, therefore, is fraught with absurdity and uncertainty. This book's sense of postmodernism largely agrees with McHale's formulation, although a provisional definition is possible. Postmodernism, for the purposes of this argument, is the literary, social, and cultural movement that embraces alienation, ambiguity, ambivalence, fragmentation, heterogeneity, incoherence, instability, nonlinearity, and doubt as unavoidable aspects of postwar (meaning post–World War II) human life. The triumph of advanced technology and corporate capitalism makes the postmodern era one of uneasy transition. Human beings no longer know exactly how to conceptualize their historical roots, their present existence, or their future lives. Postmodernism, in fact, sometimes manifests a startling ahistoricism that, in literature, provides authors with opportunities to create nonchronological and nonhistorical fiction that juxtaposes disparate genres into a jumbled (even incoherent) pastiche of older literary forms.

This lack of historical memory, moreover, stresses the extreme doubt that characterizes postmodernism. The loss of secure political, economic, and cultural footholds—what amounts to a pervasive sense of becoming uncoupled from historical truths, narratives, and certainties—challenges humanism's belief in individual autonomy, agency, and identity. Postmodernism may not fully reject reason's capacity to improve human life, but it repeatedly questions reason's significance in an age where war, economic injustice, political oppression, and ecological devastation underscore the failures of rationality, progress, and hope.

No matter how dismal this formulation may seem, postmodernism also embraces an escape from literary, cultural, and aesthetic convention. Postmodern authors frequently delight in combining older literary forms without worrying about generic boundaries or origins. Postmodern literature plays with literary traditions by provocatively melding different modes, genres, and media. Post-modern authors, therefore, engage in literary bricolage that reflects the postwar period's cultural ambivalence. The fragmentation and alienation of human identity, to say nothing of institutional, political, economic, and cultural decline, appear so frequently in postmodern literature that secure judgments seem impossible. The carnivalesque attitude that these phenomena produce reconfigures literature as a field of play that creates its own conventions as much as it conforms to traditional boundaries. Postmodern literature, in other words, does not obey rigid rules or trite formulations; it exceeds, transgresses, and ignores the borders that earlier literary forms follow.

Dick's fiction is remarkable in its ability to yoke postmodern transgres-sion to humanist principles. This characteristic connects Dick's writing with three authors who accomplish a similar feat: Franz Kafka, Jorge Luis Borges, and Italo Calvino. All four men are fascinated by how the failures of social, political, economic, artistic, and technological progress not only transform but also disrupt humanity's ability to affect the always-changing world that industrialism, war, and scientific advancement have ushered into existence. The challenge to human agency posed by this more complicated world is one of Dick's, Kafka's, Borges's, and Calvino's primary concerns.

This book argues not only that Kafka's art heavily influenced Dick's liter-ary response to these historical developments, but also that Dick's postmod-ern humanism developed within a cultural matrix that includes Borges's and Calvino's fiction. Neither Borges nor Calvino affected Dick as directly as Kafka, but their writing shares with Dick's fiction prevalent anxieties about progress, industrialization, mass culture, and technology. Although literary scholars normally classify Kafka as a modernist author, this book demon-strates how Kafka's fictional fascination with alienation, fragmentation, and uncertainty makes him a significant precursor to postmodern literature. Issues of classification and nomenclature, however, are less intriguing than the literary relationships between Dick, Kafka, Borges, and Calvino. Study-ing the final three authors' fiction more clearly exposes Dick's contribution to postmodern literature, while studying Dick's writing provokes previously unsuspected readings of Kafka, Borges, and Calvino to enhance the reader's appreciation for their non-American perspectives. This mutually reinforcing process, in turn, deepens the complex literary interchange between all four authors.

Dick, although an American writer, participates in a tradition of inter-national postmodern literature that includes Kafka, Borges, and Calvino.

These men, along with their American cousin, come from divergent literary backgrounds and traditions, meaning that their fiction consistently questions the nature of foreignness. Unknown, mysterious, and alien presences populate the writing of Dick, Kafka, Borges, and Calvino to depict how human consciousness reacts to the foreign aspects of daily life. Distorted perception, political mendacity, economic oppression, and social instability force each writer's characters (as well as their readers) to reconsider the political, economic, and social narratives that support their understanding of the world. Progress, freedom, and individual choice in Dick's, Kafka's, Borges's, and Calvino's fiction frequently give way to stasis, repression, and bureaucratic domination. Human agency, therefore, is fragile.

The foreign elements that threaten autonomy, agency, and identity in Kafka's, Borges's, Calvino's, and Dick's writing, however, also characterize the worlds inhabited by their protagonists. Incorporating alien forms and ideas into his characters' quotidian lives allows each author to create bizarre and mystifying narrative contexts that draw out the mysteries, ambiguities, and horrors of mundane reality. The subsequent inability of Dick's, Kafka's, Borges's, and Calvino's protagonists to locate firm social, economic, and political foundations leaves their readers unanchored. The insecure narrative worlds that these authors create paradoxically unite all four men across the geographical, historical, and linguistic barriers that divide them.

These convergences make Dick an important practitioner of postmodern humanism. Dick employs the conventions of American science fiction to write novels and short stories that recognize the complex aspects of postmodern life without attempting to resolve the contradictions that inevitably arise. Kafka, Borges, and Calvino accomplish a similar goal. They emphasize the problem of authentic and autonomous subjectivity as much as Dick does. Each author's contribution to postmodern humanism, however, is unique. Dick does not universally represent American literature (or even American science fiction) any more than Kafka universally represents German literature; Borges, Argentinean literature; or Calvino, Italian literature. Each writer participates in the literary traditions of his home country, but they all also contribute to the international phenomenon of postmodern humanism.

Dick, Kafka, Borges, and Calvino, in other words, cannot be contained by the national literatures of their own countries, even if they emblematize certain tendencies of those literatures. Their fiction illustrates the fusion of national literary traditions that makes postmodern humanism such a provocative mode (and genre). Dick's American science fiction, therefore, illuminates the cross-cultural and transhistorical concerns that characterize Kafka's, Borges's, and Calvino's writing. Although these authors never met in person during the course of their lives, their literary similarities testify to the simultaneous national and global concerns that each man struggled to negotiate during his artistic career.

The themes most commonly associated with Dick—ontological doubt, epistemological uncertainty, the necessity of creative art, the dehumanizing aspects of technological proliferation, the ambiguity of human identity, and the inability to distinguish reality from fiction—are also significant themes for Kafka, Borges, and Calvino. Comparing these four authors will reveal how their fiction explores common motifs, issues, and anxieties.

Chapter 1 of this study, "The Metamorphosis of Science Fiction: Kafka, Dick, and Postmodern Humanism," considers how Kafka's fiction and Dick's writing generate startlingly comparable yet fundamentally different characterization. Two specific types of fiction—the animal allegory and the bureaucratic bestiary—allow each author to probe the contradictions, limitations, and uncertainties of twentieth-century human experience from the perspective of an alien (animal) consciousness or from the perspective of a human being whose identity comes to resemble animal consciousness. Two pairs of related Kafka and Dick stories form the heart of this analysis. The complications of Kafka's 1922 tale "Investigations of a Dog" and Dick's 1953 short story "Roog" demonstrate how both authors create humanist stories with postmodern contexts, while the impact of bodily transformation upon human identity drives the nightmarish postmodernism of Kafka's most famous story, *The Metamorphosis* (1915), and Dick's witty 1964 antiwar story, "Oh, to Be a Blobel!"

Chapter 2, "Parallel Minds, Alternate Worlds: Borges, Dick, and the Politics of Oppression," argues that Dick's fascination with alternate-world tales is emblematic of his political sensibilities of the 1950s. Borges's seminal 1940 story "Tlön, Uqbar, Orbis Tertius" provides the launching point for this analysis of Dick's political fiction not only because Borges's story influenced Dick's writing, but also because its premise of an independent fictional world that obscures (and supplants) the narrator's own existence speaks to Dick's thematic fascination with the relationship between reality and fantasy. Dick, as his 1950s fiction makes clear, feared the possibility that the United States, during the Cold War, would become a more repressive and totalitarian society. The nuclear hysteria and governmental scrutiny of private lives that began with McCarthyism but continued throughout the Vietnam War saw several of Dick's most basic fears realized. Much of Dick's writing during this time reflects not only his political dismay, but also his penetrating social analysis of an era in which governmental power skillfully manipulated America's civic consciousness. *Eye in the Sky* (1957) and *Time Out of Joint*

(1959) are the most useful texts in this regard, although Dick's 1953 short story "The Defenders" will help unravel his bleak portrait of humanity's militant tendencies. Dick destabilizes the reader's perception of history by proposing alternate worlds that question the security of historical judgments and humanist values.

Chapter 3, "Divine Textualities: Calvino, Dick, and Authoring Creation," examines how both authors tackle divine subjects and explore human spirituality in their fiction. Calvino's outrageous short-story collections *Cosmicomics* (1965) and *t zero* (1967) recount the adventures of Qwfwq, an entity present at the moment of the universe's creation, in a fascinating amalgam of science and spiritualism. Although Calvino's *If on a winter's night a traveler* (1979) does not directly address spiritual concerns, this novel's characters, plots, and themes probe the intellectual processes of reading and writing to suggest spiritual (meaning scriptural) interpretations. Calvino's textual reworking of spiritual themes, in fact, links him with Dick's divine fiction. Examining Dick's *The Three Stigmata of Palmer Eldritch* (1964), "Faith of Our Fathers" (1967), and the first two novels of Dick's self-described VALIS trilogy—*VALIS* and *The Divine Invasion* (both 1981), but not *The Transmigration of Timothy Archer* (1982)—will reveal how Dick integrated Gnostic themes and principles into an intriguing contemplation of humanity's place in a fallen universe of pain and suffering. The postmodern implications of Dick's vision, as well as his humanist horror at the Gnostic principle that the universe was created by a powerful yet wounded demiurge who is debilitated by amnesia, expose Dick's complicated notions of religious and spiritual life. These ideas, in fact, informed much of Dick's thinking during his final decade. Dick's knowledge of religious and spiritual history also reveals science fiction's ability to deal intelligently with religious themes.

Chapter 4, "Time, Love, and Narcosis: The Importance of *Now Wait for Last Year*," reassesses the significance of Dick's beautiful and tragic 1966 novel. This book includes every theme that absorbed Dick during his most productive period, 1962–1968: time travel, drug abuse, extraterrestrial invasion, parallel realities, advanced technology, barren future landscapes, and, most notably, a marriage in crisis. The list of Dick's best work rarely contains *Now Wait for Last Year* even though the other novels of its period—*The Man in the High Castle* (1962), *Martian Time-Slip* (1964), *The Three Stigmata of Palmer Eldritch* (1964), *Do Androids Dream of Electric Sheep?* (1968), and *Ubik* (1969)—are not only acclaimed as some of his best work, but also are considered to be some of the finest SF novels produced by a twentieth-century American author. *Now Wait for Last Year*'s focus on the slyly named Dr. Eric Sweetscent's travels to the future after ingesting a narcotic, JJ-180, is only one aspect of this complicated story. Sweetscent works as a doctor who ministers to the health of United Nations Secretary General Gino Molinari, Earth's supreme leader, as Molinari conducts a war between Earth and the extraterrestrial, insectlike reegs while simultaneously trying to placate the inhabitants of Lilistar, humanoid extraterrestrial allies who act more like conquerors than wartime colleagues. The novel's center, however, is its remarkable portrait of Eric Sweetscent's deteriorating marriage to his wife, Kathy, who suffers neurological damage as a result of her addiction to JJ-180. *Now Wait for Last Year* effortlessly melds SF conventions, tropes, and characters not only to acknowledge the painful realities of male-female sexual relationships, but also to explore the difficulties of defining human identity in an uncertain and hostile colonial world. *Now Wait for Last Year* combines Dick's postmodern, humanist, and spiritual impulses to create a novel that is important to his oeuvre and to science fiction's development as a legitimate, worthwhile, and sophisticated literary genre. It displays all of Dick's narrative talents, particularly his emotionally complex characters, to become persuasive evidence for his inclusion in the ranks of the best postmodern American novelists of the last half of the twentieth century.

This book, therefore, proposes a goal that it can reach only after significant effort: determining why and how Philip K. Dick is a worthwhile contributor to postmodern fiction. Dick's work stands on its own merit but owes debts to the fiction of Franz Kafka, Jorge Luis Borges, and Italo Calvino. These three writers' literary exploration of the ambiguous borders between postmodernism and humanism enriches the critical reader's appreciation of Dick's authorial voice. This investigation, therefore, shall begin with Franz Kafka, whose tales of nightmarish bureaucracy foretell Dick's depressing fiction in the same manner that Jorge Luis Borges believes "the poem 'Fear and Scruples' by Browning foretells Kafka's work."[8] For Borges, reading Kafka "perceptibly sharpens and deflects our reading of the poem,"[9] just as reading Dick will sharpen the reader's understanding of Kafka, Borges, and Calvino.

Notes

1. Lawrence Sutin, *Divine Invasions: A Life of Philip K. Dick* (New York: Citadel-Carol, 1989), 1.

2. Sutin, *Divine Invasions*, 1.

3. Istvan Csicsery-Ronay Jr., "Pilgrims in Pandemonium: Philip K. Dick and the Critics," in *On Philip K. Dick: 40 Articles from Science-Fiction Studies*, ed. R. D. Mullen et al. (Terre Haute, IN: SF-TH, 1992), vi.

4. M. Keith Booker, *Monsters, Mushroom Clouds, and the Cold War: American Science Fiction and the Roots of Postmodernism, 1946–1964*, Contributions to the Study of Science Fiction and Fantasy, no. 95 (Westport, CT: Greenwood, 2001), 20.

5. Jean-François Lyotard, in *The Postmodern Condition: A Report on Knowledge*, trans. Geoff Bennington and Brian Massumi, Theory and History of Literature, vol. 10 (1979; Minneapolis: University of Minnesota Press, 1984), and Matei Calinescu, in *Five Faces of Modernity: Modernism, Avant-Garde, Decadence, Kitsch, Postmodernism* (Durham, NC: Duke University Press, 1987), discuss how the collapse of the grand ordering systems of the past (what Lyotard terms the "metanarratives" that sustained Europe's and America's belief in rationality, progress, and freedom) makes postmodernism an uncertain, ambivalent, and anxious era. Postmodernism fragments these metanarratives to produce competing perspectives and opposing viewpoints. The historical, political, economic, and social cacophony that results is both chaotic and liberating by allowing artists to indulge pastiche and bricolage to produce disjointed, even incoherent works. Lyotard's and Calinescu's analyses of postmodernism are among the most significant scholarly works of the past thirty years.

6. In addition to Booker's *Monsters, Mushroom Clouds, and the Cold War*, see Damien Broderick's *Reading by Starlight: Postmodern Science Fiction* (London: Routledge, 1995), Linda Hutcheon's *The Politics of Postmodernism* (London: Routledge, 1989), and Brian McHale's *Postmodernist Fiction* (New York: Methuen, 1987) for their useful discussions, definitions, and delineations of postmodernism.

7. McHale, *Postmodernist Fiction*, 3–4.

8. Jorge Luis Borges, *Labyrinths: Selected Stories and Other Writings*, ed. Donald A. Yates and James E. Irby (New York: New Directions, 1964), 201.

9. Borges, *Labyrinths*, 201.

~

CHAPTER ONE

The Metamorphosis of Science Fiction: Kafka, Dick, and Postmodern Humanism

Kafka's and Dick's Fictional Affinities

If, as George Steiner asserts, "in more than one hundred languages, the epithet 'kafkaesque' attaches to the central images, to the constants of inhumanity and absurdity in our times,"[1] then Kafka's fiction and Dick's writing have eerie similarities. While the terms "Dickian" and "Phildickian" may not yet be recognizable in one hundred languages, they have appeared in literary scholarship and mainstream journalism so frequently since the mid-1970s that these words now constitute critical shorthand for describing a fragmentary fictional world of uncertain identities, heartless bureaucracy, unexplainable occurrences, barren landscapes, and mordant wit. Dick's writing shares many concerns, qualities, and anxieties with Kafka's, which is hardly surprising in light of Kafka's extraordinary influence on modernist, postmodernist, and humanist fiction. Steiner correctly notes that Kafka's importance transcends the literary world, pervading American and European culture so extensively that even people who have never read Kafka are aware of his work. "Kafkaesque" is now a term of political, cultural, and social import, attesting to the broader significance of Kafka's fiction.

Dick's writing may not hold such relevance, but his criticisms of bureaucratic absurdity, political manipulation, spiritual enervation, and human ugliness are as lacerating as Kafka's. Dick, in his letters and critical essays, rarely refers to Kafka by name, preferring to credit other authors (Gustave Flaubert, Guy de Maupassant, James Joyce, A. E. Van Vogt) as precursors of his own work. Dick, however, writes in a 1975 letter that "the middle initial in my name stands for Kindred, my mother's maiden name. Kafka would be more apt, perhaps."[2] Dick's acknowledgment of Kafka's influence is no accident, even if Dick fails to explore this literary lineage in detail. Ray Faraday Nelson, a close friend of Dick's who cowrote *The Ganymede Takeover* with him, claimed that "Dick could quote such authors as Heine, Rilke, and Kafka from memory" and that Dick had "been reading Kafka at the time he wrote *The Three Stigmata of Palmer Eldritch*."[3] Based on Nelson's comments, Dick biographer Gregg Rickman surmises that Dick's "first exposure to the master of nameless dread may postdate the late '40s."[4]

Dick's intimate knowledge of Kafka also reflects Dick's lifelong fascination with (and admiration for) German art. Nelson once remarked that Dick used the term "influence" exclusively for "authors who were (a) dead and (b) German,"[5] with Goethe and Schiller being important to Dick's appreciation of German Romanticism. Contemporary German literature also inspired Dick, who considered Erich Maria Remarque's novel *All Quiet on the Western Front* (1922), Ernst Junger's anti-Nazi novel *On the Marble Cliffs* (1939), and Hans Fallada's novel of life in the Weimar Republic, *Little Man, What Now?* (1933), to be valuable works of art.[6] Dick's fondness for Germany was not confined to literature, either. One of his most obsessive enthusiasms was classical music, particularly the work of Wagner and Beethoven. From an early age, Dick immersed himself in German art forms, and must certainly have been aware of Kafka's contribution to German culture before reading him.

Even so, several pertinent questions about prospective correspondences between Kafka's and Dick's fiction are important to any comparison of these authors. What significant similarities, if any, do they share? What importance do parallels between the two writers hold for our understanding of each man's fiction? What can we learn about modernist, postmodernist, and humanist literature by examining two men living in vastly different historical circumstances? Is such a comparison fair, especially considering the different literary reputations of the two authors? Kafka, after all, has long been considered one of the twentieth century's leading literary practitioners, while Dick is a relatively recent entrant into critical discussions about worthwhile American fiction. These questions, of course, implicitly endorse the canonical view of each writer. Kafka, in this assessment, is a literary artist, while Dick is a literary hack. Examining two notable aspects of each man's work, however, will illuminate their fundamental compatibility. The first feature is "animal allegory," a symbolic literary form that portrays human behavior from a radically different perspective by ascribing human characteristics to animal protagonists. The second feature is the "bureaucratic bestiary," a subgenre of fantastic storytelling that features political bureaucracies, social injustices, and economic realities so repressive that human characters, by losing track of their own identities, transform into animalized versions of themselves. The specific inflections that these tropes achieve in Kafka's and Dick's writing demonstrate how well fantastic fiction can capture the predominant political, social, economic, and artistic anxieties of twentieth-century European and American life. These animal allegories and bureaucratic bestiaries, in short, are mature evocations of how human beings endure, but rarely resolve, the twentieth century's predominant cultural tensions.

Dog Days

Animal protagonists allow Kafka and Dick to metaphorically explore human venality. Walter Benjamin best summarizes Kafka's animal allegories by noting the artfulness with which Kafka constructs them:

> It is possible to read Kafka's animal stories for quite a while without realizing that they are not about human beings at all. When one encounters the name of the creature—monkey, dog, mole—one looks up in fright and realizes that one is already far away from the continent of man. But it is always Kafka; he divests the human gesture of its traditional supports and then has a subject for reflection without end.[7]

This fright resonates with Darko Suvin's seminal conception of science fiction as a method of "cognitive estrangement" in which alternate fictional realms become capable of reflecting back upon our shared experiential world.[8] Kafka's animal allegories, particularly "Investigations of a Dog" (1922), operate in precisely this manner by positing an alternate society (dogdom) comprised of thinking, feeling, sentient members. The story's first-person narrator observes the world around him, and then, in complete (and often elegant) sentences, speculates upon the philosophical, political, and aesthetic implications of the narrated events. This literate self-awareness seduces even a reader mindful of the narrator's animal status into an unusual, complicated relationship with the story's speaking voice, whose intelligence and verbal dexterity resemble human thought far more than the simplified mentality normally ascribed to animals.

The contrast represented by Dick's 1953 short story "Roog," therefore, might appear extreme. "Investigations of a Dog," however, does not merely lead us toward Dick's fiction, but insistently points to the earliest stage of Dick's professional writing career. The first story Dick sold, in October or November 1951 (to editor Anthony Boucher of the *Magazine of Fantasy and Science Fiction*),[9] was "Roog," an animal allegory—Dick calls it "a tiny fantasy"[10]—about a family dog's fearful encounter with garbage collectors. Boris, Dick's canine protagonist, perceives these trash men as ominous alien entities who illicitly consume the contents of his family's metal "offering urns."[11] Boris's attempt to alert his owners, Alf and Mrs. Cardossi, to the Roogs' presence by whimpering, whining, and screaming the word "roog" only convinces the Cardossis that the dog's behavior is insufferably erratic. The story builds to a point of tremendous dread, as Boris angrily barks at the Roogs, who, while collecting trash on Friday morning, laugh at the dog's discomfort.

Many differences between "Roog" and "Investigations of a Dog" are apparent. Dick's story is extraordinarily short, in contrast to Kafka's extensively narrated tale. Dick employs a third-person narrator, while Kafka adopts a first-person point of view. The long, sometimes rambling confessional tone of Kafka's canine narrator is absent from Dick's portrait of Boris, who never experiences an internal monologue. The philosophical ruminations about science, music, and progress in Kafka's story, more significantly, appear nowhere in Dick's stripped-down tale.

Critical readers, therefore, can legitimately question any comparison between "Investigations of a Dog" and "Roog," particularly in light of Istvan Csicsery-Ronay Jr.'s thoughts about Kafka's influence on science fiction:

> Little has been written about the way Kafka's fiction contains an implicit critique of the ruling mythology of our culture—namely, scientism: the faith that all knowledge worth having can be given adequate causal formulation through quantification; and hence, that the greatest human faculty is positive rationality, the capacity to know progressively more things for certain through an understanding of these formalized causal laws. Many writers of scientific fantasy have not only recognized the critique of scientism latent in Kafka's fiction, but have derived models from it for writing critical science fiction appropriate for their social and national audiences.[12]

Kafka's critique of scientism in "Investigations of a Dog" is hardly latent, but Csicsery-Ronay's comments demonstrate how deeply implicated Kafka is in science fiction's project to explore alternate societies, histories, and perspectives. Dick shares enough of Kafka's scientific, modernist, postmodernist, and humanist doubts for the careful reader to recognize that Dick derived, knowingly or unknowingly, models of critical science fiction from Kafka, even if no one knows which of Kafka's tales most influenced Dick.

Both authors utilize the animal allegory and the bureaucratic bestiary to dislocate human subjectivity. Hybridizing a human perspective with an animal's consciousness, for Kafka and for Dick, illustrates the ambivalent nature of human language, ontology, and epistemology. Decentering subjectivity, moreover, allows each author to criticize the repressive aspects of industrial capitalism, to parody the structures of capitalist authority that exploit human subjects, and to highlight important modern and postmodern literary strategies that fracture human consciousness.

Human Voices, Animal Narrators

Kafka and Dick, as befits their individual temperaments, go about these projects in different ways. Kafka creates a paradoxical illusion in his animal allegories (animals speak as human beings would speak if humanity were the subject of the story), while Dick often prevents his animal characters from talking at all (forcing the reader to develop a sense of their internal lives from purely external details). This difference does not mean that Kafka uses animal characters as thin stand-ins for human characteristics. Indeed, Kafka alerts the reader of "Investigations of a Dog" to its narrator's nonhuman status often enough to prevent mistaking the story's animal society for humanity. A purely symbolic reading of dogdom as a metaphor for human culture is obviated by reminders that, no matter how much the reader may want to reduce this animal society to a human model, its animal subjects are distinct, unique, and inhuman. This development produces the bewilderment of Benjamin's realization that the reader "is already far away from the continent of man."[13] Benjamin's geographical metaphor also instructively extends Kafka's incongruity: humanity, physically separated from the story's animal society, inhabits a separate continent despite the intellectual proximity (conveyed through language, cognition, and emotion) that the animal narrator shares with a human perspective. Kafka confounds his reader's perception of the animal narrator, its society, and its biography by destabilizing the boundary between human and animal subjectivities. This confusion induces perplexity, fear, and cognitive dissonance (or estrangement) that undermine four dichotomies important to Western philosophy: human/animal, culture/nature, individual/community, and intelligence/mindlessness.

"Roog," through a much different narrative process, also unseats the division between human and animal consciousness to generate fear, confusion, and estrangement. Dick never provides direct access to Boris's thoughts, but compels the reader to induce the dog's motivations and anxieties from an external vantage point. This externality permits multiple readings of the story's central question: Are the garbage collectors that Boris dreads actually extraterrestrial creatures bent on stealing trash for an unknown (and suspicious) purpose, or are they merely ordinary human beings whom the dog misperceives? To answer this question, considering two possible interpretations of "Roog's" plot will disrupt the same dichotomies that "Investigations of a Dog" deconstructs.

The modernist implications of this erosion between previously stable binaries are well known. The loss of intellectual certainty about the world; the resulting ambiguity about how to define oneself (and to act) within this ambivalent field; and the sometimes severe emotional, epistemological, and ontological shock that attends these developments can be found in Ezra Pound's *Cantos*, T. S. Eliot's *The Waste Land*, Virginia Woolf's *Mrs. Dalloway*, and a host of other canonical modernist texts. Kafka's animal allegories embody these anxieties by proposing a world that, although animal, seems human. Rather than explicitly commenting upon the equivocal fate of humanity in the industrialized, heavily bureaucratized states that developed in late nineteenth-century Europe and America, Kafka indicates a subtle, yet profound, shift in human consciousness. Examining dogdom from the internal perspective of an animal narrator (one who employs human language to criticize his own society) creates a simultaneously intimate and alien reflection upon the consensual world shared by Kafka and his reader. This narrative estrangement upsets all comfortable knowledge about how the world operates.

Dick, on the other hand, places Boris within an initially mundane setting—a 1950s American small town—not only to contrast canine and human perspectives, but also to expose this quotidian world as a disturbingly alien place. The conflict between these perspectives creates the story's dramatic tension, allowing Dick to portray three divergent mind-sets: Boris, his human owners (the Cardossis), and the potentially alien Roogs. This multifocal narration, in which objectivity comprises competing subjectivities, alters the humanist belief in the integrity of individual consciousness to disrupt the secure unitary personality that stories like "Investigations of a Dog" exhibit. Dick's fractured narration also achieves a more kinetic sense of plot, theme, and character than Kafka displays. "Investigations of a Dog" unveils an extraordinary intellectual landscape for the reader to digest, while "Roog" requires intellectual effort merely to understand what happens to its protagonist. These different narrative enterprises not only illustrate a key difference between Kafka's modern sensibilities and Dick's postmodern impulses, but also reveal the ability of animal allegory to combine modernist and postmodernist viewpoints into a humanist perspective that, by failing to consolidate consciousness into a single subjectivity, mourns the loss of the secure identity that it finally disrupts.

Kafka's and Dick's different narrative projects, moreover, employ black humor to blend modernism's uncertainty about the past with postmodernism's disinterest in history. This amalgamation produces humanist anxiety about the validity, integrity, and reliability of historical narratives that cannot be ignored or resolved. For Kafka, the canine narrator's confessional analysis of his own biography produces an earnest examination of dogdom's history that lampoons faith in the nineteenth century's most significant structuring concepts: reason, progress, science, art, and the individual's ability to meaningfully understand what has gone before him or her. For Dick, whose story is not as outwardly funny as Kafka's, Boris's frantic attempts to warn the Cardossis about the Roogs' dangerous presence engage limited historical memory. The dog, after all, fails to realize that the garbage collectors who appear every Friday morning are not extraterrestrial entities, but rather civil servants discharging their occupational duty. Boris's inability to comprehend this simple truth makes his emotional distress perversely humorous, although the possibility that the dog's senses are more finely tuned than those of his human owners gives "Roog" an ambivalent edge. Dick's tale may not seem as formally impressive as Kafka's, but it reveals greater depth than its pulp-fiction roots imply. Reading "Investigations of a Dog" prepares us for the melancholy situation "Roog" poses, implicating both stories in the idiosyncratically humanist sensibility that characterizes each author.

Dog's-Eye View

"Investigations of a Dog" is a confessional exploration of its canine narrator's uncertainties about his society's cultural, political, and artistic roots. The paradoxical dualities of modern life—and of modernism's response to twentieth-century humanity's fundamentally ambiguous experience—are prevalent from the story's opening lines:

> How much my life has changed, and yet how unchanged it has remained at bottom! When I think back and recall the time when I was still a member of the canine community, sharing in all its preoccupations, a dog among dogs, I find on closer examination that from the very beginning I sensed some discrepancy, some little maladjustment, causing a slight feeling of discomfort which not even the most decorous public functions could eliminate; more, that sometimes, no, not sometimes, but very often, the mere look of some fellow dog of my own circle that I was fond of, the mere look of him, as if I had just caught it for the first time, would fill me with helpless embarrassment and fear, even with despair.[14]

A better introduction to the nameless dread Rickman senses in Kafka's fiction is difficult to locate. The narrator cannot define the changeless change that characterizes his life, but realizes that a genial relationship with his society is now impossible. His social position has diminished (he is no longer "a dog among dogs") because the narrator's priorities have shifted from the canine community's normal preoccupations to his individual concerns, permitting the narrator a privileged vantage point from which to confess his new worries. Public functions cannot calm the narrator's apprehension about existing apart from mass society, but rather exacerbate his fear of difference to paranoiac levels. Even a once-trusted compatriot's facial expression now causes suspicion, discomfort, and unhappiness; this dog, as the passage implies, silently reproaches the narrator. An initially limited sense of unease, moreover, takes only a few lines to grow into embarrassment, fear, and despair. Kafka, in a passage of remarkable expressive power, indicates a complex welter of emotions that upends the narrator's social equilibrium.

Despite the complicated human feelings expressed by Kafka's prose, the reader cannot forget (even if Benjamin does) that the story recounts an animal's experience. The narrator's canine status, in a pattern that recurs throughout "Investigations of a Dog," remains ever present. The quoted passage contains three explicit references to dogs, the last of which ("a dog among dogs") stresses the narrator's simultaneous membership in the canine community and his alienation from his own social class. Kafka does not equate dogdom with humanity here, since the narrator refers to his social equal as "some fellow *dog* of my circle" rather than just "some *fellow* of my own circle." The border between the human and canine realms, therefore, is less permeable than it might seem. The reader remains far from the continent of man, as the narrator notes in four significant examples: (1) "For it must not be assumed that, for all my peculiarities, which lie open to the day, I am so very different from the rest of my species";[15] (2) "no creatures to my knowledge live in such wide dispersion as we dogs";[16] (3) "I have preserved my childlike qualities, and in spite of that have grown to be an old dog";[17] and (4) "the ordinary dogs themselves set science right here without knowing it."[18] These passages demonstrate the narrator's consistent identification of his species as unique, praiseworthy, and nonhuman.

Still, Kafka's reader cannot ignore the essential truth of Benjamin's observation that, in spite of these reminders about the narrator's canine existence, he speaks like an educated, bourgeois, European human being. The simple discontinuity of a dog using language (whether the German of Kafka's original prose or the English of the Muir translation) rises to the level of absurdity in an exquisitely comic passage that both celebrates and satirizes the narrator's intellectual prowess:

I have all the respect for knowledge that it deserves, but to increase knowledge I lack the equipment, the diligence, the leisure, and—not least, and particularly during the past few years—the desire as well. I swallow down my food, but the slightest preliminary methodical politico-economical observation of it does not seem to me worth while [sic]. In this connection the essence of all knowledge is enough for me, the simple rule with which the mother weans her young ones from her teats and sends them out into the world: "Water the ground as much as you can." And in this sentence is not almost everything contained? What has scientific inquiry, ever since our first fathers inaugurated it, of decisive importance to add to this? Mere details, mere details, and how uncertain they are: but this rule will remain as long as we are dogs.[19]

The narrator, perhaps unwittingly, ridicules the notion of scientific progress even as he promotes its virtues. Knowledge becomes an elusive goal, its pursuit is no better than urinating on the earth. This realization, furthermore, is not a complex intellectual process, but rather simple obedience to a maternal injunction that prevents infant suckling. Scientific progress, in one of the passage's most withering commentaries, is unavoidably tied to the bodily processes of consumption and excretion,[20] with the narrator identifying the essence of knowledge as sufficient compensation for the impoverished, faintly Marxist political-economic analysis (of the act of swallowing food) that he indulges. This explicit rejection of abstract thinking in favor of fleshly essences (defecation is implicit in the sequence of consumption, digestion, and urination invoked by the narrator) is wedded to the narrator's *lack* of desire for learning. Scientific progress, therefore, becomes a form of sexual impotence.

Csicsery-Ronay's attitude about Kafka's contribution to science fiction here plays a useful role in understanding the convergences between Kafka and Dick. Csicsery-Ronay recognizes that Kafka's fiction indicts scientism, the belief that proper knowledge comes through quantification and "that the greatest human faculty is positive rationality, the capacity to know progressively more things for certain through an understanding of these formalized causal laws."[21] Formalized causal laws, however, have only limited application in "Investigations of a Dog" and play no explicit role in "Roog." This fact has significant implications for Dick's place as a successor to Kafka. In Dick's story, as in Kafka's, the canine protagonist's awareness so differs from that of the "people" (whether human or canine) most familiar to him that it forces the reader to interrogate the causal (meaning narrative) laws that structure the story's world. These laws threaten to break down or to lapse entirely, providing Dick's fiction with its characteristic fear, doom, and gloom.

The psychological uneasiness of reading a Dick story is, like reading Kafka, the result of recognizing that the protagonist's consciousness cannot attach itself to stable foundations of thought, image, or symbol. This process upsets the rational events, as well as the unitary subjectivities, that characterize traditional humanism.

Csicsery-Ronay sees explicit connections between Kafka and Dick: "The influence of Kafka on Dick's work is unmistakable. Dick was intoxicated with the arbitrary transformations of ontological categories, the metaphysical double-binds, and the deadpan elaboration of paradoxical premises that are typical traits of the Kafkaesque."[22] Do such grand claims apply to "Roog," Dick's tiny fantasy about a dog who misperceives trash men as alien thieves? The answer lies not only in the implicit fragmentation of "Roog's" narrative, but also in the failed communication of its characters. A lack of mutual understanding seals the dog Boris, the human Cardossis, and the alien Roogs into individually bounded worlds to which only the reader has full access.

Dick's use of a third-person narrator in "Roog" might deflect the intimacy of Kafka's first-person account, but the story's opening lines immediately convey Boris's perspective:

> "Roog!" the dog said. He rested his paws on the top of the fence and looked around him.
> The Roog came running into the yard.
> It was early morning, and the sun had not really come up yet. The air was cold and gray, and the walls of the house were damp with moisture. The dog opened his jaws a little as he watched, his big black paws clutching the wood of the fence.
> The Roog stood by the open gate, looking into the yard. He was a small Roog, thin and white, on wobbly legs. The Roog blinked at the dog, and the dog showed his teeth.
> "Roog!" he said again.[23]

The reader becomes privy to Boris's conceptualization of the world around him. Two more pages elapse before Mrs. Cardossi explicitly identifies the Roogs as garbagemen, leaving the reader to induce their identity from the sparse clues provided by Dick's narrative. The Roog himself—thin, white, and wobbly—might be a white-furred animal with an unsteady gait, since Dick fails to identify the creature as bipedal. The story's sensory details are quotidian, even dull: cold and gray air, damp walls, Boris's black paws, a typical yard. Dick introduces a single foreign element—the unknown term "Roog"—into an otherwise normal scene to emphasize his story's realistic environment. The locale is not exotic, but one of the most banal possible: a small-town American home.

Other details, however, are subtly foreign. Boris speaks English, calling the Roog by name rather than onomatopoetically "woofing" or "barking." He first rests his paws atop the fence, standing on his two hind legs, but then clutches the fence in a gesture that closely resembles human hands. This visual impression reminds the reader of a person who casually leans against the fence to observe the Roog, then becomes more agitated until he shakes the barrier in frustration. Boris's upright body position underscores this parallel human stature, momentarily blurring the line between canine and *Homo sapiens*. When Boris shows his teeth, it might be a smile, but more likely indicates a dog about to growl. Dick, however, immediately switches perspectives when Boris *speaks* (rather than *barks*), confusing the reader's perspective. Does the story illustrate a human or a canine viewpoint? Which world does Boris inhabit? Which perspective is primary? The reader, despite Boris's canine existence, cannot be entirely certain because Dick skillfully manipulates everyday details to obscure the boundary between each domain. Apart from the unfamiliar word "Roog," this scene is mundane. The divergences from everyday reality—a talking dog, a funny name for a strange creature, paws that function like hands—manifest themselves quietly. The reader, consequently, might forget that the dog's perspective controls this story.

Whereas Kafka's narrator calls attention to his nonhuman status, Boris obscures the differences between canine and human viewpoints. Kafka, however, develops comparable confusion between the human world and the canine realm due to his extreme skepticism about the nature, or even the possibility, of progress. "Investigations of a Dog" reflects suspicions about the benefits of scientific research that appeared in Europe following the savagery of World War I, in which technological horrors such as trench warfare, mustard gas, incendiary bombs, and efficient firearms left traumatic impressions on virtually all aspects of European culture.[24] Kafka's tale, however—especially its narrator's disquisition about the oral, urinary, and scatological processes that form the basis of all knowledge—becomes a darkly humorous reaction to the wartime abuse of science and technology. Kafka lampoons the intellectual tendency to elevate the smallest, most vulgar elements of daily life into events of cosmic significance. Invoking an abstract bromide such as the "essence of knowledge," for instance, may transform the narrator's matronly cliché about pissing on the ground into the basis of all learning, but the narrator's attempt at sophisticated critical discernment—at distinguishing between quotidian necessities (such as urination) and philosophical values (such as knowledge)—cannot be taken seriously. Science can add only "mere details" to the narrator's universalizing maxim about urination. This snide comment not only pokes fun at the intellectual tendency to mistake trivial ideas for profound truths, but also reveals Kafka's talent for absurdity.

The narrator's articulate control of language, consequently, allows him to talk himself into any opinion. Progress becomes not so much a matter of scientific advance as a semantic game dependent upon verbal flourishes, dubious analogies, and irrational deductions. Kafka's witty burlesque unseats his reader's faith in progress by exposing the arbitrary linguistic means by which the essence of knowledge—rather than comprehensive understanding—is achievable. The "essence of all knowledge," therefore, simply magnifies maternal advice about frequent urination ("Water the ground as much as you can")[25] into the nucleus of advanced intellectual activity. That the narrator does not perceive the foolishness of this magnification only stresses Kafka's skill at constructing ludicrous juxtapositions.

Language is equally important, albeit ambiguous, in "Roog." After Boris races to his yard's fence in an effort to frighten away the first Roog, Dick introduces the Cardossis with minimal transition:

> The dog lay silently, his eyes bright and black. The day was beginning to come. The sky turned a little whiter, and from all around the sounds of people echoed through the morning air. Lights popped on behind shades. In the chilly dawn a window was opened.
> The dog did not move. He watched the path.
> In the kitchen Mrs. Cardossi poured water into the coffee pot. Steam rose from the water, blinding her. She set the pot down on the edge of the stove and went into the pantry. When she came back Alf was standing at the door of the kitchen. He put his glasses on.
> "You bring the paper?" he said.
> "It's outside."[26]

Dick moves from a canine to a human viewpoint by linking the human world's appearance in the story with the rising sun. As the light brightens, the noise of people beginning their morning routine emphasizes the humdrum reality of Mrs. Cardossi's breakfast chores. The reader requires no extensive description of husband or wife, who are so banal that they verge on stereotype: The good housewife prepares coffee, while her husband only wishes to read his morning newspaper.

This depiction of an ordinary 1950s married couple resonates with what M. Keith Booker, in *Monsters, Mushroom Clouds, and the Cold War*, summarizes as "the reputation of the decade for conservatism and conformity."[27] Booker finds this reputation misleading, since the social, political, and economic foment of the 1950s found its most public expression in the era's well-known anti-Communist hysteria. The structure of Dick's plot even implicates the unsuspecting Cardossis in looming, yet invisible, paranoia: The story begins with Boris's dislike of the as yet unidentified Roogs before evoking a pleasant morning for his human characters. The Cardossis' ignorance of the danger embodied by the Roogs causes the reader not only to question the dog's perception, but also to dismiss his misgivings as nothing more than the family pet's overprotective instincts. Alf infers as much when, stepping outside to retrieve his newspaper, he sees Boris lying near the fence:

> The dog and the man looked at one another. The dog whined. His eyes were bright and feverish.
> "Roog!" he said softly.
> "What?" Alf looked around. "Someone coming? The paperboy come?"
> The dog stared at him, his mouth open.
> "You certainly upset these days," Alf said. "You better take it easy. We both getting too old for excitement."
> He went inside the house.[28]

Communication lapses in this brief exchange. Alf, not understanding Boris's statement, ascribes the dog's distress to advancing age. Furthermore, whether Alf has actually heard Boris speak the word "Roog," as Dick indicates in the attribution "he [Boris] *said* softly," or has simply heard a dog's bark is unclear. Boris's comprehension of Alf's speech is especially ambiguous. The dog says nothing more, frustrated by his failure to alert Alf to the threat posed by the Roogs. The two characters lack a common language, leaving them both dissatisfied by their inability to communicate.

As with "Investigations of a Dog," "Roog" presents its canine protagonist as enduring interruptions to his normal environment. Dick, however, diverges from Kafka's model by accenting the fundamental poverty of language (specifically English), or its incapacity to convey crucial information. This setback, by extending the dog's isolation, destroys all hope of community. Where Kafka's loquacious narrator speaks volubly about how his intellectual pursuits alienate him from society, Boris speaks only one word throughout Dick's story. Boris, tellingly, has no society, since no other dogs are present. The only community that he might claim—the Cardossi family—cannot understand his apprehension. Boris, as a result, is not an intellectual. If he has any complex thoughts, the reader never encounters them.

The postmodern fascination with alienation, fragmentation, and confinement that Boris's simplistic mentality indicates relates, but by no means confines itself, to the story's 1950s setting. Dick's use of the past in "Roog" lacks the firm historical grounding that characterizes "Investigations of a Dog" because only the barest shared experiences between Boris and Alf Cardossi emerge. Dick's human characters, unlike Kafka's canine narrator, never think in historical detail. This lack of explicit intellectual activity (and the restriction of perspective that it implies) counters the self-indulgent monologue of Kafka's canine narrator to underscore the slippery nature of historical memory. Kafka satirizes the tendency to overanalyze past events, while Dick parodies the opposing inclination toward superficial historical thinking. Kafka and Dick, by highlighting the poverty of both positions, create narrators whose interior life (or lack thereof) points us toward the animal allegory's most postmodern quality: its ability to subvert human viewpoints, ideologies, and beliefs by examining them from an alien perspective that, finally, is not nearly so foreign as it appears.

Inner Spaces

To understand this point, the effects of Kafka's and Dick's distinct narrative strategies become relevant. Dick's third-person narration in "Roog" limits the reader's access to Boris's mental life, just as the Cardossis cannot get inside the dog's mind to understand his erratic behavior. The story's narrator describes Boris's reactions in unadorned prose that fails to probe the dog's deeper motivations, unlike the internal dissent that characterizes Kafka's canine protagonist. Boris's psychological simplicity does not indicate that he—or "Roog"—is an uncomplicated fictional creation, but rather that Dick's fascination with external particulars fragments the story's narrative perspective. Andrew Gibson considers such fragmentation to be unavoidably postmodern: "Narrative space is now plastic and manipulable. It has become heterogeneous, ambiguous, pluralised. Its inhabitants no longer appear to have an irrefutable or essential relation to any particular space. Rather, space opens up as a variable and finally indeterminate feature of [the] given narrative 'world.'"[29] Dick's reader, in other words, must not only keep track of Boris's and the Cardossis' competing subjectivities, but must also induce these characters' divergent motivations from scant narrative information. The subtlety with which the story's unnamed narrator moves from Boris's viewpoint to the Cardossis' perspective creates two separate yet contiguous spaces: the canine and the human.

These zones, as "Roog" unfolds, intersect without intermingling. Alf senses Boris's distress, but never fully comprehends it. These heterogeneous spaces, as Gibson suggests, blur when man and dog can perceive (however dimly) each other's emotional state, but cannot communicate a lucid message. The reader is never completely inside Boris's or the Cardossis' perspective, resulting in a variable, pluralized narrative that shifts from viewpoint to viewpoint without significant coherence. The reader, therefore, never mistakes Boris's perspective for a human outlook.

The extended monologue of "Investigations of a Dog," by contrast, creates an undivided subjectivity that easily slips from a canine perspective into a human viewpoint. No reader can be faulted for seeing dogdom as a metaphor for humanity in Kafka's long tale. The story's philosophically trenchant analysis of modernist uncertainty illuminates this point:

> True, knowledge provides the rules one must follow, but even to grasp them imperfectly and in rough outline is by no means easy, and when one has actually grasped them the real difficulty remains, namely to apply them to local conditions—here almost nobody can help, almost every hour brings new tasks, and every new patch of earth its specific problems; no one can maintain that he has settled everything for good and that henceforth his life will go on, so to speak, of itself, not even I myself, though my needs shrink literally from day to day.[30]

The difference between knowledge and experience, the gulf between theory and praxis, robs the narrator of security, comfort, and understanding. He exists in a bleak landscape of shrinking needs and limited possibilities whose barrenness seems thoroughly human. This passage, more melancholy than satirical, not only evokes a sense of permanent (even insurmountable) loss, but also misdirects the reader into believing that the loquacious narrator is more intelligent than the average dog.

The allegory of "Investigations of a Dog," therefore, seems clear: Humanity fruitlessly struggles toward greater comprehension of the world, only to discover that humanity's animal nature betrays the possibility of historical, scientific, and philosophical achievement. This allegory, however, is far from a somber philosophical disquisition because the narrator, rather than observing humanity, refers to dogdom. Kafka, through his canine narrator, parodies the reader's earnest attempt to discover lessons about human society. Placing the reader within a dog's consciousness, then communicating that dog's thoughts in human language, combines two radically different worldviews into a single narrative consciousness that Kafka plays for comic effect. Readers cannot help but question how the canine narrator's observations reflect their own lives. The dog's speculations about science and culture, therefore, demonstrate the limitations of his canine consciousness even as they parody his intellectual ambitions. Kafka melds these opposing tendencies into a humanist allegory that subverts reason by elevating the capacity for rational thought into the grandest intellectual aspiration of a dog that will never attain it.

The narrator's scientific quest to comprehend the world around him, in one of the story's most telling details, involves a fundamental misprision. He wishes to discover natural laws that might explain how food magically appears on the ground every day:

> My personal observation tells me that the earth, when it is watered and scratched according to the rules of science, extrudes nourishment, and moreover in such quality, in such abundance, in such ways, in such places, at such hours as the laws partially or completely established by science demand. I accept all this; my question, however, is the following: "Whence does the earth procure this food?"[31]

The narrator's subsequent experiments cannot provide the answer that Kafka's readers know from the beginning: A human hand places food on the ground, which, as Matthew Olsham notes, "is beyond the conceptual grasp of the dog, whose deadpan insistence on the most rigorous 'scientific' method for his investigations is the straight man in the story's comedy."[32] Kafka's story reduces the laws of science to instinctual canine behavior: The narrator believes that scratching the ground in order to cover the area of its urination results in an abundant harvest. This food, of course, is the treat a dog receives for successfully performing an assigned task, not a well-tended crop. The narrator's earnest scientific investigation contradicts the dog's inevitable failure to comprehend the truth of his world. This contrast, for Olsham, is where "the comedy of the story exists, and also its horror."[33]

Olsham's comment also returns us to Benjamin's territory of fright and despair, far from the continent of humanity, to provoke a fundamental question about dogdom: Does it function as a metaphor for humanity? The explicit reminders of the narrator's canine existence make this metaphor problematic, for they do not relent as "Investigations of a Dog" continues. The reader, as a result, cannot easily equate dogs with humans, particularly considering the narrator's philosophical musings about his relationship with his own species. Four extracts prove this point: (1) "I understand my fellow dogs, am flesh of their flesh, of their miserable, ever-renewed, ever-desirous flesh";[34] (2) "every dog has like me the impulse to question, and I have like every dog the impulse not to answer";[35] (3) "the only strange thing about me is my nature, yet even that, as I am always careful to remember, has its foundation in universal dog nature";[36] and (4) "consolingly in my ears rang the assurance that no matter how great the effect of my inquiries might be, and indeed the greater the better, I would not be lost to ordinary dog life."[37] These comments not only drive the division between the canine world and the human realm ridiculously high, but also construct the narrator as a thoughtful (if pretentious) member of the former world. These intellectual and emotional struggles, although Kafka renders them in achingly human terms, remain the reflections of a lowly dog.

As such, the humor and the horror of "Investigations of a Dog" lie in the constant discrepancy between the narrator's desire to understand larger issues that will forever elude him—particularly the progress of science—and the prosaic explanations that Kafka's readers easily recognize. The story's canine narrator attempts to explain his social isolation from other dogs by contrasting his personal history (as well as the history of his species) with present-day events. This historicizing project, however, reveals the inadequacy of the narrator's analytical pretensions. His canine consciousness, the story makes clear, is not capable of fully comprehending the world around him. Kafka's narrative displacement of bourgeois intellectual processes into an animal speaker mocks humanist attempts to comprehend the difficult, ambiguous, and uncertain historical circumstances that confront the narrator. Kafka also satirizes the postmodern impulse of rejecting all efforts at understanding the past as doomed to failure. The human and canine worlds neither fully consolidate nor cleanly separate in "Investigations of a Dog," transforming the story into an animal allegory that not only depicts the ambiguity of historical memory, but also illustrates reason's inability to reveal the truth about nature, science, progress, and human psychology.

The Secret Lives of Dogs

This complex relationship between the human and canine worlds more closely connects "Investigations of a Dog" to "Roog," especially in light of the divergences between the two stories' protagonists. Kafka's narrator doubts the possibility of historical and scientific progress, while Boris holds primitive doubts about the Roogs' identity. The linguistic oddities of Dick's story become paramount, for Boris's second encounter with the Roogs is even stranger than the first. The sun has risen on a peaceful, lazy day:

> He was standing under the tree when he saw two Roogs sitting on the fence, watching him.
> "He's big," the first Roog said. "Most Guardians aren't as big as this."

The other Roog nodded, his head wobbling on his neck. Boris watched them without moving, his body stiff and hard. The Roogs were silent, now, looking at the big dog with his shaggy ruff of white around his neck.

"How is the offering urn?" the first Roog said. "Is it almost full?"

"Yes." The other nodded. "Almost ready."

"You, there!" the first Roog said, raising his voice. "Do you hear me? We've decided to accept the offering, this time. So you remember to let us in. No nonsense, now."

"Don't forget," the other added. "It won't be long."

Boris said nothing.

The two Roogs leaped off the fence and went over together just beyond the walk. One of them brought out a map and they studied it.

"This area really is none too good for a first trial," the first Roog said. "Too many Guardians . . . Now, the northside area—"

"*They* decided," the other Roog said. "There are so many factors—"

"Of course." They glanced at Boris and moved back farther from the fence. He could not hear the rest of what they were saying.[38]

Communication appears to improve in this passage. Boris understands not only the Roogs' conversation, but also the rough outlines of their secret plan to "test" the neighborhood (a machination controlled, the Roogs imply, by the mysterious leaders of an unnamed organization). The Roogs employ unconventional terms (Guardians, offering urns) instead of common designations (dogs, trash cans) to emphasize their foreignness. They do not conform to their quotidian surroundings, at least as Boris perceives these surroundings. The Roogs openly taunt the dog, assuming that he can do little to prevent them from "accepting the offering," a phrase with religious (or at least church-going) resonance in an otherwise secular story. Boris's silence, moreover, signals the Roogs' narrative eminence. Their perspective dominates this passage, providing the protagonist (and the reader) with information about the Roogs' murky intentions. The narrator refuses to reveal important details about Boris's and the Roogs' inner lives, focusing instead on their outer mannerisms, actions, and words. The reader's incomplete knowledge of the Roogs' identity mirrors Boris's confusion, although their shadowy plot to conduct an unspecified "trial" lends credence to the dog's earlier, angry response at seeing them.

At least two explanations about the Roogs' identity are possible. First, the Roogs may be extraterrestrial creatures that gather the Cardossis' garbage for an unknown purpose. "The trial" might refer to a scientific, military, or commercial test of the neighborhood's suitability as a source of trash, which, for unknown reasons, remains crucial to the Roogs' plan. Boris, however, somehow perceives the Roogs' true nature, thereby threatening to upset the trial. This improbable explanation of the story's plot makes certain mysteries clearer. If the Roogs are terrestrial, why do they upset Boris? He does not perceive Alf as a small, thin, wobbly figure, indicating that the dog can distinguish between human beings and other living creatures.

The possibility that Boris barks at unfamiliar human garbage collectors, whom he misperceives as suspicious alien entities, becomes less significant when Alf Cardossi discusses the dog's behavior with his wife. Boris whines and whimpers when Alf approaches, but the dog cannot express his anxiety about the Roogs in human terms. Alf, visibly worried about his dog, goes into the house for lunch:

> "What's the matter?" Mrs. Cardossi said.
> "The dog got to stop making all that noise, barking. The neighbors going to complain to the police again."
> "I hope we don't have to give him to your brother," Mrs. Cardossi said, folding her arms. "But he sure goes crazy, especially on Friday morning, when the garbage men come."
> "Maybe he'll calm down," Alf said. He lit his pipe and smoked solemnly. "He didn't used to be that way. Maybe he'll get better, like he was."
> "We'll see," Mrs. Cardossi said.[39]

The garbagemen, this exchange implies, collect trash every Friday morning, but Boris's reaction to them has changed. One fanciful explanation for this behavioral adaptation suggests that the human trash collectors have been replaced by Roogs, but that only Boris, with his finely calibrated canine senses, can perceive the alteration. This plot—of extraterrestrial creatures supplanting human beings—became so common in 1950s American science fiction that Booker calls it the "aliens-are-already-among-us" tale,[40] citing Robert Heinlein's 1951 novel *The Puppet Masters* and Jack Finney's 1954 novel *Body Snatchers* (as well as Don Siegel's 1956 film adaptation of Finney's book, *Invasion of the Body Snatchers*) as exemplars of this tradition. The irrational possibility that extraterrestrial garbagemen have invaded the Cardossis' neighborhood, no matter how unbelievable, helps clarify "Roog's" linguistic contradictions. Boris's attempt to communicate his fear of the Roogs to Alf initially fails, causing the dog to listen intently as the Roogs discuss the upcoming trial. The Roogs then move out of earshot when they notice Boris's silent attention, leading the reader to wonder how Boris can comprehend the Roogs, but not Alf.

Boris, like many pets, may understand (or *seem* to understand) rudimentary English, even if he cannot speak it. The Roogs, alternatively, may speak a language that Boris, but not human beings, can comprehend. If so, the narrator translates the Roogs' foreign tongue into English for the reader's benefit. Dick's story, however, neither mentions nor implies this translation, plunging the reader into a perplexing perceptual tangle about the precise nature of Boris's linguistic comprehension.

These ambiguities underscore Dick's fragmentary narrative. Its deceptively straightforward plot unveils competing perceptions, perspectives, and possibilities. Boris does not occupy the same mental, linguistic, or perceptual space as his owners. The dog may indicate his distress about the Roogs by whining, whimpering, and barking, but Boris's inability to clearly communicate with Alf Cardossi traps the dog in a nightmarish realm of escalating tension. When the Roogs arrive to collect their offering, Boris cannot restrain himself. The story concludes on a note of unbearable tension:

> "ROOG!" Boris screamed, and he came toward them, dancing with fury and dismay. Reluctantly, the Roogs turned away from the window. They went out through the gate, closing it behind them.
>
> "Look at him," the last Roog said with contempt . . . . Boris strained against the fence, his mouth open, snapping wildly. The biggest Roog began to wave his arms furiously and Boris retreated. He settled down at the bottom of the porch steps, his mouth still open, and from the depths of him an unhappy, terrible moan issued forth, a wail of misery and despair. . . .
>
> All the Roogs laughed.
>
> They went on up the path, carrying the offering in the dirty, sagging blanket.[41]

Boris's anger, in the end, is little more than the occasion for the Roogs' mockery. Dick's canine protagonist ends "Roog" emotionally drained, defeated, and powerless. The story features one of Dick's most depressing conclusions, for the reader cannot determine whether Boris understands the Roogs' language, whether the Roogs abscond with the Cardossis' trash, whether the dog misperceives their identity, or whether Boris (due to age or illness) has taken leave of his senses. The reader may question, but cannot resolve, these narrative disjunctions.

By fracturing the reader's certainty about the story's events, this multifocal narration blocks decisive interpretation. Neither the story's characters nor its audience can be certain that the Roogs are real, that Boris's anger is justified, or that the Cardossis' annoyance at Boris's behavior is unwarranted. The absurd possibility that Boris's suspicions are accurate, however, permits a more plausible (and perversely funny) explanation.[42]

This second interpretation of "Roog" distinguishes it from the aesthetic accomplishment of Kafka's "Investigations of a Dog" by observing that Dick's story, without Kafka's narrative subtlety, merely recounts the mistaken cognition of an emotionally unstable family dog. The narrator's absurd portrayal of Boris's inability to recognize the garbage collectors as human beings mocks the reader who finds narrative complexity in "Roog." Such a reading becomes an example of literary overinterpretation in Umberto Eco's sense of this term: "the overestimation of the importance of clues is often born of a propensity to consider the most immediately apparent elements as significant, whereas the very fact that they are apparent should allow us to recognize that they are explicable in much more economical terms."[43]

Dick's story, in this reading, is aesthetically inferior to Kafka's elegantly written tale. Discerning intellectual maturity in "Roog" becomes a mistake that locates bogus significance in a story that cannot hope to match the linguistic sophistication of "Investigations of a Dog." Dick, as if to support this perspective, acknowledged the limitations of his early fiction during a 1976 radio interview by revealing that his initial draft of "Roog" was much longer than the published version. Dick significantly revised this draft at the behest of Anthony Boucher, editor of the *Magazine of Fantasy and Science Fiction*: "Tony Boucher said, 'If you rewrite along these lines, you will have a worthwhile piece of fiction.' . . . I had sent him eight or nine thousand words, and I cut it down to about two thousand words. That was a story called 'Roog.'"[44] Boucher, a notoriously tough critic, became what Ray Faraday Nelson once called "the only influence [Dick] ever talked about at length, because Boucher taught him how to put together a short story."[45] Less was apparently more for Boucher, whose advice suggests that Dick's first draft was overwritten.

"Roog's" brevity excludes the long philosophical passages that characterize "Investigations of a Dog." The artistry of Dick's story lies in its linguistic concision. His prose, as spare as Kafka's is verbose, still manages to convey how differently Boris perceives the world from the Cardossis and from the Roogs. This epistemological disparity underscores the story's competing subjectivities, even if the reader has no access to the characters' internal lives. This strangely mediated position accumulates external details to suggest, rather than to depict, their turbulent psyches. By eliminating interior monologues and explicit philosophizing, Dick's story accrues sensory details to establish "Roog" as a different type of animal allegory than "Investigations of a Dog": one that relies on narrative subtext, but that, like Kafka's tale, emphasizes a humanist outlook.

Boris's behavior becomes more frantic as "Roog" unfolds, but does not significantly change. His protective impulses carry the day, just as the philosophizing tendencies of Kafka's canine narrator carry "Investigations of a Dog" to its sober conclusion. Both characters, however, allegorize human potential. Kafka's allegory subverts easy faith in scientific, social, and political progress, while Dick's allegory employs limited canine consciousness to question reality's epistemological basis. The Cardossis' perspective may anchor the story in recognizably human elements, emotions, and language, but "Roog" is not the simplistic story that it initially appears. "Roog," unlike "Investigations of a Dog," indirectly illustrates ambiguities of identity and existence rather than propounding them in long, discursive meditations. Both Kafka's and Dick's animal allegories, however, successfully parody human foibles, pretensions, and ideologies.

Man, Animal, Allegory

"Investigations of a Dog" and "Roog" are satirical animal allegories. Kafka and Dick emphasize bleak, yet perverse, humor that mocks their protagonists' inability to understand the contexts, the possibilities, and the limits of their own experience. Neither Boris nor Kafka's narrator will ever understand the perplexing circumstances of his own life. Boris inhabits a living nightmare of undiminished anxiety, while Kafka's canine protagonist philosophizes so abstractly that he cannot comfortably relate to his own society. Both stories, despite their radical differences, displace human inadequacies into animal characters that allegorize the difficulties of living in the modern and postmodern eras.

These animal allegories, therefore, externalize their readers' normal experience to underscore the absurd strangeness of human behavior. Adopting another creature's worldview not only estranges the reader from his or her known world, but also reconfigures that world as a foreign, often ridiculous place. Kafka's and Dick's animal allegories become literary hybrids that graft the modernist mistrust of scientific, cultural, and historical progress onto the postmodernist acceptance of scientific, cultural, and historical uncertainty. These odd tales provoke humanist anxiety about the impossibility of securely defining one's identity in a world that can no longer be fully comprehended. Kafka's and Dick's animal allegories represent the quotidian world as a place of ambiguous, inauthentic, and fearful black comedy. Their readers move from errant hopefulness, through gloom, to wicked pleasure in the disappointments that characterize each protagonist. The overall impact of these animal allegories leads Kafka's and Dick's readers, in Walter Benjamin's evocative metaphor, "far away from the continent of man,"[46] only to suggest that they never escaped this territory. Kafka's and Dick's readers have simply misapprehended, from the start, the world that they presumed to know so well.

This pessimistic conclusion recalls Kafka's upsetting, yet strangely reassuring, attitude about hope. Max Brod once told Kafka about the Gnostic view of life, which sees God as evil and the world as a fallen creation. As Benjamin recounts the story, "'Oh no,' said Kafka, 'our world is only a bad mood of God, a bad day of his.' 'Then there is hope outside this manifestation of the world that we know,' [Brod replied]. He [Kafka] smiled. 'Oh, plenty of hope, an infinite amount of hope—but not for us.'"[47] This marvelously succinct formulation of humanism's lament for an earlier, simpler, and more secure era summarizes the canine protagonist of "Investigations of a Dog" better than any scholarly analysis. The dog's only reassurance is hollow, cynical faith in the ability of his intellect to liberate him from the tyranny of progress. "Roog" features no such comfort. Boris ends in emotional disarray, with two unenviable prospects: continued distress (provoked by the Roogs' weekly visits) or living with another family. Dick shatters all pretense of hope, reducing Kafka's ironic conclusion to blatant depression. For both authors, the world—of humans, of dogs, and, most importantly, of their readers—becomes an insoluble quagmire of helpless despair. Kafka and Dick defer hope to emphasize the tenuous stability of human subjectivity. This grim result, when coupled with the unavoidable—yet strangely pleasurable—aesthetic discomforts that characterize Kafka's and Dick's fiction, illuminates their SF allegories as valuable assessments of postmodern humanism.

Animal allegory also leads us to Kafka's and Dick's use of the "bureaucratic bestiary." Kafka's *The Metamorphosis* (1915) and Dick's "Oh, to Be a Blobel!" (1964) are potent examples of this narrative form. These hybrid texts blend the alienness of animal allegory with the oppressive bureaucracy of traditional dystopia to establish a unique literary subgenre. Kafka's and Dick's bureaucratic bestiaries portray the radical bodily transformations that result when invasive bureaucracies control the most intimate aspects of their protagonists' mental, physical, and spiritual lives. The metamorphosis of human characters into thinking animals permits both authors to mercilessly satirize the social conditions that drive their protagonists to regret, to despair, and to madness.

Bugs, Blobels, and Bureaucracy

So much has been written about *The Metamorphosis* that even a cursory review of the available criticism tempts us to apply George Steiner's cynical assessment of scholarship about Kafka's 1925 novel *The Trial* to the story of Gregor Samsa's horrific transformation: "The secondary literature is cancerous. It multiplies daily in the academy, in *belles-lettres* and literary journalism. It is parasitic on every element (one is tempted to say 'every paragraph') of this inexhaustible text."[48] Steiner's reaction to the proliferation of Kafka scholarship may be overstated, but his impatience with the morass of critical opinion that surrounds *The Trial*—and that forces the inquisitive reader to hack through it en route to understanding this fundamentally mysterious book—is understandable. Encountering the numerous, widely divergent readings of *The Metamorphosis* may convince the discerning reader that they, too, are inexhaustible. The question of Gregor Samsa's transmutation continues to fascinate Kafka's readers and critics, resulting in innumerable competing interpretations. The suspicion that coherently comprehending *The Metamorphosis* is impossible looms large over this vexing tale of a common man who becomes a giant insect.

Although a comprehensive reading of *The Metamorphosis* may be unattainable, the writing of Stanley Corngold, Walter H. Sokel, William J. Dodd, Evelyn Beck, and Michael P. Ryan offers stimulating analyses of this fascinating text. *The Metamorphosis*'s many layers make it an exemplary "bureaucratic bestiary" that melds the animal allegory of "Investigations of a Dog" with the dystopian bureaucracy exemplified by *The Trial*. The bureaucratic bestiary, consequently, is a hybrid text that combines elements from both parent genres: The protagonist sees him- or herself as nonhuman, while oppressive bureaucratic interference constitutes the major feature of his or her life. The bureaucratic bestiary's fusion of fantasy and paranoia removes its reader from the constraints of naturalist narrative, even as the story subjects its characters to the vicissitudes of a thoroughly human world marked by increasingly bureaucratized political conditions. *The Metamorphosis*, indeed, illustrates bureaucracy's reductive power from its earliest moments. The story's famous opening line casts the reader into immediate confusion: "As Gregor Samsa awoke one morning from uneasy dreams he found himself transformed in his bed into a gigantic insect."[49] The protagonist is no mere animal, but a lowly vermin. The story's tone then fluctuates between terror, horror, despair, and gallows humor to demonstrate Kafka's masterful ability to navigate the enigmatic emotional terrain confronted by his pitiful protagonist.

Gregor occupies an unenviable narrative position. His newfound animal form frightens his family, yet his human consciousness remains intact, allowing Gregor to feel the sting of that rejection. The resulting alienation provokes sorrow, envy, and anger when Gregor's father, mother, and sister Grete usurp his position as the family's sole breadwinner. Gregor, deprived of his occupation and human form, adjusts to life as an invalid: Sequestered in his bedroom, Gregor becomes dependent upon his family for food and for care. Gregor has little to do beyond thinking about his newly outcast status, his diminished future, and his regrets about allowing the life of a traveling salesman to interfere with more important goals. Perhaps the most touching scene in *The Metamorphosis*, if not in all of Kafka, comes when a forlorn Gregor gazes out his bedroom window: "He nerved himself to the great effort of pushing an armchair to the window, then crawled up over the window sill and, braced against the chair, leaned against the windowpanes, obviously in some recollection of the sense of freedom that looking out of a window always used to give him."[50] This passage's palpable loss indicates that, as Gregor's sight dims, so do the chances of his transformation reversing itself. Gregor cannot escape the physical containment of his room or his new body, causing his psyche to deteriorate into lonely suffering. When death comes to Gregor, it is almost as much a relief for the reader as it is for Gregor's exasperated family.

Dick's "Oh, to Be a Blobel!" seems a great deal lighter, but no less upsetting. To the uninitiated reader, this story, about George Munster, a veteran of Earth's war against the Blobels (an amoeba-like extraterrestrial life form), can readily be mistaken for pure comedy. George visits a "homeostatic psychoanalyst,"[51] or mechanical therapist, named Dr. Jones to receive professional advice about his unusual problem. George's battlefield heroism earned him a position as a Terran intelligence agent sent to spy on the Blobels. In order to infiltrate this alien society, George underwent a medical procedure that extracted a high price. "You had to relinquish your human form and assume the repellent form of a Blobel,"[52] Dr. Jones realizes during his first session with George, outlining the story's central tension. George's humanity is nebulous because, as the narrator informs the reader, "for almost twelve hours out of the day he reverted, despite all the efforts of himself and the Veterans' Hospitalization Agency of the UN, to his old war-time Blobel shape. To a formless unicellular-like blob, right in the middle of his own apartment."[53] This transformation may not seem funny, but the narrator's droll recitation underscores its tragicomic implications: "His financial resources consisted of a small pension from the War Office; finding a job was impossible, because as soon as he was hired the strain caused him to revert there on the spot, in plain sight of his new employer and fellow workers. It did not assist in forming successful work-relationships."[54]

Like Gregor Samsa's, George Munster's isolation forces him to rely on the charity of others to survive. Dick's humor in this story is dark, witty, and mordant. George's surname is a prime example of Dick's satirical intent:

"Munster" is a pun on George's status as a monster.[55] The image of a man publicly transforming into a large, amorphous blob may be ridiculous, but Dick, by acknowledging the story's absurd premise, also satirizes the fundamental pointlessness of war, as well as the plight of veterans who are forgotten by the governments that demand their loyalty and sacrifice. Dick's humor, like Kafka's, prevents George's dilemma from becoming too painful to read. By maintaining enough sympathy with the protagonist to ground their stories in genuine sympathy, Kafka and Dick question the nature, the limits, and the unity of human subjectivity.

Gregor Samsa and George Munster, therefore, become liminal characters. The narrative implications of Gregor's animalized existence are especially significant. Gregor is and is not human, is and is not animal, is and is not definable by the measure of a single identity. His personality before the metamorphosis, as depicted in the first of the story's three sections (or chapters), is that of a bourgeois salesman whose commercial occupation affords him little pleasure. Gregor's bureaucratic mentality is so strong that, rather than feeling shocked by his transformation, Gregor worries about how his new insect body will affect his career. Gregor frets about losing his job if he arrives at work late because, as *The Metamorphosis* soon makes clear, Gregor's meager income must support a family that was financially ruined when his father's business went bankrupt five years before the story begins.

Gregor, curiously, never asks the questions that would surely beset a person afflicted by his bizarre condition: How did this metamorphosis occur? What is its purpose, if any? Why has it happened to *me*? Most importantly, can it be reversed? Rather than considering these possibilities or mourning the loss of his human form, Gregor rises from bed too hastily and slightly injures his lower half. Gregor then explains the resulting pain in mundane, even banal, terms: "He remembered that often enough in bed he had felt small aches and pains, probably caused by awkward postures, which had proved purely imaginary once he got up, and he looked forward eagerly to seeing this morning's delusions gradually fall away."[56] Gregor, the reader quickly recognizes, considers the metamorphosis to be a bad dream. He does not probe the transformation's absurd reality beyond its ability to prevent a full day's work.

Gregor, in fact, is so diligent in his commercial duties that transforming into a giant insect fails to dampen his professional commitment. This situation, as ludicrous as it is tragic, caused Kafka himself to laugh uproariously while reading the story aloud to friends.[57] The metamorphosis is important to Gregor only insofar as it offers a valid excuse for his tardiness. The chief clerk of Gregor's firm, to drive home this point, soon arrives to ask about Gregor's absence from work. Gregor, in a supremely comic passage, believes his transformation to be a legitimate mitigating factor: "At the moment, true, he was lying on the carpet and no one who knew the condition he was in could seriously expect him to admit the chief clerk. But for such a small discourtesy, which could plausibly be explained away somehow later on, Gregor could hardly be dismissed on the spot."[58] Kafka's flair for absurdity forces Gregor to argue that his metamorphosis into a giant insect is grounds for taking a legitimate sick day. This pragmatic reaction to his newfound condition also suggests that Gregor's animal existence does not fully destroy his human consciousness. Gregor's identity, now caught between two worlds, becomes unstable.

This instability, evoked by Kafka's metaphorical alteration of Gregor's body, results in the subjective ambiguity Stanley Corngold recognizes in *The Metamorphosis*:

> The metamorphosis of Gregor Samsa into a vermin metaphor is disturbing, not only or not mainly because a large vermin—man or beast—is unsettling, but because the unstable, fluid movement within the metaphor of human tenor and animal vehicle is disturbing. At one moment, Gregor is pure rapture, another very nearly pure dung beetle, at times grossly human, at times daintily buglike. In shifting incessantly the relation of Gregor's mind and body, Kafka shatters the so-called unity of ideal tenor (man) and bodily vehicle (bug) within the metaphor.[59]

This oscillation between human and animal recalls the uncertain identities of the canine narrators of Kafka's "Investigations of a Dog" and Dick's "Roog." The human and animal worlds merge to suggest that unitary consciousness is impossible. The reader empathizes with Gregor's unexpected conversion to a monstrous form, but also recognizes his intellectual limitations by wondering, as Gregor does not, how and why he has become a giant insect. Gregor's human identity, so constrained by his profession's bureaucratic obsession with punctuality, is incapable of feeling shock, anger, or sorrow about his monumental transformation. The fluctuation between body and mind that Corngold confines to the metaphor of metamorphosis now spills into every other part of the story. Whether Gregor is human, insect, or a strange amalgam of both, he becomes a reclusive, increasingly unstable prisoner of frustrated desires.

Insider Perspectives

These desires reveal themselves through Kafka's intimate third-person narration, which explores Gregor's human consciousness as he resists, reacts to, and adapts to his startling transformation. Kafka, to illustrate Gregor's slippery subjectivity, switches from third- to first-person voice:

> He slid down again into his former position. This getting up early, he thought, makes one quite stupid. A man needs his sleep. Other commercials live like harem women. For instance, when I come back to the hotel of a morning to write up the orders I've got, these others are only sitting down to the breakfast. Let me just try that with my chief; I'd be sacked on the spot. Anyhow, that might be quite a good thing for me, who can tell? If I didn't have to hold my hand because of my parents I'd have given notice long ago, I'd have gone to the chief and told him exactly what I think of him.[60]

This passage's frustrated didacticism recalls the canine narrator of "Investigations of a Dog." Gregor accentuates the other salesmen's lethargy while confidently lecturing the reader. Indeed, the professorial interpolation "for instance" indicates that Gregor, rather than indulging uninterrupted interior monologue, explains himself to an unseen audience (that implicitly includes Gregor himself and *The Metamorphosis*'s reader). Gregor's pedantic tone underscores Kafka's affinity for mixing different viewpoints to reveal more information about his protagonist than a first- or third-person account, by itself, could. The narrator so subtly segues from an objective account of Gregor's physical movement to the man's subjective reflections that the reader might miss this transition.

Roy Pascal recognizes this narrative shift as an example of free indirect speech (*style indirect libre*). Pascal's analysis of Kafka's fiction notes that "free indirect speech . . . can alternate very freely, from sentence to sentence, with objective narrative, so that we cannot always be sure which is intended."[61] Pascal believes that this fluctuation between subjectivity and objectivity characterizes nineteenth-century European novels, although *The Metamorphosis*'s *style indirect libre* focuses the plot on Gregor's unfolding consciousness. Kafka does not halt *The Metamorphosis* for Gregor's interior monologue, but fluidly alternates between first- and third-person voices to expose his protagonist's past, to explore Gregor's personality, and to emphasize Gregor's limited mentality (obsessed, as the reader discovers, by financial debt and professional obligation). By doing so, Kafka stresses the importance of psychological transformation. Gregor's stubborn refusal to acknowledge his physical metamorphosis, however, demonstrates that such change is difficult (if not impossible) to attain. The careful reader, thanks to Kafka's narrative sophistication, understands that Gregor cannot escape (or ignore) his physiological alteration no matter how much he wishes he could.

Dick' narration of "Oh, to Be a Blobel!" not only embraces *style indirect libre*, but also depicts humanity even more pessimistically than *The Metamorphosis*. Humanity in Dick's futuristic world is an aggressive, imperialistic, and xenophobic species that prosecutes an immoral war against the Blobels. Dick's description of this conflict (and of George Munster's reaction to its hostilities) so memorably outlines the story's major tensions that it deserves extensive quotation:

> "I fought three years in that war," Munster said, nervously smoothing his long, black, thinning hair. "I hated the Blobels and I volunteered; I was only nineteen and I had a good job—but the crusade to clear the Sol System of Blobels came first in my mind." . . .
>
> The Blobels had emigrated originally from another star system, probably Proxima. Several thousand years ago they had settled on Mars and on Titan, doing very well at agrarian pursuits. They were developments of the original unicellular amoeba, quite large and with a highly-organized nervous system, but still amoeba, with pseudopodia, reproducing by binary fission, and in the main offensive to Terran settlers.
>
> The war itself had broken out over ecological considerations. It had been the desire of the Foreign Aid Department of the UN to change the atmosphere on Mars, making it more usable for Terran settlers. This change, however, had made it unpalatable for the Blobel colonies already there; hence the squabble. . . .
>
> Within a period of ten years the altered atmosphere had diffused throughout the planet, bringing suffering—at least so they alleged—to the Blobels. In retaliation, a Blobel armada had approached Terra and had put into orbit a series of technically sophisticated satellites designed eventually to alter the atmosphere of Terra. This alteration never came about because of course the War Office of the UN had gone into action; the satellites had been detonated by self-instructing missiles . . . and the war was on.[62]

George mentions Terra's crusade to exterminate the Blobels so casually that this pursuit's genocidal implications seem negligible. The narrator also cannot resist endorsing Terra's racist disdain for Blobels, whose intelligence (even sentience) cannot negate their physically disgusting appearance. Associating Blobels with unicellular life justifies George's prejudice because the Blobels' radically different physiology and culture distress him: The Blobels have pseudopodia, not arms; they reproduce by fission, not sexual intimacy; and they are farmers, not advanced scientific beings (an unfounded bias considering that the Blobels colonize planets outside their own solar system long before humanity). The narrator also doubts Blobel sovereignty—their prior claim to Mars—by nonchalantly dismissing the possibility that changing Mars's atmosphere will deleteriously affect Blobel health. The passage repudiates Blobel suffering as an unproven allegation. The Blobels' attempt at poetic retaliation—altering Earth's atmosphere—provokes a war that results from Terra's racist aggression. "Oh, to Be a Blobel!" amplifies Dick's lifelong anxieties about imperialistic militarism to cosmic extremes that demonstrate how universally destructive war can be.[63]

The parallels between "Oh, to Be a Blobel!" and *The Metamorphosis* are striking. War provides the context for Dick's story of George Munster's physical transformation, just as economic ruin provides the context for Kafka's tale of Gregor Samsa's physiological transmutation. George cannot develop meaningful relationships with other people because his Blobel appearance disturbs them; Gregor's family relationships deteriorate after his transformation into an insect. Dick even provides a passage in which George, reverting to Blobel form, gazes out his window:

> Sighing, Munster flowed back across the carpet, to the window, where he rose into a high pillar in order to see the view beyond; there was a light-sensitive spot on his outer surface, and although he did not possess a true lens he was able to appreciate—nostalgically—the sight of San Francisco Bay, the Golden Gate Bridge, the playground for small children which was Alcatraz Island.[64]

George's forlorn nostalgia for a vista that he can barely see so powerfully recalls Gregor's melancholy regard while gazing at the hospital behind his apartment that the reader may wonder if Dick deliberately rewrites *The Metamorphosis* for an SF audience. No evidence from Dick's biographies or correspondence confirms this possibility, but the affinities between *The Metamorphosis* and "Oh, to Be a Blobel!" illustrate how Dick's fiction reproduces Kafka's most significant themes.

The Alien and the Human

Dick deploys alienation, the most important theme for both authors, to different effect than Kafka. Whereas Gregor's isolation only increases, George Munster eventually marries Vivian Arrasmith, a Blobel woman who spied for her side during the war and who now reverts to human form for several hours each day. Dr. Jones, the mechanical therapist, arranges their first meeting, then bluntly summarizes their mutual problem: "Both of you are outcasts in either civilization; both of you are stateless and hence gradually suffering a loss of ego-identity. I predict for both of you a gradual deterioration ending finally in severe mental illness. Unless you two can develop a rapprochement."[65] Although this diagnosis perfectly describes the outcast, stateless, and pathetic Gregor Samsa, Kafka's protagonist finds no comfort in other people. His abject loneliness forestalls romantic relationships with women, but George Munster commiserates with a former enemy who has also endured shameful solitude. Dr. Jones's solution offers George and Vivian the possibility of embracing one another and of dissipating their loathsome solitude. The alien bodies that repulse George and Vivian, Dr. Jones implies, might paradoxically unite them in a beneficial relationship. Dick literalizes the metaphor of alienation by allowing two characters who become extra-terrestrials to lose their native identities. Dr. Jones's intervention, however, offers George and Vivian the opportunity to accept their alien status by becoming romantically involved with a person who understands the other's suffering. As Vivian tells George, "[W]e can enjoy [the] time together, no longer in wretched isolation."[66]

Had Dick ended "Oh, to Be a Blobel!" here, his story of wartime reconciliation would have made an obvious point: Human beings must welcome their enemies, perhaps even adopt certain qualities of their enemies, to achieve personal and political peace. This humanist philosophy, no matter how commendable, is hardly original. Advising people to love one another for the greater good was, by the time of the story's 1964 publication, an example of undistinguished—even hackneyed—social analysis.[67] Dick, however, does not conclude "Oh, to Be a Blobel!" so mundanely. George's self-loathing, along with his unresolved hatred of the Blobels, transforms the story from a simple parable about war into a complicated hybrid text that, like *The Metamorphosis*, illuminates the despair of human beings caught inside a bestial bureaucracy.

A Bug's Life

Dick hybridizes human and animal perspectives in "Oh, to Be a Blobel!" differently than Kafka does in *The Metamorphosis*. Gregor, for instance, cannot fully comprehend the reality of his physical transformation. This partial understanding mirrors an insect's limited mentality, permitting Kafka to metaphorically explore human stupidity, venality, and vice. *The Metamorphosis* recounts the story of a human being who, despite his transmutation into an insect, never fully loses his human subjectivity. Gregor retains the capacity to think and to feel even as his body expires from starvation: "He thought of his family with tenderness and love. The decision that he must disappear was one that he held to even more strongly than his sister, if that were possible."[68] The dehumanization produced by Gregor's isolation destroys his ability to endure the sufferings and indignities of daily life. Gregor, before the metamorphosis, is exceptional only in the bourgeois banality of his unremarkable existence. He dies as a filthy, burdensome bug that regards its own death as a sacrifice that will improve the Samsa family's fortunes.

The fact that Gregor's family benefits from both his disability and his death only deepens the tragedy of Gregor's life. *The Metamorphosis* concludes with Gregor's father, mother, and sister taking a trip to the country. Gregor's parents, while enjoying the bucolic locale's fresh air and sunshine, admire Grete's pretty figure: "And it was like a confirmation of their new dreams and excellent intentions that at the end of their journey their daughter sprang to her feet first and stretched her young body."[69] Gregor's financial support, this conclusion reveals, has not only made his relatives dependent upon him, but has also retarded their enthusiasm for living. The terms Kafka chooses—"new dreams," "excellent intentions," "the end of their journey"— indicate regeneration and redemption after Gregor's metamorphosis ends his economic dominance. Gregor's death, in this light, is not a sacrifice so much as a renewal of the family's traditional structure. Gregor, by assuming his father's duty as breadwinner, infantilizes the family. No character in the story may understand this truth, but Gregor's father, mother, and sister profit from the man's transformation by assuming control of their own lives. In simpler language, they become adults.

The most vexing question for Kafka's story, in light of this ironic result, is: What causes the metamorphosis? Walter H. Sokel takes the transformation as proof of Gregor's alienation, of Gregor "[finding] himself in a fundamental sense estranged from himself"[70] due to his work's instrumental, impersonal, and restrictive nature. Sokel's Marxist analysis, for all its complicated reasoning, asserts that the Samsa family's economic difficulties drive Gregor to his monstrous transformation.

Michael P. Ryan, on the other hand, finds spiritual resonances in *The Metamorphosis*, observing that "Kafka is perhaps saying that . . . traveling from one existence to another . . . Gregor *is Samsara*; he embodies rebirth and its consequent suffering."[71] Ryan considers *The Metamorphosis* to be the middle story of a trilogy that begins with "The Judgment" (1912) and concludes with "In the Penal Colony" (1919). These tales are "shackled together by the concept of metempsychosis"[72] to assert a Schopenhauerian view of life as a dreary cycle of birth, suffering, sickness, death, and rebirth. Gregor's transformation, in Ryan's reading, is merely one step in this unending process.

J. Brooks Bouson, in his harsher assessment, identifies Gregor as a "narcissistically defective individual suffering from a fragmenting, enfeebled sense of self"[73] whose low self-confidence and emotionally distant home life feed his psychosis. Bouson employs Heinz Kohut's studies of narcissistic personality disorder to argue that Gregor's metamorphosis is a grandiose fantasy that counters his psychic vulnerability. Gregor lacks "a stable cohesive self, subject to what Kohut calls 'disintegration anxiety'—'dread of the loss' of the self."[74] Gregor's transformation, in other words, exists only in his mind, resulting from the psychological instability provoked by familial dysfunction.

These divergent explanations for the metamorphosis expose possible underlying causes, but offer little more than articulate conjecture. Kafka never discusses the etiology of Gregor's transformation, directly mentioning the metamorphosis only once, in the story's first line. This narrative silence indicates that no theory sufficiently explicates the story's opening fantastic occurrence, thereby preserving the metamorphosis's metaphorical ambiguity. No empirical explanation is possible because Gregor's physical transfiguration transcends scientific discourse. *The Metamorphosis* depicts human-insect hybridity as a puzzling response to bureaucratic oppression, private trauma, and familial tension that, finally, is inexplicable.

"Oh, to Be a Blobel," by contrast, identifies unchecked militarism as the cause of George Munster's metamorphosis, as the man himself reveals in an early passage:

> *Dammit,* [George] thought bitterly. *I can't marry; I can't live a genuine human existence, reverting this way to the form the War Office bigshots forced me into back in the war times.* . . .
>
> He had not known then, when he accepted the mission, that it would leave this permanent effect. They had assured him it was "only temporary, for the duration," or some such glib phrase. *Duration my ass,* Munster thought with furious, impotent resentment. *It's been* eleven *years, now.*[75]

The military, acting on behalf of the United Nations, transforms George into Blobel form, then abdicates its responsibility to reverse the process once the war concludes. Earth's global bureaucracy, as well as Dick's narrative, dehumanizes George in literal fashion: He loses his body, his self-respect, and his native identity. "I can't live a genuine human existence," George realizes, stressing an irreversible link between bodily integrity and human subjectivity. George's oscillation between man and Blobel, in a crucial development, also destroys his masculinity. He cannot marry or have a sexual life. His bestial form, therefore, prevents George from living as an authentic human being.

George is not alone in his suffering. Sixty other men who were transformed into Blobel spies also survive the war. As George tells Dr. Jones, "[N]ow there's an organization called Veterans of Unnatural Wars of which fifty are members. I'm a member. We meet twice a month, revert in unison."[76] Little camaraderie results from this shared experience, since altercations between the veterans who meet at the VUW's dilapidated headquarters are common. George remains an outcast hybrid who cannot pursue a normal human life until he meets Vivian, discovering, much to his surprise, that he can marry and have children. These developments occur outside bureaucratic sanction, striking a blow for self-determination that promises George and Vivian some measure of personal autonomy.

Their unnatural status, however, prevents a happy relationship. Six years after George and Vivian marry, Dr. Jones receives a phone call from the UN Legal Department informing him that the custody of the Munsters' four children raises a thorny legal issue now that George and Vivian have decided to divorce. These children, it seems, follow Mendel's genetic laws (one child is a fully Blobel girl, one is a hybrid boy, one is a hybrid girl, and the fourth is a fully Terran girl). The UN expert tells Dr. Jones that "the legal problem arises in that the Blobel Supreme Council claims the pure-blooded Blobel girl as a citizen of Titan and also suggests that one of the two hybrids be donated to the Council's jurisdiction."[77] Bureaucratic regulations, not personal concern for the Munsters' emotional health, predominate. The children become either pure-blooded pets to be coddled or, more objectionably, property to be owned (a hybrid child can be "donated" to Titan rather than offered citizenship). Governmental authority defines the Munster offspring (and, retroactively, the Munster marriage) as alien. George and Vivian's miscegenation distinguishes them from "pure-blooded" couples that presumably fall outside the UN legal department's strict scrutiny. The fact that the United Nations is even aware of the Munsters' marital difficulties suggests an all-consuming bureaucracy that monitors every aspect of its constituents' lives. Dick needs no explicit narrative comment to underscore this point, while the story's disdain for political authorities that marginalize those citizens considered to be abnormal is evident. "Oh, to Be a Blobel!" does not belabor this narrative reality. The story instead focuses on more personal needs and concerns.

These private matters cover the same territory that Kafka mines so effectively in *The Metamorphosis*. Kafka's interest in the effects, rather than the causes, of Gregor's transformation foretells the generic fusion of "Oh, to Be a Blobel!" (Dick's tale, as we shall see, combines realistic family tragedy with SF allegory). *The Metamorphosis* melds domestic melodrama with what Darko Suvin calls "an SF parable [that] uses a mythological bestiary"[78] to complicate the most sophisticated hypotheses about Gregor's transformation. By highlighting physical matters (such as how Gregor's new body challenges mundane activities like arising from bed), Kafka suggests that material conditions matter more than metaphysical explanations for the metamorphosis's origin. Gregor's family, in a shocking turn of events, regards his transformation as an economic disaster: "In the course of the very first day Gregor's father explained the family's financial position and prospects to both his mother and his sister."[79] The refusal to question, or even to mourn, Gregor's disability indicates that he is little more than a meal ticket: "Gregor had earned so much money that he was able to meet the expenses of the whole household and did so. They had simply got used to it, both the family and Gregor; the money was gratefully accepted and gladly given, but there was no special uprush of warm feeling."[80] Gregor becomes the instrument of his family's survival rather than a valued son and brother.

Bouson's assertion that "Gregor does become dehumanized, not because he is at the mercy of a self-destructive economic system but because of his underlying self-disorder and because he exists in a non-empathic milieu"[81] is, therefore, problematic because Gregor's underlying disorder results from the five years he spends in debt slavery to his firm, working long and tedious hours to repay his father's creditors. Bouson correctly notes that Gregor's professional and private circumstances do not emotionally sustain the man, but Gregor's self-destruction is primarily a function of economic anxiety.

Even so, the socioeconomic system that characterizes *The Metamorphosis* remains unclear. Gregor works as a salesman for an unnamed firm in an unnamed city in an unnamed country. The reader never learns exactly what Gregor sells, how much money he earns, or how much debt his family owes (beyond the fact that he must work five or six more years to erase it).[82] Although Gregor's firm seems to participate in a capitalist economy, the firm's relationship to the state's governing authority is ambiguous. The reader, who does not know whether the company is a state-run business or an independent corporation, learns little about the world outside Gregor's bedroom beyond the fact that his family resides in Charlotte Street across from a hospital that Gregor, before his transfiguration, "used to execrate for being all too often before his eyes."[83] Kafka withholds details about the story's social, cultural, and political setting to restrict the reader's perspective to Gregor's limited outlook. Bouson notes that the narrator "serves as an extension of Gregor's consciousness, making Gregor, interestingly enough, the focal point and dominant over the reader's perceptions."[84] This development prevents the reader from fully understanding why Gregor must repay a burdensome debt that is not even his.

The Metamorphosis's bureaucratic absurdities are particularly evident in its first chapter. Upon waking, Gregor obsesses about the consequences of his tardiness. His paranoia is well founded, since the firm's chief clerk visits him to inquire about his absence only ten minutes after the office opens for business. Gregor's reaction to the chief clerk's arrival illustrates the petty concerns that now determine the course of his life:

> What a fate, to be condemned to work for a firm where the smallest omission at once gave rise to the gravest suspicion! Were all employees in a body nothing but scoundrels, was there not among them one single loyal devoted man who, had he wasted only an hour or so of the firm's time in a morning, was so tormented by conscience as to be driven out of his mind and actually incapable of leaving his bed?[85]

This passage, more than any other, identifies Gregor's oppressive working environment as the catalyst for his metamorphosis. Although Gregor thinks he is being driven out of his mind, his physical transformation demonstrates that economic oppression has driven his body into a monstrous new form. The resulting dystopia becomes so bleak that it threatens to erase the emotional distance between reader and protagonist that Ritchie Robertson believes to be the story's saving grace. This distance, in Robertson's words, is the only factor that "keeps [Gregor's] sufferings from being unbearably painful to read."[86] The story's mounting horror results from its stark contrast between the fertile detail of Gregor's personality and the arid abstraction of his society's pernicious bureaucracy. This disparity emphasizes the humanist fear of vast and unfathomable controlling agencies that seek to destroy personal freedom. Knowing so much about Gregor's transformed subjectivity emphasizes the tragedy of his alienation, humiliation, and dehumanization by an impersonal, instrumental, and inescapable bureaucratic system. *The Metamorphosis*, therefore, hybridizes its protagonist's human and animal qualities to trap Gregor, like the insect he comes to resemble, in a web of meaningless tedium that only his death can alleviate.

Walter H. Sokel, therefore, is correct to comment that the bureaucratic nightmare sketched by Kafka in *The Metamorphosis* is one where "the worker is dehumanized wherever his work fails to involve his creative urge and desire."[87] *The Metamorphosis* merges animal allegory with bureaucratic dystopia to produce a depressing hybrid text that offers death as the only remedy for the subjugation of human creativity by soul-crushing utilitarianism. Kafka's bureaucratic bestiary grafts two sovereign genres into one, illuminating his pessimistic vision of individuality's destiny in the emerging superstates of early twentieth-century Europe and America. Gregor Samsa, finally, is an exterminated insect. This vulgar, obscene, yet perfectly formulated metaphor lingers in the mind long after the story concludes, sketching the inevitable fate of a common man—of all common people—in the impersonal, uncaring, and industrialized bureaucracies that characterize the modern and postmodern eras.

My Enemy, My Ally

Kafka's paranoid depiction of industrialized capitalism resonates with Dick's concern in "Oh, to Be a Blobel!" about the personal tragedies that result from pursuing wealth. Dick's story indicts the economic motives of the oppressive government that changes George Munster from a human being into an animalized version of himself. "Oh, to Be a Blobel!" is, in truth, a domestic melodrama that functions equally well as a humanist satire of postmodern capitalism. M. Keith Booker cogently defines postmodernism as "a reflection of the increasing ideological hegemony of capitalism in the [1950s], as the last remnants of agrarian alternatives to capitalism were swept from the American scene once and for all."[88] George reproduces this ideological hegemony by indulging racist and sexist attitudes about Blobels as he pursues get-rich-quick schemes that dismally fail. The first such venture, notably, is an absurd agrarian idea: George attempts to raise Jovian bullfrogs for use in competitive frog racing, only to find that "in the relatively feeble Terran gravity the frogs were capable of enormous leaps, and the basement proved too small for them; they ricocheted from wall to wall like green ping pong balls and soon died."[89] George's personal failure, therefore, has political resonance: George's money-losing scheme causes marital tension with Vivian, much as the Blobels' agrarian pursuits on Mars cause tension with Earth.

George's marital woes and insecure masculinity demonstrate capitalism's deleterious effect upon human identity. George's reversion to Blobel form precludes regular employment, making Vivian the household breadwinner: "His pension comprised an amount only one-fourth that of his wife's salary and he felt it keenly. To augment it, he had searched for a way of earning money at home."[90] His wife's earning power threatens George's masculinity, while the birth of their first child, a fully Blobel girl, reveals his latent racism:

> "How can I consider it my child?" he asked [Vivian]. "It's—an alien life form to me." He was discouraged and even horrified. "Dr. Jones should have foreseen this; maybe it's *your* child—it looks just like you."

Tears filled Vivian's eyes. "You mean that insultingly."

"Damn right I do. We fought you creatures—we used to consider you no better than Portuguese sting-rays."[91]

This misdirected (and unbridled) xenophobia illustrates how much George loathes the alien form that he assumes every day. George's hybridity, the reader now understands, results in social alienation and self-hatred.[92] George's reversion to Blobel form fosters enough professional, personal, and economic impotence to unman him, causing George to reject his wife and child. George later requires Vivian's financial assistance to fund a profit-making scheme to transport luck-generating stones to Earth from Titan. When this venture fails as miserably as the Jovian frog-jumping enterprise, the result is emotional devastation: "*I'm a failure*,' George said to himself."[93]

This loss of secure identity, of course, is not exclusively George's fault. His conflicting desires, drives, and prejudices all stem from governmental intrusion into his life. George's hatred of the Blobels, his conversion into Blobel form, and his meager government pension grind George into a resentful, bitter, and unhappy outcast. Dick's cynical portrayal of George's postwar life excoriates the bureaucratic heartlessness of brazenly animalizing a man who sacrifices his loyalty, his future, and his humanity to the state. "Oh, to Be a Blobel!" suggests that large governments do not wish to improve, but only to exploit, the lives of the citizens under their control. Dick's terrible postmodern future depicts a government that abandons the people who defend and consolidate its power when these individuals no longer serve a useful purpose.

This utilitarian regard for human beings is why Andrew P. Hoberek declares that many of "Dick's critics have, following Fredric Jameson's influential lead, seen him as a precocious theorist of late capitalism."[94] Dick is not a self-conscious theorist in "Oh, to Be a Blobel!" but his take on late capitalism is remarkably subversive for so short a tale. George, in the story's twist ending, becomes a self-described industrial tycoon "making and selling a complex electronic reducing gadget which Vivian had helped him design; it was based in principle on a Blobel device popular on Titan but unknown on Terra."[95]

Financial success, however, cannot salvage the Munster marriage. George at one point wishes that he and Vivian could "find a new society somewhere on a remote moon . . . neither Terran nor Blobel,"[96] but this dream's impossibility reinforces the bitter truth that, without Vivian, George would be nothing more than a lonely, pathetic human-Blobel hybrid. George contemplates suicide, but refrains when Vivian persuades him that "you have so much to offer the children."[97] He then takes the wife of a fellow VUW member as his mistress before reconsidering his hybrid status: "If UN taxes had been reasonable he would by now be a wealthy man . . . brooding on that, George wondered what the tax rate was in Blobel-run lands, on Io, for instance. Maybe he ought to look into it."[98] This comment reveals the extent of George's self-hatred. He seems willing to accept his Blobel heritage out of economic greed, not because he embraces the fundamental equality of all life forms. Blobels become better business for George, making industrial capitalism, not humanist sympathy, the savior of George's professional, personal, and masculine vigor. George, in the story's most ironic development, rejects the Earth government that has abandoned him, moving from suicidal despair over his outcast status to renewed faith (in himself and in Blobel citizenship) with astonishing speed. George's identity, torn between human and alien subjectivities, now favors his extraterrestrial physiology because it may secure him wealth.

The darkly hilarious altercation between George and his mistress Nina's husband underscores George's changing perspective:

> One night at VUW Headquarters he discussed the subject [of relocating to Io] with Reinholt, Nina's husband, who of course was ignorant of the modus vivendi between George and Nina.
>
> "Reinholt," George said with difficulty, as he drank his beer, "I've got big plans. This cradle-to-grave socialism the UN operates . . . it's not for me. It's cramping me. The Munster Magic Magnetic Belt is—" He gestured. "More than Terran civilization can support. You get me?"
>
> Coldly, Reinholt said, "But George, you are a Terran; if you emigrate to Blobel-run territory with your factory you'll be betraying your—"
>
> "Listen," George told him, "I've got one authentic Blobel child, two half-Blobel children, and a fourth on the way. I've got strong *emotional* ties with those people out there on Titan and Io."
>
> "You're a traitor," Reinholt said, and punched him in the mouth. "And not only that," he continued, punching George in the stomach, "you're running around with my wife. I'm going to kill you."
>
> To escape, George reverted to Blobel form; Reinholt's blows passed harmlessly deep into his moist, jelly-like substance. Reinholt then reverted too, and flowed into him murderously, trying to consume and absorb George's nucleus.
>
> Fortunately fellow veterans pried their two bodies apart before any permanent harm was done.[99]

This passage's shifting tone—from cautious revelation to traitorous accusations to murderous rage—may engage serious issues of political honor, integrity, and betrayal, but its lacerating gallows humor adulterates any attempt at solemnity by presenting the image of two giant, squabbling amoebae as a moment of unexpected slapstick comedy.

George's invocation of "cradle-to-grave socialism" also extends the story's socioeconomic satire. His newfound belief in market capitalism results from the Earth government's cruelty in destroying George's humanity, then discarding him after the war concludes. George, therefore, resists his own exploitation by becoming what his government most despises: a Blobel. This development prepares George for a materially wealthier, yet spiritually empty, future that is as bleakly tragic as Gregor Samsa's death.

Dick's narrative coup de grâce comes when George discovers that he must become a full Ionan citizen (meaning he must become fully Blobel) in order to relocate. He does not protest when his attorney, Hank Ramarau, informs him of this requirement: "'Hmmm,' George said. 'This is bad. But we'll overcome it, somehow. Listen, Hank, I've got an appointment with Eddy Fullbright, my medical coordinator; I'll talk to you after, okay?' He rang off and then sat scowling and rubbing his jaw. *Well*, he decided, *if it has to be it has to be. Facts are facts, and we can't let them stand in our way.*"[100] George voluntarily ends his human existence, relocates to Io, and sets himself on the path to enormous wealth. He has overcome all the obstacles before him, triumphing over the Earth bureaucracy that has ruined his life to achieve extraordinary success.

This denouement is heartbreakingly ironic because George must renounce Vivian and his children to become a rich man. The breezy pace and tone of the story's final half sees George waver in his family commitments. After the fight with Reinholt, a shaken George pleads with Vivian to emigrate to Io with him: "'I love you,' [George said]. 'You and the children—plus the belt business, naturally—are my complete life.'"[101] Yet a few weeks later, when Dr. Jones calls George to try to save the Munster marriage, George brusquely dismisses the idea:

> "Bah," George said contemptuously. "That woman? Never. Listen, Doctor, I have to ring off; we're in the process of finalizing on some basic business strategy, here at Munster, Incorporated."
> "Mr. Munster," Dr. Jones asked, "is there another woman?"
> "There's another Blobel," George said, "if that's what you mean." And he hung up the phone. *Two Blobels are better than none*, he said to himself.[102]

George has transformed his body, his perspective, and his beliefs to accept Blobel physiology, culture, and economic policy. The Blobel bureaucracy, by only allowing full Blobels to become citizens, essentializes its residents even more than Earth does. George reproduces this prejudice by refusing to call his Blobel mistress a woman. "Two Blobels are better than none" is a witty reversal of George's disgust at Blobel physiology, raising the story's cynical irony to ruthless mockery. Only George's desire for wealth makes his change of heart possible, meaning that imperialistic capitalism, which provoked war with the Blobels, becomes George's personal salvation.

"Oh, to Be a Blobel!" is not satisfied with even this perverted conclusion. Vivian has Blobel doctors stabilize her human form so that George will accept her. As she tells Dr. Jones, "[I]t's because I love George so much, even more than I love my own people or my planet. . . . I've renounced my natural form in order to keep my marriage with George."[103] He, however, has already stabilized his Blobel form before emigrating to Io. George, in fact, feels joy when the groundbreaking ceremony for Munster, Incorporated's new Ionan headquarters (and, significantly, "Oh, to Be a Blobel!") ends:

> "This is a proud day in my life," George Munster informed them, and began to ooze by degrees back to his car, where his chauffeur waited to drive him to his permanent hotel room at Io City.
>
> Someday he would own the hotel. He was putting the profits from his business in local real estate; it was the patriotic—and profitable—thing to do, other Ionans, other Blobels, had told him.
>
> "I'm finally a successful man," George Munster thought-radiated to all close enough to pick up his emanations.
>
> Amid frenzied cheers he oozed up the ramp and into his Titan-made car.[104]

This wicked conclusion punctures the humanist themes invoked by Dick's story: (1) war's futility, (2) humanity's goodness, (3) love's power to dispel xenophobia, and (4) capitalism's compatibility with meaningful family life. George, in other words, must sacrifice his humanity to become a successful man. The story's humor, therefore, could not be more desolate. The only way for George to defeat Terran bureaucracy is to accept permanent exile from his homeland by becoming a hated alien Other.

George therefore embraces his enemy's equally xenophobic culture. "Oh, to Be a Blobel!" extrapolates industrial capitalism's global reach into an interplanetary force that consumes human identity along with natural resources. Dick's statement against war is no clichéd leftist attack on militarism, but rather a mature SF parable about the political, economic, and cultural imperialism that reinforces aggressive militarism. His story demonstrates how bureaucracies become bestial: They constrain, oppress, and finally destroy human subjectivity. "Oh, to Be a Blobel!" follows George Munster to his death: not the literal death of Gregor Samsa, but a more pernicious end in which George murders his own humanity without realizing this act's terrible cost.

Conclusion

The bureaucratic bestiaries of Kafka's *The Metamorphosis* and Dick's "Oh, to Be a Blobel!" pessimistically explore humanism's failure to offer solace in the face of postmodern doubt, just as the animal allegories of Kafka's "Investigations of a Dog" and Dick's "Roog" recognize humanism's incapacity to resolve the paradoxes of modern life. Kafka and Dick remain apprehensive about the survival of political, intellectual, and emotional freedom in the economically oppressive states birthed by late nineteenth-century Europe and America. Neither man trusts bureaucracy, nor does either promote the social, technological, and cultural "progress" so often trumpeted as the twentieth century's undisputed contribution to human civilization. These anxieties result in unique narrative forms—animal allegories and bureaucratic bestiaries—that demolish humanist platitudes about social advancement.

One factor, therefore, unites Kafka's distinguished fiction with Dick's subversive writing: Each author questions, unhinges, and dismantles the humanist certainties of twentieth-century European and American life. Even so, Kafka and Dick are not antihumanist thinkers. The territory that they chart is ambiguous, ambivalent, even paradoxical. The reader may not expect humor from such unsettling fiction, but Kafka and Dick, by injecting soul-sustaining black comedy into their work, acknowledge the difficulties humanism faces when political, economic, and technological resources reduce human beings to commodities.

Both men understand that humanism, although irrelevant to the twentieth century's gargantuan bureaucracies, has never been more necessary. Kafka and Dick lampoon the bureaucratic excesses that typify the modern and postmodern eras, but they never dismiss as insignificant the human or animal characters that struggle to exist as free, independent, and autonomous agents. Kafka's and Dick's profound compassion, as welcome as it is unexpected, marks them as conflicted humanist writers. They cannot, in the end, dismiss humanism, no matter how inadequately it responds to the vicissitudes, the savageries, and the absurdities of twentieth-century life. Humanism, for Kafka and for Dick, is an unsustainable ideology, an imperfect basis for personal salvation, and, finally, the only hope.

Each author's animal allegories and bureaucratic bestiaries create characters that embody these humanist paradoxes. Kafka and Dick depict the fractured lives and petty tyrannies that result from the development of heartless postmodern bureaucracies. Neither man creates a humanist utopia or a comfortable space for his characters to spend their uncertain days. Readers are left with the suspicion that, for Kafka and for Dick, life comprises little more than conflict, sorrow, and pain. Such is the destiny of humanism's (perhaps naive) celebration of the individual's significance to the modern and postmodern eras. Humanistic verities surround Kafka's and Dick's readers no less than their characters. Freedom, autonomy, and self-determination hang in the air all around Gregor Samsa, George Munster, Boris the dog, the unnamed narrator of "Investigations of a Dog," and, finally, we readers. These values are always present. They insist on making themselves known. But they simply are not for us.

The fate of humanism, in the fiction of Franz Kafka and Philip K. Dick, is therefore unenviable. Humanism becomes untenable, unbelievable, always just out of reach. It also remains crucial to preserving the humanity of Kafka's and Dick's characters, even when those characters are not human. This contradiction is not easy to comprehend or to resolve, but it animates the animal allegories and bureaucratic bestiaries that Kafka and Dick skillfully narrate. Both authors, with honesty, humor, and empathy, evoke postmodernism's fearful anxieties about human freedom, identity, and integrity. This accomplishment, more than any other, explains why each man's fiction has remained valuable long after his death.

Notes

1. George Steiner, introduction to *The Trial: The Definitive Edition*, by Franz Kafka, trans. Willa and Edwin Muir with E.M. Butler (1925; New York: Schocken, 1984), vii.

2. Philip K. Dick, *The Selected Letters of Philip K. Dick, Volume 2: 1972–1973* (Novato: Underwood-Miller, 1993), 126. The letter is addressed to Göran Bengston.

3. Gregg Rickman, *To the High Castle: Philip K. Dick: A Life 1928–1962* (Long Beach, CA: Fragments West/Valentine, 1989), 210.

4. Rickman, *To the High Castle*, 210.

5. Rickman, *To the High Castle*, 209.

6. Rickman, *To the High Castle*, 209.

7. Walter Benjamin, *Illuminations*, ed. Hannah Arendt, trans. Harry Zohn (1955; New York: Schocken, 1968), 122.

8. Darko Suvin, *Metamorphoses of Science Fiction: On the Poetics and History of a Literary Genre* (New Haven, CT: Yale University Press, 1979), 4–8.

9. The exact date of "Roog's" composition is a matter of minor disagreement. In his 1968 "Self Portrait" (published in *The Shifting Realities of Philip K. Dick: Selected*

Literary and Philosophical Writings, ed. Lawrence Sutin [New York: Vintage-Random, 1995]), Dick states that "[i]n October of 1951, when I was twenty-one years old, I sold my first story: a tiny fantasy to *F&SF*, the magazine that Tony Boucher edited" (14). Gregg Rickman, however, says in *To the High Castle* that the story might have been written in November 1951 (based mostly on a letter that Dick wrote on November 8, 1951, that thanks *F&SF* for accepting the story). Since Boucher required several drafts of "Roog" before publishing it, and Dick did not become a client of the Scott Meredith Literary Agency until spring 1952, precise records are unavailable. Boucher printed the story in *F&SF*'s February 1953 issue, so it is likely that, after Dick wrote the initial draft in October 1951, Boucher quickly accepted "Roog." Then a long process of revision began. Whatever the exact sequence of events, "Roog," Dick's first professional sale, was a major accomplishment for the young author.

10. Dick, *The Shifting Realities of Philip K. Dick*, 14.

11. Philip K. Dick, *The Collected Stories of Philip K. Dick, Volume One: The Short, Happy Life of the Brown Oxford* (New York: Citadel-Kensington, 1987), 14.

12. Istvan Csicsery-Ronay Jr., "Kafka and Science Fiction," *Newsletter of the Kafka Society of America* 7, no. 1 (1983): 5.

13. Benjamin, *Illuminations*, 122.

14. Franz Kafka, *The Complete Stories*, ed. Nahum N. Glatzer (New York: Schocken, 1971), 278. "Investigations of a Dog" was translated by Willa and Edwin Muir.

15. Kafka, *Complete Stories*, 279.

16. Kafka, *Complete Stories*, 279.

17. Kafka, *Complete Stories*, 286.

18. Kafka, *Complete Stories*, 304.

19. Kafka, *Complete Stories*, 287.

20. Stanley Corngold's "Allotria and Excreta in 'In the Penal Colony,'" *Modernism/Modernity* 8.2 (2001): 281–93, offers an intriguing analysis of the effects of bodily waste upon the symbolic, semiotic, and allegoric narrative strata of "In the Penal Colony." Corngold, in one of the article's most important passages, declares that the "excremental speaks for itself—or does it? In this story—and in the history of its versions—the process of excretion functions as a species of speech . . . uncannily: it is the body's mute howl of pain, its resistance to being evacuated of its substance" (285). Although "Investigations of a Dog" does not feature the mute howl of bodily pain that "In the Penal Colony's" apparatus provokes in its victims, "Investigations," by aligning progress with the bodily processes of consumption and excretion, becomes a different species of speech altogether. Speech, in "Investigations," is voluble, extensive, and comical. Kafka employs excretion metaphorically to make a vulgar point: belief in progress is tantamount to a body expelling feces, removing almost all significance from it.

21. Csicsery-Ronay, "Kafka and Science Fiction," 5.

22. Csicsery-Ronay, "Kafka and Science Fiction," 8.

23. Dick, *Collected Stories, Volume One*, 13.

24. See Paul Fussell's *The Great War and Modern Memory* (Oxford: Oxford University Press, 1975) for a thorough examination of how the technological advances of World War I were culturally conceived. Fussell not only notes that what "we can call gross dichotomizing is a persisting imaginative habit of modern times, traceable, it would seem, to the actualities of the Great War" (75), but also identifies paranoid melodrama as "a primary mode of modern writing" (76). Although "Investigations of a Dog" is not a melodrama of domestic tension, the narrator's continual dichotomizing—he divorces himself from society to comment upon dogdom's nature—is a melodramatic parody of the monographs, prevalent at the time of the story's composition, that purported to analyze entire societies (Oswald Spengler's *Decline of the West*, ed. Helmut Werner, trans. Charles F. Atkinson [1918–1923; Oxford: Oxford University Press, 1991] may be the most famous such publication). The narrator's concern with his own identity's integrity approaches paranoia when he questions the opinions of other dogs, the suitability of his own choices, and the error of his ways. Based on Fussell's criteria, "Investigations of a Dog" is an exemplary modern text, even though war is not its subject.

For more information about how World War I affected European culture, see Vera Brittain's *Testament of Youth: An Autobiographical Study of the Years 1900–1925* (New York: Macmillan, 1933) and *Testament of Experience: An Autobiographical Story of the Years 1925–1950* (New York: Macmillan, 1957); Robert Graves's *Goodbye to All That* (1929; London: Folio Society, 1981); Liddell Hart's *The History of the First World War, 1914–1918* (Boston: Little, Brown, 1935); and Oliver Lyttelton Chandos's *From Peace to War: A Study in Contrast, 1857–1918* (London: Bodley Head, 1968).

25. Kafka, *Complete Stories*, 287.

26. Dick, *Collected Stories, Volume One*, 13–14.

27. M. Keith Booker, *Monsters, Mushroom Clouds, and the Cold War: American Science Fiction and the Roots of Postmodernism, 1946–1964*, Contributions to the Study of Science Fiction and Fantasy, no. 95 (Westport, CT: Greenwood, 2001), 6.

28. Dick, *Collected Stories, Volume One*, 14.

29. Andrew Gibson, *Towards a Postmodern Theory of Narrative* (Edinburgh: Edinburgh University Press, 1996), 12. Gibson specifically discusses what he calls interactive fiction (IF) when he comments upon the genre's postmodern implications. For Gibson, IF includes "participant" novels, films, and computer games: "IF allows the reader a certain freedom of movement within the story. But it does so in producing narrative as a system of forking paths or what [David] Graves calls 'decision-trees.' There are multiple sequences of events in IF which the participant may or may not elect to pursue" (11). "Choose your own adventure" books, marketed almost exclusively to children, may be the most obvious literary example of IF. Gibson then constructs a new theory of postmodern narrative that criticizes classical narratology's geometrical/geographical references to narrative spaces, spheres, and areas.

30. Kafka, *Complete Stories*, 299.

31. Kafka, *Complete Stories*, 288.

32. Matthew Olsham, "Franz Kafka: The Unsinging Singer," in *Modern Jewish Mythologies*, ed. Glenda Abramson (Cincinnati: Hebrew Union College Press, 2000), 180.

33. Olsham, "Franz Kafka," 180.

34. Kafka, *Complete Stories*, 291.

35. Kafka, *Complete Stories*, 293.

36. Kafka, *Complete Stories*, 297.

37. Kafka, *Complete Stories*, 308.

38. Dick, *Collected Stories, Volume One*, 14–15. The emphasis is Dick's.

39. Dick, *Collected Stories, Volume One*, 15.

40. Booker, *Monsters*, 126.

41. Dick, *Collected Stories, Volume One*, 16–17.

42. A more abstruse interpretation of "Roog" is possible. Dick elliptically engages the "aliens are already among us" plot that M. Keith Booker finds fundamental to American science fiction's response to the growing anti-Communist movement of the 1940s and 1950s. This political and social backlash culminated in two related events: the House Un-American Activities Committee (HUAC) investigations of Communist infiltration into the film industry and, even more famously, Senator Joseph McCarthy's manipulation of the Senate Committee on Government Operations to initiate a well-known campaign against suspected Communist influence in politics, literature, and education. Dick was a politically sensitive writer whose short stories, especially during the 1950s, reflect many of America's prevalent concerns about the Cold War (see "Impostor"), the Red Scare ("Second Variety"), and the atomic bomb ("The Defenders").

"Roog" satirizes the anti-Communist sentiment that, by the time of the story's composition, had grown into fervent hysteria. HUAC, as John Belton recounts in *American Cinema/American Culture* (New York: McGraw-Hill, 1994), had begun its first hearings about a "Red menace" in Hollywood by 1947. A group of witnesses that became collectively known as the Hollywood Ten refused to identify any potential (or actual) Communist sympathizers. The Ten, originally consisting of eleven "unfriendly witnesses," lost one member when modernist German playwright Bertolt Brecht fled the United States the day after testifying that he had never been a member of the Communist Party. Further hearings led to the now-famous Hollywood Blacklist, in which uncooperative HUAC witnesses were refused work by the major movie studios. McCarthy's crusade against all forms of Communism, beginning in February 1950, became a witch-hunt of nearly unparalleled proportions in the history of American government, generating a widespread fear of invasion by unknown (and unknowable) Communist agents (Belton 233–56).

Dick lampoons this hysteria by assigning it to a canine character. Boris suspects the Roogs of nefarious dealings, while their comments about "the Guardians" and "the first trial" only exacerbate his paranoia. Boris's uncertainty about the Roogs' true identity evokes the intangible fear that Communism provoked in the lives of 1950s Americans. Boris's fright, however, becomes wickedly funny when the reader recalls the implicit absurdity of narrating this story from a dog's viewpoint. Dick compares the hysterical political foment of the early 1950s to a dog's overzealous concerns about Roogs stealing garbage. Animalizing the fear of unseen infiltration not only distances the reader from this possibility, but also makes it ridiculous. Boris becomes a metaphor for the small-minded, melodramatic, and thoughtless paranoia that allowed McCarthyism to flourish until the Senate censured McCarthy in December 1954 (Belton 242–43).

Such distancing is a key component of David Seed's analysis of American science fiction's narrative discourse about the Cold War. Declaring that "the Cold War was a metaphor," Seed writes in his well-considered book *American Science Fiction and the Cold War* (Edinburgh: Edinburgh University Press, 1999) "that the US perception of the Cold War was structured around key metaphors, like the analogy between the Soviet Union and 'dangerous predators.' Such metaphors carried their own narrative with them—here primarily of attack—which postwar science fiction repeatedly actualised" (1). In "Roog," the dangerous predators are trash men whose physical abnormalities—thin white bodies and wobbly legs—suggest foreign aggression, untrustworthiness, and deformity. By creating such unusual characters, Dick accomplishes one of science fiction's greatest narrative potentials: estrangement. As Seed notes, "Being less tied to prescriptive conventions of representation than realism, science fiction can defamiliarise metaphors of the times by rendering them as concrete metonyms. . . . The fiction uses narrative to interrogate the key metaphors within Cold War discourse" (2).

This defamiliarization also allows "Roog" to become a Red Scare satire that privileges Boris's viewpoint. The story interrogates the metaphors of paranoia and infiltration common to Cold War discourse, but defers final judgment about these metaphors' legitimacy. "Roog's" political subtext, therefore, is just that: a subtext that acknowledges the anti-Communist anxieties of its era, but never emerges into a fully rounded discourse.

Belton's chapter on the Cold War is an excellent primer for investigating this prolonged conflict's influence on American culture, especially as it affected the film industry of the 1950s. Other useful texts in this regard are Booker's *Monsters, Mushroom Clouds, and the Cold War*; Larry Ceplair and Steven Englund's *The Inquisition in Hollywood: Politics in the Film Community, 1930–1960* (Berkeley and Los Angeles: University of California Press, 1983); John Lewis Gaddis's *The United States and the Origins of the Cold War, 1941–1947*, Contemporary American History Series (New York: Columbia University Press, 1972); David Halberstam's *The Fifties* (New York: Fawcett, 1994); Lynn Hinds and Theodore Windt's *The Cold War as Rhetoric: The Beginnings, 1945–1950*, Praeger Series in Political Communication (New York: Praeger, 1991); Mary Kaldor's *The Imaginary War: Understanding the East-West Conflict* (Oxford: Basil Blackwell, 1990); and David Rees's *The Age of Containment: The Cold War 1945–1965* (London: Macmillan, 1967).

43. Umberto Eco et al., *Interpretation and Overinterpretation*, ed. Stefan Collini (Cambridge: Cambridge University Press, 1992), 49.

44. Philip K Dick, interview by Mike Hodel, *Hour 25*, KPFK, North Hollywood, June 26, 1976. A transcript of this interview, edited by Frank C. Bertrand, can be found at http://www.philipkdickfans.com/frank/hour25.htm. It includes a link to an audio recording of Dick's full interview.

45. Rickman, *To the High Castle*, 253.

46. Benjamin, *Illuminations*, 122.

47. Benjamin, *Illuminations*, 116.

48. Steiner, introduction to Kafka's *Complete Stories*, vii.

49. Kafka, *Complete Stories*, 89.

50. Kafka, *Complete Stories*, 112.

51. Philip K. Dick, *The Collected Stories of Philip K. Dick, Volume Four: The Minority Report* (1987; New York: Citadel-Carol, 1991), 359.

52. Dick, *Collected Stories, Volume Four*, 360.

53. Dick, *Collected Stories, Volume Four*, 361.

54. Dick, *Collected Stories, Volume Four*, 361.

55. A common misconception about "Oh, to Be a Blobel!" is that Dick chose George's surname as an intertextual reference to CBS's 1964–1966 sitcom *The Munsters*. This television series relentlessly parodied horror-film plots, characters, and themes, along with suburban American life, by placing a ghoulish family headed by Herman Munster (Fred Gwynne) in an otherwise bright, even utopian, small-town neighborhood. Gwynne's character is clearly inspired by Boris Karloff's portrayal of Frankenstein's creature in three Universal films of the 1930s and 1940s, while Munster's wife, son, and father-in-law are vampires. The series premiered on September 24, 1964, but "Oh, to Be a Blobel!" first appeared in the February 1964 edition of *Galaxy*. Dick's story manuscript, moreover, was received by the Scott Meredith Literary Agency on May 6, 1963, predating *The Munsters's* arrival on television by nearly eighteen months. Dick's choice of the surname "Munster," therefore, seems only to be a coincidence.

56. Kafka, *Complete Stories*, 92.

57. See John Updike's forward to Glatzer's edition of Kafka's *Complete Stories* and Max Brod's biography, *Franz Kafka*, trans. G. Humphreys Roberts and Richard Winston, 2nd ed. (New York: Schocken, 1960), for more information about how Kafka's laughter frequently interrupted his own readings.

58. Kafka, *Complete Stories*, 96.

59. Stanley Corngold, "Kafka's Other Metamorphosis," *Kafka and the Contemporary Critical Performance: Centenary Readings*, ed. Alan Udoff (Bloomington: Indiana University Press, 1987), 45. The emphasis is Corngold's.

60. Kafka, *Complete Stories*, 90.

61. Roy Pascal, *Kafka's Narrators: A Study of His Stories and Sketches*, Anglica Germanica Series, no. 2 (Cambridge: Cambridge University Press, 1982), 25. Pascal helpfully analyzes how Kafka adopts different narrative stances to create character intimacy. Pascal's cogent discussion of *style indirect libre* nicely explores how this narrative style affects both *The Metamorphosis* and "The Judgment."

62. Dick, *Collected Stories, Volume Four*, 359–60.

63. Parallels to American military involvement in Vietnam, especially the invasion of agrarian natives by a technically advanced (and militaristic) foreign power, are difficult to ignore. The extreme physical disparity between humans and Blobels can be read as a physiological metaphor for the ideological differences between the United States' commitment to democratic individuality and Vietnam's official policy of Communist collectivism. George Munster's comment that the Blobels' pliable physiology causes them "to fuse together and unfuse confusingly" (Dick, *Collected Stories, Volume Four* 360) strengthens the story's Cold War discourse. George implies that no real differences exist among the unicellular Blobels, just as 1950s and 1960s Americans often conceptualized Communists as people whose individual personalities were secondary to the unitary collectivism of the state. Communism, at least in American minds, threatened human identity, individuality, and freedom.

Dick himself disavows specifically referring to Vietnam while writing "Oh, to Be a Blobel!": "I wasn't thinking of the Viet Nam War [*sic*] but war in general; in particular, how a war forces you to become like your enemy. Hitler had once said that the true victory of the Nazis would be to force its enemies, the United States in particular, to become like the Third Reich—i.e. a totalitarian society—in order to win" (*Collected Stories, Volume Four* 379). Even so, "Oh, to Be a Blobel's" fictional rendering of military conflict's ecological costs so resembles American, European, and Asian demonstrations against the war's destruction of the Vietnamese countryside that Dick's reader cannot mistake the immediate context of his 1964 short story.

64. Dick, *Collected Stories, Volume Four*, 361.

65. Dick, *Collected Stories, Volume Four*, 364.

66. Dick, *Collected Stories, Volume Four*, 364.

67. This philosophy, no matter how laudable, was naive even in 1964, when President Lyndon B. Johnson's escalation of the Vietnam War demonstrated that simple expressions of goodwill could not end America's military presence in Southeast Asia. Dick's political pessimism about Vietnam becomes evident in his 1979 headnote to "Oh, to Be a Blobel!": "As I watched the American military-industrial complex grow after World War Two I kept remembering Hitler's analysis [about turning America into a totalitarian state], and I kept thinking how right the son of a bitch was" (*Collected Stories, Volume Four* 379). Dick's gloomy view of his own country's militaristic tendencies prevents him from happily concluding "Oh, to Be a Blobel!"

68. Kafka, *Complete Stories*, 135.

69. Kafka, *Complete Stories*, 139.

70. Walter H. Sokel, "From Marx to Myth: The Structure and Function of Self-Alienation in Kafka's *Metamorphosis*," *Literary Review* 26, no. 4 (1983): 485.

71. Michael P. Ryan, "Samsa and *Samsara*: Suffering, Death, and Rebirth in 'The Metamorphosis,'" *German Quarterly* 72, no. 2 (1999): 140. The emphasis is Ryan's.

72. Ryan, "Samsa and *Samsara*," 138.

73. J. Brooks Bouson, "The Repressed Grandiosity of Gregor Samsa: A Kohutian Reading of Kafka's *Metamorphosis*," in *Narcissism and the Text: Studies in Literature and*

the Psychology of Self, ed. Lynne Layton and Barbara Ann Schapiro (New York: New York University Press, 1986): 192.

74. Bouson, "Repressed Grandiosity of Gregor Samsa," 193.

75. Dick, *Collected Stories, Volume Four*, 361. The emphasis is Dick's.

76. Dick, *Collected Stories, Volume Four*, 362.

77. Dick, *Collected Stories, Volume Four*, 365.

78. Suvin, *Metamorphoses of Science Fiction*, 26.

79. Kafka, *Complete Stories*, 110.

80. Kafka, *Complete Stories*, 110–11.

81. Bouson, "Repressed Grandiosity of Gregor Samsa," 193.

82. Kafka, *Complete Stories*, 90.

83. Kafka, *Complete Stories*, 112.

84. Bouson, "Repressed Grandiosity of Gregor Samsa," 196. Or, as Ritchie Robertson says in *Kafka: Judaism, Politics and Literature* (Oxford: Clarendon, 1985), "By confining the reader to the narrative perspective of the protagonist, Kafka obliges him to share the latter's development and induces a similar sense of confinement" (76).

85. Kafka, *Complete Stories*, 94–95.

86. Robertson, *Kafka: Judaism, Politics and Literature*, 76.

87. Sokel, "From Marx to Myth," 486.

88. Booker, *Monsters*, 4.

89. Dick, *Collected Stories, Volume Four*, 366.

90. Dick, *Collected Stories, Volume Four*, 365–366.

91. Dick, *Collected Stories, Volume Four*, 366. The emphasis is Dick's.

92. One of the story's most potent subtexts is its frank acknowledgment of the racist American attitudes toward miscegenation that not only deplored mixed African American/Caucasian couples (and their children), but that also shunned the Amerasian children born to American servicemen romantically linked with Vietnamese women.

93. Dick, *Collected Stories, Volume Four*, 367. The emphasis is Dick's. This aspect of "Oh, to Be a Blobel!" resonates with Dick's biography. He divorced his second wife, Kleo Apostolides, in 1959 so that he could marry Anne Williams Rubenstein, the widow of the recently deceased poet Richard Rubenstein. Dick and Anne had been conducting a secret affair almost since he and Kleo moved to Point Reyes Station, California, in September 1958. Anne, after marrying Dick, started a jewelry-making business in which Dick initially took an active interest. Anne's financial success became a sore point for the author for two reasons: (1) none of Dick's realist novels had sold and (2) his income from publishing SF novels was paltry. Dick, who had always been sensitive about his small income, was also unimpressed by the comparatively ornate lifestyle that his new wife and her first husband had enjoyed (Richard came from a prosperous family, while his large Point Reyes Station home was luxurious compared to Dick's Berkeley house). These factors battered Dick's self-confidence, as is evident to any reader of his 1959–1964 fiction (written while married to Anne). *Confessions of a Crap Artist* (1975), *The Man in the High Castle*

(1962), and *Clans of the Alphane Moon* (1964) all feature male characters demoralized by their ambitious and successful wives, their lowly occupations, or both. The portrait in "Oh, to Be a Blobel" of George and Vivian Munster's rocky relationship reflects Dick's marital anxieties, although strict biographical correlations should be avoided. The similarities between Dick's life and the story's plot, however, suggest the fractious marital tensions that resulted in Dick's contentious divorce from Anne in 1964. Dick's insecure feelings about Anne's more lucrative occupation, it seems clear, questioned his role as the Dick household's primary breadwinner.

94. Andrew P. Hoberek, "The 'Work' of Science Fiction: Philip K. Dick and Occupational Masculinity in the Post–World War II United States," *Modern Fiction Studies* 43, no.2 (1997): 375. Hoberek's fascinating article offers the single best analysis of Dick's problematic understanding of his writing career's masculine legitimacy by focusing on *Time Out of Joint*'s depiction of proper male labor. Hoberek analyzes "the experiential and ideological matrix through which Dick's model of late capitalist/postmodern culture gets channeled" to demonstrate "the limits of totalizing theories of postmodernity" (375). This formulation is a fruitful contribution to frequently staid Marxist evaluations of Dick's economic satire.

95. Dick, *Collected Stories, Volume Four*, 368.

96. Dick, *Collected Stories, Volume Four*, 367.

97. Dick, *Collected Stories, Volume Four*, 369.

98. Dick, *Collected Stories, Volume Four*, 369.

99. Dick, *Collected Stories, Volume Four*, 369–70. The emphasis is Dick's.

100. Dick, *Collected Stories, Volume Four*, 372. The emphasis is Dick's.

101. Dick, *Collected Stories, Volume Four*, 370.

102. Dick, *Collected Stories, Volume Four*, 371. The emphasis is Dick's.

103. Dick, *Collected Stories, Volume Four*, 373.

104. Dick, *Collected Stories, Volume Four*, 373.

CHAPTER TWO

~

Parallel Minds, Alternate Worlds: Borges, Dick, and the Politics of Oppression

Openings

Ursula K. Le Guin, friendly correspondent of Philip K. Dick (and noted SF author in her own right), makes explicit the link between Dick and Jorge Luis Borges in her suggestively titled 1976 *New Republic* article, "Science Fiction as Prophesy."[1] She does so in an effort to raise Dick's reputation from cheap SF novelist to resonant, meaningful author:

> [Dick's] inventive, intricate plots move on so easily and entertainingly that the reader, guided without effort through the maze, may put the book down believing that he's read a clever sci-fi thriller and nothing more. The fact that what Dick is entertaining us about is reality and madness, time and death, sin and salvation—this has escaped most readers and critics. Nobody notices; nobody notices that we have our own homegrown Borges, and have had him for 30 years.[2]

This final sentence has been quoted so often that comparing Dick to the Argentinean fabulist no longer shocks or surprises literary scholars. Le Guin has succeeded in getting Dick noticed as a Borgesian successor (even claiming, "I think I'm the first to bring up Borges"[3] relative to Dick), but her efforts have produced few critical reflections about the two authors' intimate literary connections.[4]

Borges's and Dick's fiction, however, shares intriguing themes, unexpected humor, and disturbing imagery. The fragmentation of reality into a confusing maze of contradictory perspectives is a favorite theme of both authors, bespeaking their fascination with bizarre textual, physical, and psychological deformations. Both writers are politically subversive humanists who criticize, satirize, and parody political oppression. Borges and Dick not only acknowledge the dangers of Nazism, Communism, and fascism, but also fictionally demonstrate how easily democratic nations can become totalitarian states. Resisting political repression, for Borges and for Dick, fails when humanism's misplaced faith in individual autonomy underestimates the power of government, industry, and the military to control the destinies of entire populations. Political engagement for both authors, consequently, is a literary as much as pragmatic arena.

Borges and Dick accomplish this goal by engaging what SF critics commonly call the alternate-world tale. By positing realities similar to, but sufficiently different from, the experiential worlds shared by reader and author, alternate-world tales place their readers in disturbingly foreign, yet oddly familiar, settings. The alternate-world (or parallel-reality) story, therefore, gives its author wide latitude to explore the consensual world that readers presume to know so well. Possibilities for thoughtful analysis, witty satire, wild speculation, extended extrapolation, and unabashed polemic characterize the alternate-world tale's ability to distort quotidian reality, thereby exposing the cultural, economic, and political inequities of daily life that mainstream genres gloss over, sanitize, or ignore. Merging the world of consensual experience with fiction helps reformulate that world's parameters to suit the author's political, social, and satirical intent. By doing so, the alternate-world tale also traffics in postmodern humanism. Borges's artistry in this form, particularly in one of his most important stories, "Tlön, Uqbar, Orbis Tertius" (1940), provides a crucial backdrop for Dick's dystopian alternate worlds of the 1950s, especially the manner by which Dick's 1953 short story "The Defenders," his 1957 novel *Eye in the Sky*, and his 1959 novel *Time Out of Joint* examine the Cold War's totalitarian and antihumanist ideologies. The alternate-world tale, in the hands of Borges and Dick, becomes a potent fictional rendezvous with political oppression that also expresses each author's unique yet complementary brand of postmodern humanism.

Political Realities, Fictional Discriminations

Focusing on Dick's 1950s alternate-world fiction is strategic, for, in this decade, he produced some of the most political writing of any twentieth-century American novelist. This analysis ignores the book generally regarded as one of the best alternate-world novels in the American SF tradition (and, significantly, as one of Dick's most impressive fictions): *The Man in the High Castle* (1962). Dick's Hugo Award–winning novel features a fertile, alternative-historical premise: The Axis Powers have won World War II. Germany and Japan share joint control of the United States, with Germany ruling the eastern half of the country and Japan ruling the Pacific States of America. The Nazis are much less sympathetic occupiers than the Japanese, having legalized slavery, constructed extermination camps, applied the Final Solution to the entire continent of Africa, and developed a vigorous space-exploration program. The novel follows five American characters as they deal with this new political order's social, cultural, and economic complexities. Scholars of Dick's fiction customarily refer to *High Castle* as the author's earliest masterpiece. Kim Stanley Robinson, in a famous critical evaluation, claims that this novel single-handedly improved the entire SF genre:

> It was a tremendous leap in the quality of Dick's novels, comparable to the shift from *The Beautiful and the Damned* to *The Great Gatsby* in Fitzgerald's career—except, in Dick's case, he was writing in a genre in which the great majority of the works were at the level of *The Beautiful and the Damned* (or below it), so that in this case he helped draw up an entire genre with him.[5]

The fact that *The Man in the High Castle* won the 1962 Hugo Award supports Robinson's high praise, although other commentators find the novel's assumption that Japanese totalitarianism is less cruel than German fascism to be politically naive.[6] Even so, the prevailing critical consensus agrees with Robinson's evaluation, finding *High Castle* to be a fascinating, complex, and worthwhile alternate-world/alternative-history tale. The novel's unconventional narration, plotting, and characters contribute to this assessment. Rather than depicting resistance to the Japanese and German occupation of America, *High Castle* traces the moral, ethical, and political difficulties of its five protagonists' daily lives. Dick's fine rendering of how occupation alters traditional American notions of democracy, freedom, and art results in a provocative analysis of American politics that Robinson, John Rieder, and Carl D. Malmgren perceptively explore in their scholarship.[7]

High Castle's political stance, however, fundamentally differs from Dick's 1950s fiction, making it less amenable to comparison with Borges's "Tlön, Uqbar, Orbis Tertius." *High Castle* not only comprehensively illustrates how colonial oppression reformulates the colonized individual's identity, but also forcefully demonstrates how fascism debilitates the colonized individual's ability to resist its restrictive ideology. The novel, in short, depicts how fascist oppression provokes self-doubt, self-loathing, and self-hatred. The fact that all five of *High Castle*'s protagonists imperil themselves to privately struggle against German and Japanese fascism provides hope within the novel's otherwise gloomy political landscape.

Dick's 1950s fiction, by contrast, is more pessimistic. His protagonists, if not forced to endure systems of government that recapitulate the paranoid conservatism of Eisenhower-era America, die as a result of political repression. Dick's 1950s fiction also acknowledges four political realities that *High Castle* elliptically references: the Cold War, the Red Scare, McCarthyism, and the arms race. This fifties fiction, therefore, has been unjustly overlooked as the precursor to the novels that Dick published between 1962 and 1968 (a group that includes *Martian Time-Slip* and *Do Androids Dream of Electric Sheep?*). This oversight results in the mistaken belief that Dick's 1950s short stories are not as politically astute as his later novels or, even worse, that they simply pave the way for those books.

This impression is incorrect because the Cold War tensions Dick examines in "The Defenders," *Eye in the Sky*, and *Time Out of Joint* reproduce the most important economic, cultural, and ideological anxieties of the 1950s. These works, rather than illustrating the turmoil of Vietnam-era America exemplified by Dick's sixties novels, inscribe the Cold War, the Red Scare, McCarthyism, and the arms race into paranoid alternate worlds that collapse their protagonists' reality in the same manner that the false reality depicted in Borges's "Tlön, Uqbar, Orbis Tertius" destroys its narrator's daily experience.

Dick's 1950s fiction, therefore, closely recalls Borges's use of the alternate-world genre. Dick's publishing history also justifies examining his 1950s fiction as a cohesive period of artistic growth. After *Time Out of Joint*'s 1959 release, Dick published only two minor novels in 1960. No new fiction appeared until *The Man in the High Castle* was published in 1962. This two-year gap was mostly the result of Dick's complicated personal life. He moved from Berkeley to Point Reyes Station, California, in 1958 before divorcing his second wife, Kleo Apostolides. Dick married his third wife, Anne Williams Rubinstein, in 1959. Becoming father to Anne's three daughters, plus seeing his first child, Laura, born in 1960, changed Dick's life.

These new responsibilities altered Dick's personal and political attitudes at a crucial juncture in American history. John F. Kennedy's 1960 ascent to the presidency created energetic optimism about the nation's future that, as the decade unfolded, could not sustain itself. In addition, the United States' involvement in Vietnam, which had begun covertly during the Truman and Eisenhower administrations, changed the nation's regard for Communism.

The overwhelming hysteria of the McCarthy years waned as the war's increasing casualties provoked many Americans to question their nation's aggressive opposition to Soviet Communism. Dick was affected by these events, as was his 1960s writing, especially *The Man in the High Castle*. The skepticism of Cold War ideology that characterizes Dick's fifties fiction becomes outright hostility during his sixties novels. The ideological ambivalence of Dick's 1950s writing, therefore, dissipates as the specter of Vietnam begins to haunt his 1960s oeuvre. Borges's "Tlön, Uqbar, Orbis Tertius," therefore, is closer in spirit to Dick's fifties fiction, making a sustained comparison of these authors' writing a productive venture.

Textual Themes, Ideological Inscriptions

Both writers' alternate-world fiction deals with restrictive political ideologies. Neither Borges nor Dick, however, offers an extensive treatise about political oppression (even if the academic tone adopted by "Tlön, Uqbar, Orbis Tertius" suggests otherwise). Borges and Dick instead create fictional worlds beholden to overwhelming political bureaucracies that disrupt the reader's attempts to rationally understand the methods by which authoritarian regimes maintain their dominance. Borges's and Dick's alternate-world fiction keeps its protagonists (and its readers) off balance to illustrate that pervasive ideological consolidation not only destroys an individual's autonomy, but also subverts that individual's subjectivity. Four fundamental themes connect Borges's and Dick's alternate-world fiction:

1. *Politically powerless protagonists/narrators*: These characters find themselves (in Borges's and Dick's fiction of this era, the protagonist is always male) at the mercy of politically repressive bureaucracies that erase individual autonomy and subjectivity. Pervasive antihumanist policies and ideologies destabilize the protagonist's identity as a free, independent, and autonomous individual. Anxiety and doubt proliferate when the protagonist realizes that he cannot trust any person, policy, or institution. The resulting alienation pushes the protagonist to resist the limitations imposed upon him by external forces, but he nearly always fails. Human subjectivity, shackled by institutional authority, cannot transcend ideological limitations to exhibit the freedom, self-determination, and autonomy that characterize humanist practices.

2. *Politically powerful oligarchies*: Borges's and Dick's alternate-world fiction frequently features a cabal (of human beings, extraterrestrials, or robots) that secretly controls the world by generating an illusion of

freedom, democracy, and/or autonomy that prevents its subjects from realizing their own oppression. This ruling elite's active (if invisible) power over its subjects creates enormous institutional bureaucracies that control the most intimate aspects of these subjects' lives: their historical memory, their intellectual development, and their political liberty. The powerless protagonist does not initially recognize the extent, or even the existence, of this cabal's power, which accounts for the humanist disaffection that characterizes Borges's and Dick's alternate-world fiction. Once the protagonist suspects that he does not control his own life, his world radically transforms, his reality breaks down, and his existence becomes unstable.

3. *Reality breakdowns*: The dismantling of consensual reality is the theme that most closely links Borges's and Dick's alternate-world fiction. The protagonist's world begins obeying previously unknown rules, eventually transforming into a foreign locale. This postmodern theme makes Borges's and Dick's alternate-world stories curious amalgamations of humanist and antihumanist principles, especially after the protagonist realizes that his world is an artificial (and largely narrative) construction. This recognition underscores the fluid relationship between reality and fiction. The protagonist, unable to distinguish fact from fantasy, then questions whether his original world (meaning the world that begins the novel or short story) was real, fictional, or an amorphous combination of these two states. Borges's and Dick's alternate-world tales, by suggesting that the protagonist inhabits worlds that infinitely regress (or defer) onto one another, also imply that intellectual, emotional, and philosophical chaos awaits the protagonist, whose awareness of the world's instability fragments his consciousness. The protagonist's life, therefore, comes to resemble that of a fictional character, subject to the control of unknown (and unseen) creators who might change the narrative rules at a moment's notice. These invisible creators often secretly control the protagonist's world (or worlds), testifying to the politically subversive tone of Borges's and Dick's alternate-world stories.

4. *Language mediates the story's political, ideological, and humanist concerns*: Borges and Dick both emphasize their fictional worlds' verbal artifice. Their alternate-world tales are unavoidably linguistic, with language becoming the prism through which all political, ideological, and humanist concerns pass. The manipulation of words and images, therefore, becomes the primary means of political and ideological control in Borges's and Dick's alternate-world fiction. These tales, as a result, have numerous twentieth-century cognates, with McCarthy-

ist propaganda characterizing so much of Dick's 1950s fiction that his protagonists often fail to resist its polarizing tendencies.

These four themes compose "the ideology of inscription" because ideology's textuality is unavoidable in Borges's and Dick's alternate-world fiction. The political realm, in fact, becomes part of ideology's linguistic basis, narrative sophistication, and verbal dexterity. This conceptualization recalls Slavoj Zizek's paradoxical consideration of ideology's basis. Zizek, in one of *The Sublime Object of Ideology*'s most pregnant passages, recognizes that ideology depends upon its invisibility to the subjects whom it rules:

> The social effectivity of the exchange process is a kind of reality which is possible only on condition that the individuals partaking in it are *not* aware of its proper logic; that is, a kind of reality *whose very ontological consistency implies a certain non-knowledge of its participants*—if we come to "know too much," to pierce the true function of social reality, this reality would dissolve itself.[8]

This formulation perfectly describes the slippery ontologies of Borges's and Dick's fictional alternate worlds. It also raises the disquieting possibility that ideology comprises nothing more than false representations utilized by authority figures to dupe their subjects into believing that individual agency, autonomy, and liberty are political realities. This illusion, in turn, covertly controls subjects who believe themselves to be autonomous agents, but who are in reality unwitting drones.

Borges's and Dick's alternate-world fiction is ideological insofar as reality dissolves precisely as Zizek predicts when their protagonists "know too much," or learn that reality is controlled by invisible forces. For Zizek, ideology is not simply an enabling illusion, but a sophisticated means of manipulating reality:

> This is probably the fundamental dimension of "ideology": ideology is not simply a "false consciousness," an illusory representation of reality, it is rather this reality itself which is already to be conceived as "ideological"—"*ideological*" *is a social reality whose very existence implies the non-knowledge of its participants as to its essence*—that is, the social effectivity, the very reproduction of which implies that the individuals "do not know what they are doing." "*Ideological*" *is not the "false consciousness" of a (social) being but this being itself in so far as it is supported by "false consciousness."*[9]

Zizek understands that ideology does not merely oscillate between illusion and reality, but rather cycles between representation and identity, with human subjectivity depending upon concepts of freedom, autonomy, and liberty that people take to be natural states of being. This idea is inherently textual, for language creates, maintains, and consolidates political ideology. As such, Borges's and Dick's alternate worlds are Zizekian political narratives: Their existence as verbal artifacts places ideology within fictional frameworks that can exist only because of the ideologies inscribed within them. The term "ideology of inscription," therefore, alerts us to language's power to create, to revise, and to destroy narrative worlds, with all the political and ideological ramifications that this power implies. Borges and Dick engage inscriptive ideology to generate alternate worlds whose fluid instability cannot be fully (or finally) resolved. This situation's postmodern ambiguities produce the paranoid uncertainty that readers have long associated with Borges and Dick.

The ideology of inscription also allows for the possibility of *reinscription*, in which a parallel-reality story's narrative world may be altered by its own internal elements (including its own characters). This complicated outcome prevents endless debate about which specific ideology (capitalism or Communism, democracy or totalitarianism) is superior because all ideologies depend upon their opposites for existence. The fact that competing political ideologies rely on one another for legitimacy, often promoting different social agendas by employing the same rhetorical strategies, characterizes Borges's and Dick's alternate-world fiction. Both authors understand that ideology can inscribe its worldview on paper, on history, and on human identity through sophisticated yet insidious means. Borges's "Tlön, Uqbar, Orbis Tertius" not only illustrates this narrative possibility better than any other alternate-world story, but also illuminates the ways in which Dick's 1950s fiction operates.

Tertiary Orbits

The imaginary planet that intrudes into, eventually obscures, and finally supplants human reality in "Tlön, Uqbar, Orbis Tertius" is an alternate world of apparently apolitical ideology, where, as the story's narrator (Borges himself) comments, "the nations of this planet are congenitally idealist."[10] This idealism corresponds to George Berkeley's definition of reality as the sum of mental perceptions, not as material objects that exist independently of the mind. Borges introduces this concept with remarkable concision: "Their language and the derivations of their language—religion, letters, metaphysics—all presuppose idealism. The world for them is not a concourse of objects in space;

it is a heterogeneous series of independent acts. It is successive and temporal, not spatial."[11] Borges carefully excludes political concerns from the list of Tlön's linguistic derivations, presumably because politics involves governing the material world and its inhabitants' physical desires. The independent acts that characterize Tlönian existence do not, despite their heterogeneity, admit the untidy complications of exchanging material objects because Tlön's languages have no nouns: in the southern hemisphere's "*Ursprache* . . . there are impersonal verbs, modified by monosyllabic suffixes (or prefixes) with an adverbial value,"[12] while, in the languages of Tlön's northern hemisphere, "the prime unit is not the verb, but the monosyllabic adjective. The noun is formed by an accumulation of adjectives."[13]

These linguistic oddities have far-ranging ramifications for Tlönian culture, whose literature abounds "in ideal objects, which are convoked and dissolved in a moment, according to poetic needs,"[14] a statement that accurately describes much of Borges's oeuvre. "Tlön, Uqbar, Orbis Tertius" exemplifies its author's penchant for idealist bricolage by grafting realism, fantasy, and extrapolation (of Tlön's philosophical and sociological underpinnings) into a story that features actual and imagined characters; that mutates from moment to moment; and that jumps (or at least seems to jump) haphazardly, at the narrator's whim, from one theme, character, and situation to another. The story's unexpected shift from the dramatic narrative of Borges and his (real) friend Bioy Casares's textual detective work as they seek to prove the existence of the mythical nation Uqbar (after finding it mentioned in a pirated copy of the *Encyclopaedia Britannica*) to the implausible discovery of *The First Encyclopedia of Tlön*, the fictional history of a nonexistent place, typifies Borges's continual disruption of mimetic narrative devices. Tlön, it seems, is twice removed from the narrator's reality: "Only one trait is worthy of recollection," Borges says of the *Britannica*'s interpolated entry on Uqbar: "The literature of Uqbar was one of fantasy . . . its epics and legends never referred to reality, but to the two imaginary regions of Mlejnas and Tlön."[15] Since Borges and Casares can locate the Uqbar entry in only one copy of one volume of a single set of the *Britannica* (all other volumes they consult mysteriously omit this information), they presume that Casares's edition contains information about Uqbar that has been forged, not simply pirated. Tlön, therefore, is the imaginary literary creation of an already fictional nation, a dream inside a dream, so to speak, that occupies a tertiary position relative to the primary level of Borges's physical actuality. Uqbar, of course, occupies the secondary level of this increasingly unreal structure, being only one step removed from Borges as he narrates the story's events.

(Un)Real Worlds

This ontological hierarchy, featuring a series of worlds (or realms) that issues from the story's primary reality, is the first important connection between Borges and Dick, whose 1957 novel *Eye in the Sky* includes four alternate worlds through which protagonist Jack Hamilton passes. Jack's 1959 primary reality is a realm of anti-Communist hysteria more nakedly political than the world of intellectual reflection and textual investigation that "Tlön's" narrator inhabits, but both texts posit a principal reality that generates newer, alternative realms. The political implications of such world creation are significant, for each new realm (whether the literary creation of Tlön or the multiple worlds through which Jack moves) remains subordinate to the principal reality from which it springs. This primary world controls its offshoots the way a centralized government rules its outlying states, by providing parameters, boundaries, and constraints within which the newer reality develops.

Both Borges (the narrator of "Tlön") and Jack discover, however, that the multiple worlds confronting them do not form a neatly arranged structure. Each realm eventually competes with its counterparts for ontological primacy. Dick's novel *Eye in the Sky* and short story "The Defenders" employ this ontological competition to interrogate American political mendacity, while Borges's "Tlön, Uqbar, Orbis Tertius" traces how the story's two worlds (Borges's primary reality and Tlön's fictional realm) share an unstable relationship that eventually reverses itself, allowing the fictional Tlön to control Borges's now secondary reality. This control, significantly, is a textual process that sees Tlön inscribe its actuality onto Borges's formerly real word, stressing the power of inscription to unseat the previously stable boundaries between fiction and reality. This theme indicates that Borges, although the protagonist of his own story, holds less narrative and political power than the reader initially presumes.

James E. Irby succinctly summarizes the difficulties confronting any reader who tries to decipher the ontological puzzles that "Tlön, Uqbar, Orbis Tertius" raises: "Already a kind of palimpsest, a many-layered paraphrase of other paraphrases, the tale tends to make any critical résumé and commentary both desperately tautological and inaccurate, for at every turn one is also faced with sly reversals and subversions of the very schemes the work sets forth."[16] Even so, Irby enthusiastically analyzes the story's philosophical, ontological, and spiritual perplexities, attesting to the intellectual richness of Borges's fictional world. Tlön's contradictory nature, as Irby points out, may be its most salient feature. The Tlönian language, for instance, lacks nouns, meaning that the inhabitants of Tlön's northern hemisphere (whose nouns, according to Borges, are little more than accumulations of adjectives) "do not say 'moon,' but rather 'round airy-light on dark' or 'pale-orange-of-the-sky' or any other such combination."[17] Even if the reader excuses the first formulation's use of "light" and "dark" as sufficiently adjectival, the second combination's invocation of "the sky" is certainly a noun. This contradiction is analogous to using a term within its own definition: The act negates its own necessity, thereby calling into question its integrity, its possibility, and its existence.

This typically Borgesian paradox diminishes political concerns by underscoring the story's existence as a literary construction. Gene H. Bell-Villada recognizes this idea as the key component of Borges's love of "the literature of unreality":[18] "For Borges, who is temperamentally averse to nineteenth-century narrative, one of the chief errors of the traditional novel was the misconceived attempt to reproduce reality. Realism, in Borges's view, mistakenly attempts to make the reader 'forget [the novel's] quality of verbal artifice' and tries to be a ready-made mirror instead of a written object."[19] Reproducing reality becomes less important than using fiction to alter reality so that a distorted reflection of the reader's mundane world emerges. Language, particularly Tlön's idealist (or nonmaterialist) language, is the only way to make sense of the perplexing ontological maze that "Tlön, Uqbar, Orbis Tertius" creates. Political considerations seem unimportant, if not impossibly banal, in this unstable fictional matrix. This instability, however, also asserts an ideology that Borges inscribes into the story's fictional portrait of a world whose reality cannot be trusted.

Tlön's linguistic paradox, therefore, is also its enabling existential agent. Borges, as author and narrator, realizes this truth without apparent guile: "The fact that no one believes in the reality of nouns paradoxically causes their number to be unending. The languages of Tlön's northern hemisphere contain all the nouns of the Indo-European languages—and many others as well."[20] The reader must accept, as simple fact, that Tlönian languages exceed their real-world counterparts despite their lack of nouns. Tlön's inscriptive ideology not only supports, but also depends upon paradox: the absence of nouns generates a linguistic fecundity that subordinates the material world to the ideal realm. According to Borges, psychology (rather than science, religion, or government) becomes Tlön's controlling ideology, but not as a method of analyzing the human mind's complicated operation. Instead, psychology becomes a unified arena of ideal awareness: "We already know," Borges says, "that in Tlön the subject of knowledge is one and eternal."[21]

The sheer constructedness of the Tlönian world, therefore, dismisses material concerns as less significant than literary creation or psychological innovation. This tendency toward unreal formulations also makes sociopolitical institutions obsolete because Tlön's ideal mental order is infinitely self-regulating. "Every mental state is irreducible," Borges tells us. "The mere fact of naming it—i.e., of classifying it—implies a falsification."[22]

Normative categories also allow material logic to shackle transcendent ideas: "The metaphysicians of Tlön do not seek for truth or even for verisimilitude, but rather for the astounding. They judge that metaphysics is a branch of fantastic literature. They know that a system is nothing more than the subordination of all aspects of the universe to any one such aspect."[23] The astounding, for Borges as much as for the Tlönian metaphysicians, escapes the constraints of quotidian reality even as it exposes that reality's material grandeur: "It can be deduced that there are no sciences on Tlön, not even reasoning. The paradoxical truth is that they do exist, and in almost uncountable number."[24]

Such paradoxes—unreasonable reason, materialistic idealism, and metaphysical physics—challenge the reader's humanist certainties. The loss of faith in science, reason, and language that characterizes postmodernism also produces ontological angst that gives way to humanist dislocation, disaffection, and fragmentation. The reader can easily forget that Tlön is the fictional creation of the already unreal nation of Uqbar because Borges slips real people and doctrines—Bioy Casares, David Hume, Berkeleian idealism—into a world that diverges from the reader's imperfect everyday experience. Tlön's improved, seductive, and entirely fictional society, with its radically different notions of time uncoupled from space and language unfettered by grammatical rules, liberates the reader's intellect from the strictures, limitations, and reservations of corporeal existence.

Simulated Inscriptions

This "freedom from the real" nonetheless depends upon the reader's knowledge of the material world, or at least the world that Borges sketches in the opening section of "Tlön, Uqbar, Orbis Tertius." The story's ideal Tlönian realm is possible only against the backdrop of a physical world that follows some organizing principle, even if Borges never precisely codifies this principle. Tlön's narrative existence, then, diverges from its author's mundane reality even while depending upon that reality for its existence. This further paradox, in which the ideal and the real meld into a strange amalgam of the old and the new, parallels Old Town, the community created by the American military featured in Dick's 1959 novel *Time Out of Joint* to dupe its protagonist, Ragle Gumm, into believing that he still lives in his fifties-era hometown. This ersatz city is not an intellectual abstraction, but then neither is Tlön once it invades Borges's actual world. Attending to Dick's literary conception of this false city, therefore, can help us comprehend exactly how Tlön functions as a symbol of unreal reality in Borges's story.

Old Town is instructive because its physical actuality—the houses, the objects, and the people who constitute it—are simulacra that support Ragle Gumm's delusional, nostalgic fantasy of a simpler time. Old Town is a retreat from Ragle's "real" 1998 world of civil war, just as Tlön retreats from the untidiness of Borges's physical actuality to purify the real world's ambiguities, anxieties, and ambivalences. Tlön, therefore, becomes a simulacrum that denies the real world's complex social, economic, and ideological tensions to indulge a utopian vision of life. The physical actuality that both Old Town and Tlön achieve compels Dick's and Borges's readers to recognize idealism as a powerful creative force.

The social consequences of this "freedom from the real" in "Tlön, Uqbar, Orbis Tertius" are extreme. Irby denies any sociological concern in Borges's story: "Here is no new social order, but rather a new natural order, a whole new epistemology, a new relationship between mind and phenomena, worked out in myriad consequences of detail."[25] Irby correctly notes that Borges's account of Tlön's composition includes no specific rules for governing the relationships between individuals. Tlön, as we have seen, requires no government in the sense of regulatory agencies that authorize some behaviors while prohibiting others. Political concerns, however, intrude in the form of *hrönir*, duplicated lost objects that become proof that "centuries and centuries of idealism have not failed to influence reality":[26]

> In the most ancient regions of Tlön, the duplication of lost objects is not infrequent. Two persons look for a pencil; the first finds it and says nothing; the second finds a second pencil, no less real, but closer to his expectations. These secondary objects are called *hrönir* and are, though awkward in form, somewhat longer. Until recently, the *hrönir* were the accidental products of distraction and forgetfulness.[27]

The fact that, in Tlön's fictional world, distraction and forgetfulness prove capable of duplicating existing objects implies an organizational structure that controls that world. Borges, however, never identifies this structure because the duplication process eclipses the original objects, much as Borges's narrative creation of Tlön (as the tertiary manifestation of Uqbar, itself the secondary fictional layer of a story that Borges writes from his primary level of authorial reality) occludes this principal stratum from the reader's consciousness.

"Tlön, Uqbar, Orbis Tertius" jumps from Borges and Casares's quest for Uqbar's textual existence to a detailed description of Tlönian culture that supplants Borges's primary reality. The temporal instability of *hrönir* alters Tlön's existence even further: "The methodical fabrication of *hrönir* . . . has performed prodigious services for archaeologists. It has made possible the interrogation and even the modification of the past, which is now no less plastic and docile than the future."[28] Modifiable time implies that human memory can shift so fundamentally that it becomes unrecognizable. This possibility emphasizes the constructed nature of Tlön's narrative existence.

Irby shrewdly notes that the story postulates an entirely new natural order, but overlooks the relationship between *hrönir* and their creators. Even if *hrönir* only exist in Tlön's ideal fiction, Borges implies that, despite Tlön's distaste for materialism, an underlying social organization acknowledges, accommodates, and regulates these objects. Irby recognizes the impact of this simultaneously real and unreal environment: "The idea of proliferation is thus abruptly juxtaposed with that of loss, and, retroactively, the idea of forgetting suggests that the preceding discussion of *hrönir* was, at least in part, an extended metaphor of the process of memory, *as well as of historiography.*"[29] The self-regulating relationships shared by Tlön's people, objects, and ideas, therefore, organize its fictional world according to rules that Borges's reader can understand.

The past, per Irby, becomes a palimpsest that Tlön erases, then reconfigures, into a more perfect world. The story, by fragmenting Borges's, Casares's, and the reader's consensual experience of time and memory, overwrites their reality with a utopian social arrangement whose objects duplicate the historical artifacts of an unreal world. This postmodern development questions the relationship between reality and fiction in the same manner that Hayden White doubts the conventional wisdom that "historical events are supposed to consist of or manifest a congeries of 'real' or 'lived' stories, which have only to be uncovered or extracted from the evidence and displayed before the reader to have their truth recognized immediately and intuitively."[30] Tlön's truth lies in its ability to inscribe a new reality upon what Borges's reader takes to be actual history, further supporting White's suspicion that historical accounts are not objective: "I regard this view of the relation between historical storytelling and historical reality as mistaken or at best misconceived. Stories, like factual statements, are linguistic entities and belong to the order of discourse."[31] So, too, does the historical veracity of the world that Borges, as narrator of "Tlön, Uqbar, Orbis Tertius," presumes to be primary. The fact that the narrator and the reader may revise this primary reality emphasizes the power inscription holds over humanity's ability to excavate the past, which, in White's crucial realization, is a discursive reconstruction rather than an unproblematic telling of historical truth.

Defending the (Un)Real

Dick's fictional manipulations of memory and historiography recall Borges's invocation of these themes. Dick's 1953 short story "The Defenders" posits a world in which robots engineer a perfect society by duping the human population into believing that nuclear war between the United States and the Soviet Union, fought exclusively by machines, rages on the terrestrial surface while humanity occupies protected underground habitats. In truth, the robots (called leadies) have not only ended the conflict, but have also restored the surface to pristine condition. The leadies transmit false television images of nuclear devastation to their subterranean creators, hoping that humanity's terrible confinement will exhaust its aggressive tendencies. The leadies promulgate false history to manipulate human politics; to alter humanity's cultural memory; and to produce a globally peaceful society that avoids militarism, warfare, and misery.

Historiography in "The Defenders," therefore, is an enormous hoax that obscures the quotidian world's sloppy and imperfect human conflicts. The leadies believe that humanity's physical suffering (in dingy, cramped, and unattractive underground living quarters) will expunge the Soviet-American tensions that ignited the war. Transcending national differences, forgetting political conflicts, and surmounting nationalist ideologies are the leadies' primary goals. These automatons hope to change human behavior by offering a dystopian alternative (of meaningless subterranean production and consumption) even more horrific than the reality of nuclear war. This dystopia also simplifies the political complexities that cause the war, for only then will an alternative future of Soviet-American cooperation seem more attractive.

The leadies' decision to deceive the human populace by manipulating mass media underscores the importance of fact and fiction (or of reality and textuality) when developing social utopias. Borges's fictional Tlönian society, as even a cursory reading confirms, is more orderly, more mannered, and more attractive than the real world, with its messy complications. Tlön's highly intellectual character also prefigures the leadies' abstract notion of a globally unified society. The fictionalizing tendencies of cultural memory and historiography, as Borges's and Dick's short stories demonstrate, produce utopias that seem impossible to realize because they can exist only in the future, away from political necessity of regulating human desires. The utopian ideology of peaceful human cooperation, in both "Tlön" and "The Defenders," inscribes itself onto the venality, vice, and corruption of the actual human world. Dystopia and utopia not only become capable of writing one another, but also emphasize the theme of *revision*. Tlön's and the leadies' imagined futures promise to refashion humanity's imperfectly divided world into political paradise, purifying the depressing actuality of human aggressiveness while depending for their existence upon that unkind reality.

Alternate Worlds, Familiar Realities

This collaboration between fact and fiction, between Borges's reality and Tlön's fantasy, makes Borges's most inventive twist in "Tlön, Uqbar, Orbis Tertius" even more politically shrewd. Tlön, the ideal fictional realm invented by Borges's fertile imagination, invades its narrator's reality to link the story more closely with Dick's science fiction. The 1947 postscript to "Tlön, Uqbar, Orbis Tertius" uncovers a letter that explains Tlön's origin: "One night in Lucerne or in London, in the early seventeenth century, the splendid history has its beginning. A secret and benevolent society (amongst whose members were Dalgarno and later George Berkeley) arose to invent a country."[32] The political implications of inventing an imagined nation (Uqbar) remain insignificant as long as that nation stays fictional, but, in typically Borgesian fashion, fiction exceeds its supposedly stable boundaries to protrude into the world of human actuality.

This process occurs only after nineteenth-century American millionaire Ezra Buckley decides to expand this enterprise's scope by inventing an entire planet (Tlön). Buckley does so for blasphemous reasons: "Buckley suggested that a methodical encyclopedia of the imaginary planet be written . . . on one condition: 'The work will make no pact with the impostor Jesus Christ.' Buckley did not believe in God, but he wanted to demonstrate to this nonexistent God that mortal man was capable of conceiving a world."[33] By rejecting belief in a divine creator, Buckley's intellectually audacious project annexes all control of Tlön to human authority. Buckley and the men he employs become oligarchs who function as the demiurgic founders of an entire planet. This metaphor for Borges's own status as the privileged (and intellectually nimble) creator of fictional worlds transforms Borges from the story's controlling agent (as both author and narrator) into a powerless protagonist who can no longer separate reality from fantasy. Previously fictional Tlönian objects begin appearing in the real world, including a compass with Tlönian writing and a cone of unknown metal that mysteriously surfaces in 1942. All forty volumes of *The First Encyclopedia of Tlön* are then discovered in a Memphis, Tennessee, library in 1944 (Memphis, significantly, is Buckley's home city).

This event occasions the story's most drastic ontological shift. The narrator recognizes that "the contact and the habit of Tlön have disintegrated this world."[34] The presence of Tlönian objects erases the more fractious, brutal, and upsetting history of the actual world, which cannot remain the story's primary reality. The narrator laments the postmodern doubt that this eradication evokes: "Already the teaching of [Tlön's] harmonious history (filled with moving episodes) has wiped out the one which governed in my childhood; already a fictitious past occupies in our memories the place of another, a past of which we know nothing with certainty—not even that it is false."[35] The narrator's political insight about this development even repudiates the new world that Tlön creates: "A scattered dynasty of solitary men has changed the face of the world. Their task continues."[36] These final passages not only indicate the danger that fiction poses to human liberty when wielded by a small group of unscrupulous men (or, in the case of Dick's "The Defenders," by a large group of well-intentioned machines), but also weave the themes of powerless protagonist, secret cabal, reality breakdown, and textual primacy into an artful whole. Little obvious totalitarian intent accompanies Buckley's project (providing that we trust the letter's assertion that the secret society creating Uqbar is benevolent, which, like almost everything else in this story, is an ambivalent position), although the narrator reveals in a footnote that "Buckley was a freethinker, a fatalist and a defender of slavery"[37] to foreshadow the enslavement of human history that Tlön finally represents.

Borges does not indict fiction itself, but rather its appropriation by a hidden elite that wishes to regulate human identity's basic constituents: memory, history, and free choice. The narrator may mourn the fact that people willingly yield to Tlön's utopian vision of a better life, but he understands the seductively political basis of their submission: "Ten years ago any symmetry with a semblance of order—dialectical materialism, anti-Semitism, Nazism—was sufficient to entrance the minds of men. How could one do other than submit to Tlön . . . ?"[38] Tlön promises a more secure and stable life, aligning it with the totalitarian ideologies that allowed Hitler and Stalin to flourish. Tlön functions as a political metaphor: Fiction becomes the potentially devastating tool of oppressive ideologies that create alternative worlds whose ideal character hides their destructive tendencies.

Borges, therefore, has not written a message story with a simple moral or a single theme. The tale's unhappy ending, in which Tlön takes control of the narrator's reality, highlights the unreliability of unitary narratives. The story becomes, in Bell-Villada's words, "a parable about the lure of self-contained ideas, the destructive appeal of fabricated selves and symmetries."[39] "Tlön, Uqbar, Orbtis Tertius" refashions its reader's conception of history not only by questioning received historical narratives, but also by distrusting the memories proffered by scholars, artists, and governmental authorities.

The story's elegiac conclusion, with the narrator saying, "I pay no attention to all this [the disintegration of his world in favor of Tlön]"[40] even though it bothers him tremendously, speaks to the conflicting tensions of postmodern life, in which fact and fiction combine so thoroughly that disentangling them becomes an impossible task. "Tlön, Uqbar, Orbis Tertius" not only illustrates the uncomfortable power of fiction to alter human consciousness, but also provokes the thoughtful reader to cast aside mindless faith in historical narratives. This perspective's cynicism not only mistrusts all ideologies, but also demonstrates the story's relevance in a world characterized by governmental improprieties and political cover-ups.

Borges's masterful performance in the alternate-world genre, as exemplified by "Tlön, Uqbar, Orbis Tertius," reveals how intelligently fantastic fiction can integrate political themes into its bizarre fictional premises. Dick wrote numerous alternate-world stories during the 1950s to comment upon the political excesses of his own time, especially the Cold War, the Red Scare, McCarthyism, and nuclear brinkmanship. Dick's novels and short stories of the 1950s may not stylistically resemble Borges's writing, but they repeatedly engage the postmodern themes of "Tlön, Uqbar, Orbis Tertius." Dick, who uses the alternate-world tale to ruthlessly satirize Eisenhower-era America's conformity, emerges as one of the decade's most intelligent political writers.

Eye on America

Dick directly confronts major political fears in his 1950s fiction. His short stories—frequently set in blasted, desolate, radiation-filled environments—are among the most starkly cynical apocalyptic writing produced by a twentieth-century American author. For Dick, the alternate-world/parallel-reality story was a congenial forum for political parody and polemic. Dick's fifties fiction reveals that this decade, despite its reputation for stultifying conservatism, was a period of social, cultural, and political foment, or what David Halberstam calls, in typically understated fashion, "a more interesting and complicated decade than most people imagine."[41]

Dick's political sympathies during the 1950s are best described as antiauthoritarian. He rejected McCarthyism and Stalinism as equally repressive ideologies, although this belief never drove him to become a political activist. Dick's second wife, Kleo Apostolides, who lived with him from 1950 to 1958, once recalled, "To the best of my knowledge he never participated in any political act."[42] Dick's friend Vincent Lusby briefly interested Dick in Henry Wallace's 1948 Progressive Party presidential candidacy, but later commented that Dick "didn't like to be dragged out anywhere—he came because I was going to be there. He didn't do anything really."[43]

Dick's time living in the openly leftist atmosphere of Berkeley, California (when the Communist Party and Marxist sympathizers were visible participants in the local political scene), has enhanced his reputation as a radical thinker, but, contrary to what some later admirers have claimed, Dick was never a street-fighting man or a person who advocated destroying the American government. In 1952, for example, Dick wrote a letter to Governor Earl Warren of California expressing respect for the United States Constitution. Warren, a moderate or liberal Republican depending upon whom was asked ("He's a Democrat and doesn't know it," Harry Truman once quipped about Warren),[44] would not become Chief Justice of the Supreme Court until 1953, where his reputation as a liberal social engineer only took hold after he spearheaded the landmark 1954 *Brown v. the Board of Education of Topeka* desegregation ruling. Warren may have attended college in Berkeley before World War I, but he was regarded as a square, proper, and dignified man—certainly not as a countercultural icon—by his constituents. Dick's admiration of Warren reflects the political moderation of an author, who, in Gregg Rickman's words, "was what he was: pro-American, in the liberal Democratic sense; hostile to the Stalinist left; hostile to McCarthyism as well."[45]

This centrist position, however, should not diminish Dick's support for Berkeley's well-known liberalism, chiefly when it came to resisting Eisenhower-era America's repressive tendencies. Kleo was more politically active than her husband, attending speeches and rallies (of often Marxist character) at Sather Gate on the University of California–Berkeley campus. Her presence at these events caused two FBI agents to visit the Dicks in 1952 or 1953[46] while searching for citizens willing to inform on their neighbors. The agents asked Kleo to identify photographs of people who had attended the rallies and, during a subsequent interview, offered to pay the Dicks' expenses to study at the University of Mexico if they would monitor student activities there; the Dicks refused this financially rewarding opportunity because they could not condone spying on other people.[47] Thus began Dick's strange, tortured relationship with the FBI, whose centralized authority he feared and eventually came to loathe.[48] This distrust strongly influenced Dick's fiction, perhaps most directly in his inventive 1957 alternate-world novel, *Eye in the Sky*.

Dick attributes *Eye in the Sky*'s basic premise—eight characters find their awareness fused together by a proton-beam mishap before inhabiting the psyche of whomever is closest to regaining full consciousness, forcing them to experience another character's private, nightmarish, and often deranged vision as a separate reality—to Frederic Brown's 1949 novel *What Mad Universe*. Dick later claimed that adapting Brown's fundamental ideas became a significant step in his (Dick's) artistic development: "I reapplied [Brown's premise]. Instead of having one fantasy universe I had a series of competing fantasy, or irreal [sic], universes. And there of course my preoccupation with irreality [sic], the fraudulent universe, begins. That's the origin right there."[49] These fraudulent universes may be unreal, but they remain recognizable. The four universes that the novel's characters inhabit before returning to their primary reality are gross distensions of their consensual world that exaggerate certain aspects of *Eye in the Sky*'s 1959 California setting almost to the point of caricature: The first realm belongs to a male religious bigot who allows God to directly punish even minor infractions of moral law; the second realm belongs to a puritanical woman who abolishes all unacceptable objects (including sex organs); the third realm reveals a female paranoiac's nightmarish suspicion that everyone is out to get her, causing a house to transform, in Lovecraftian fashion, into a living creature that attempts to ingest its inhabitants; while the fourth world belongs to a secret Communist sympathizer who imagines inhabitants incessantly spouting Stalinist slogans and continually fighting capitalist insurgents.

Eye in the Sky may be Dick's most direct attack on the anti-Communist hysteria of the 1950s. Although Joseph McCarthy had been censured by the United States Senate in December 1954 (before dying of cirrhosis in 1957), McCarthyism survived much longer than anyone predicted, with many political consequences. Halberstam notes that Harry Truman's surprise 1948 presidential defeat of Thomas Dewey embittered the Republican Party, which had hoped to reclaim the White House after sixteen years of Democratic rule: "The Republicans now faced four more years out of office. The bitterness within the party grew. So much for the high road in American politics [that Dewey had advocated]. The Communist issue would be fair game in the near future. It was the only way they knew how to fight back."[50] Lynn Boyd Hinds and Theodore Otto Windt Jr. agree with this assessment:

> After Truman's ascension to the presidency, two streams came together that would merge into a raging river of hysteria, fear, and retribution. The first stream had as its source the great spy scare of the immediate postwar years. . . . The second stream was political, pure and simple. After fourteen years of

being beaten over the head with the responsibility for the Great Depression, Republicans found an issue to do some head-bashing themselves. The issue was communism. In the [midterm] election of 1946 some Republicans made it a major issue. . . . If Republicans could be charged with not caring about the economic well-being of American citizens, Democrats could be charged with not caring about the political security of American citizens. If Republicans could be accused of leading the country into the Great Depression, Democrats could be accused of leading the country down the road to socialism, or worse, allowing America to be infiltrated with communists.[51]

The 1946 Republican victory in reclaiming both houses of Congress led Truman, in March 1947, to issue Executive Order 9835, officially titled "Prescribing Procedures for the Administration of an Employee Loyalty Program in the Executive Branch of the Government," but known more concisely as Truman's Loyalty Program. With this measure, the president attempted to undercut Republican charges of being soft on Communism by identifying, then dismissing, government employees suspected of disloyalty, a condition defined not only to include traditional acts of sabotage, espionage, treason, and sedition, but also to cover personal relationships nebulously formulated as "membership in, affiliation with or sympathetic association with any foreign or domestic organization, association, movement, group or combination of persons, designated by the Attorney General as totalitarian, fascist, communist, or subversive."[52]

This definition's broad scope legitimated HUAC's investigations into suspected Communist infiltration of Hollywood while giving the appearance of official sanction to McCarthy's later actions as a member of the Senate Committee on Government Relations. Hinds and Windt note that "it would be irresponsible to place the blame for the great fear that was to follow, the fear we now call McCarthyism, solely or even primarily on Truman. The causes of McCarthyism are more complex than that. Republicans and anti–New Deal Democrats had already raised the issue of domestic communism."[53] The first major anti-Communist movement, or Red Scare, in American history appeared as early as 1919, only two years after the Bolshevik Revolution,[54] so Truman's Loyalty Program was not the only cause of the anti-Communist hysteria that swept the nation during the 1950s. Truman's program, however, was also not blameless. The rhetoric employed by HUAC and McCarthy to insinuate Communist influence in American culture, as Hinds and Windt acknowledge, "echoed the rhetoric used by the administration in justifying its foreign policy" of opposing and containing Soviet Communism.[55]

McCarthy, therefore, became a political lightning rod. A demagogue who knew how to channel the nation's latent anxieties about the postwar world into a powerfully viable (and politically divisive) institutional paranoia, McCarthy birthed a political, cultural, and social movement that outlived him by decades. McCarthy's rhetoric of subversion was especially effective at identifying its opponents as misguided, corrupt, and treasonous. McCarthy and his followers preyed upon American fears of the Soviet Union's strengthened position after Germany's defeat, upon the public's distress over the development of atomic weaponry, upon prevalent anxieties about a possible economic downturn (that dredged up painful memories of the Great Depression), and upon new uncertainties about the country's changing social complexion as African Americans, women, and Jews began redefining their traditionally circumscribed roles within the body politic. Halberstam sees the McCarthy era as an ugly, mean-spirited time in America's national life:

> McCarthyism crystallized and politicized the anxieties of a nation living in a dangerous new era. He took people who were at the worst guilty of political naïveté and accused them of treason. He set out to do the unthinkable, and it turned out to be surprisingly thinkable.
>
> The problem with America, he was saying, was domestic subversion, as tolerated and encouraged by the Democratic party. . . . If events in the world were not as we wanted them, then something conspiratorial had happened. . . . His message was simple: the Democrats were soft on Communism. With that, he changed the nature of American politics. Our control of events was limited because sinister forces were at work against us.
>
> Democrats would spend the next thirty years proving that they were not soft on Communism, and that they would not lose a country to the Communists.[56]

The fear of subversion provoked by McCarthyism influenced America's foreign policy, domestic politics, and national consciousness for many years. This new Red Scare was a time of ascending suspicion that not even McCarthy's disgrace and death could demystify.

Eye in the Sky starkly illustrates how political paranoia destroys private lives. Its powerless protagonist (a quintessential example of this character type), Jack Hamilton, is denied security access to California Maintenance Labs, the guided-missile facility where he works as head of missile research, because his wife, Marsha, is classified as a security risk. The charges against Marsha are presented to Jack by Charley McFeyffe, "captain of the security cops who prowled around the missile plant, screening out Russian agents."[57] McFeyffe's name and occupation make him the novel's thinly disguised stand-in for McCarthy, while the pernicious character of McFeyffe's accusations against Marsha demonstrate Dick's command of McCarthyism's irrational language. Marsha, Jack is told, joined the Progressive Party in 1948, signed the Stockholm Peace Proposal, and remains a member of the American Civil Liberties Union, which, McFeyffe gamely tells Jack, can be described as pro-left:

> "What," Hamilton demanded, "does *pro-left* mean?"
>   "It means sympathetic to groups or persons sympathetic with Communism." Laboriously, McFeyffe continued. "On May 8, 1953, Mrs. Hamilton wrote a letter to the *San Francisco Chronicle* protesting the barring of Charlie Chaplin from the United States—a notorious fellow-traveler. She signed the Save the Rosenbergs Appeal: convicted traitors. In 1954 she spoke at the Alameda League of Women Voters in favor of admitting Red China to the UN—a Communist country. In 1955 she joined the Oakland branch of the International Coexistence or Death Organization, with branches in Iron Curtain Countries. And in 1956 she contributed money to the Society for the Advancement of Colored People." He translated the figure. "Forty-eight dollars and fifty-five cents."[58]

This last charge is the most damning, as revealed by McFeyffe's later comment that Marsha has "had plenty of time to make up her mind about Communism. But she still goes to these things; she still turns up when some Commie group organizes to protest a lynching in the South."[59] McFeyffe's wholesale equation of Communism with calls for racial justice, as well as his refusal to acknowledge that Marsha's passion about ending the practice of lynching is so strong that she attends a Communist-sponsored antilynching rally (even without being a member of the Party), illustrates the collapse of even basic logic that McCarthyism/McFeyffism represents in the novel.

The possibility that a person can endorse a political goal—in this case, social justice for African Americans—without endorsing all (or most) of the tenets of a political organization that supports this goal escapes McFeyffe. He also seems not to understand the differences between Stalinism and the American Communist Party, which gained support during the Depression by advocating a redistribution of resources to millions of newly impoverished Americans who found themselves without work or savings. The Party also provided food and clothing to the Depression's most destitute victims to relieve their suffering. During the 1940s, mass media outlets and political leaders repeatedly encouraged Americans to view the Soviet Union as America's ally in defeating Nazism. As John Lewis Gaddis has commented, "[T]hrough a curious kind of illogic the Russians' vigorously successful resistance to Hitler purified them ideologically in the eyes of Americans."[60] McFeyffe, however, has no time for such historical subtleties; he is hunting Communists and, despite flimsy evidence, believes he has found one in Marsha.

Jack recognizes McFeyffe's thinking for what it is: "Guilt by association. She's curious; she's interested. Does her being there prove she *agrees* with what they're saying?"[61] McFeyffe, a friend of Jack's, even claims to dislike assembling evidence against Marsha. He cannot prove Marsha's Communist sympathies, but does not care, for no proof is necessary: "We can't look into her mind—and neither can *you*. All we can judge is what she does: the groups she joins, the petitions she signs, the money she contributes. That's the only evidence we have—we've *got* to go on that."[62] McFeyffe's questionable assumptions, when combined with his refusal to ask Marsha about her actual political beliefs, reveal his capacity for mistrust (McFeyffe suspects that Marsha would simply lie by denying what are to him obvious Communist sympathies) even while foreshadowing the novel's central irony: The proton-beam accident that occurs at the Belmont Bevatron allows Jack, Marsha, and the reader to look into the mind of the novel's only real Communist, Charley McFeyffe.

Even before the mishap, an argument between Jack, Marsha, and McFeyffe underscores McFeyffe's true nature: "As the elevator ascended, Hamilton was treated to the sight of the man's fiery red neck. McFeyffe, too, was upset."[63] The dual symbolism here (of McFeyffe as a Communist and as a race-baiting redneck) is hardly delicate, but Jack does not suspect McFeyffe's Communist sympathies because of the emotional turmoil provoked by McFeyffe's accusations: "His own [Jack's] loyalty was to her, and that was a strange thing to realize. It was not really the loyalty business that bothered him; it was the idea that he and Marsha were cut off from each other, separated by what had happened."[64] Dick identifies McCarthyism's most insidious effect: The alienation evoked by unfounded suspicion tempts Jack to doubt Marsha's loyalty by hinting at her potentially subversive character. Reaffirming Jack's devotion to Marsha has a high price: He must reject Marsha if he wishes to save his job in the defense industry (itself a product of the Cold War) and to preserve his reputation as a patriotic American.

Subverting Reality

Eye in the Sky, therefore, accurately sketches the depressing ugliness of McCarthyist America before breaking into nightmarish unreality. Dick repeats this pattern in *Time Out of Joint*, although Charley McFeyffe's Communist fantasy concludes *Eye in the Sky* on a note of extraordinary paranoia. Jack, the novel's viewpoint character, initially presumes that Marsha's secret political beliefs create this absurdly dangerous world to demonstrate how destructive ideological suspicion can be in even the most intimate relationships.

McFeyffe's alternate world, however, is not a Marxist utopia, but rather a realm of empty political platitudes that destroys human liberty. Dick burlesques the sloganeering associated with political activism in general, and Communism in particular, by transforming words into dangerous physical objects. Jack and Marsha Hamilton encounter an armed militia loyal to Dr. Guy Tillingford, the president of the Electronics Development Agency in Jack's primary reality (this company, significantly, devotes itself to scientific research rather than to military applications), who, in McFeyffe's parallel reality, is a capitalist insurgent. The Hamiltons are shocked by Tillingford's changed character, but even more mystified when they see enormous letters form in the sky, "partially disintegrated slogans of comfort, written shakily across the black emptiness, for their benefit.

We Are Coming.
Hold Out.
Fighters Of Peace.
Arise."[65]

Tillingford, a friend of Jack's father in real life, has become a "bloated, blood-smeared capitalist"[66] in McFeyffe's Communist fantasy, and he suffers an unforgettable fate:

At that moment, one of the fiery slogans in the sky exploded. Bits of flaming wood cascaded down, setting the heaps of rubble on fire. Cursing, beating at his clothing, Tillingford reluctantly retreated; a section of burning rubbish had fallen on him, setting his coat on fire. To his right, his group of company toughs were half-buried under a vast, incandescent outline-portrait of Bulganin that had come loose from the sky and fallen directly on top of them.[67]

Communism's noble sentiments become lethal in Dick's outrageous satire of Stalinism's hollow rhetoric. *Eye in the Sky*'s armed conflict between Communism and capitalism reduces each ideology's proponents to urban guerrilla fighters espousing shallow doctrines that disgust Jack. He then sees the flaming word "Peace" fall from the sky to destroy his house, after which Marsha notices the word "Coexistence" coming loose from its airborne position.[68] The implication that the world is out to get them could not be clearer. The excesses of McFeyffe's Communist fantasy affect Jack as profoundly as the excesses of his anti-Communist primary reality. Dick's reader cannot miss the disturbing similarities between McFeyffe's intemperate Communist domain and the real world's democratic capitalism.

McFeyffe's fantasy in *Eye in the Sky* also offers a fascinating parallel to Tlön in Borges's "Tlön, Uqbar, Orbis Tertius." Tlön's ideal, unreal existence—its status as a textual invention—may infect Borges's world, but Tlön does not displace Borges's primary reality so much as it generates a hyperrealistic simulacrum of that reality: "Some of the incredible aspects of the Eleventh Volume [of the *First Encyclopedia of Tlön*] (for example, the multiplication of the *hrönir*) have been eliminated or attenuated in the Memphis copies; it is reasonable to imagine that these omissions follow the plan of exhibiting a world which is not too incompatible with the real world."[69] Replacing the narrator's reality with Tlön's fantasy produces an exhibit rather than a new world. Tlön's artifice transforms Borges's world into an orderly display that does not disclaim material concerns so much as it demonstrates how an ideal world might function.

Such exhibitionism characterizes the alternate-world genre. *Eye in the Sky*'s many artificial worlds suggest to the careful reader that the novel's opening, supposedly consensual world of anti-Communist suspicion may be as unreal as all the others. By positing McFeyffe's Communist fantasy as an exhibit (or living museum piece) that traps Jack, Marsha, and the other Bevatron victims in its dangerously absurd confines, Dick's novel implies that their primary reality, full of baseless accusations and unjust dismissals, is not so different. The sense of being on display looms large in each alternate realm that Jack experiences, but the paranoid fear of McFeyffe's fantasy world emphasizes its unreal tenor. Words become lethal in this alternate realm, directly inscribing ideology into *Eye in the Sky*'s fictional narrative.

Dick's reader must also wonder whether the novel's primary reality is preferable to McFeyffe's fantasy. Jack knows precisely where he stands in McFeyffe's parallel reality, yet wishes to return to the disheartening world of *Eye in the Sky*'s opening chapters, even though, in this bewildering place, traitors like McFeyffe masquerade as patriots. The novel's primary reality, therefore, is Dick's fictional exhibit of the ideological anxieties that characterized California during the 1950s. This primary world—like all the parallel realities included in *Eye in the Sky*—becomes Dick's textual representation, reflection, and exaggeration of that decade's political paranoia. McFeyffe's fantasy, more than any other alternate realm depicted in *Eye in the Sky*, forces the reader to question the reality of its "parent world" (the 1959 California setting that begins the novel), just as Tlön forces Borges's reader to doubt the reality of the narrator's primary world in "Tlön, Uqbar, Orbis Tertius."

This development illustrates how Borges's brand of intellectual, linguistic, and abstract unreality becomes terrifyingly tactile in Dick's novel. *Eye in the Sky* is a literary descendent of "Tlön, Uqbar, Orbis Tertius" that resembles, without reproducing, the narrative parameters of Borges's short story. Both texts, however, demonstrate the political and humanist dangers of fictionalizing an entire culture's history.[70]

Worlds Apart?

Eye in the Sky conflates Marxism with Communism and Communism with McCarthyism to parody the Cold War rhetoric that characterized 1950s America. Jack Hamilton, who believes that Marsha's imagination is responsible for the Communist fantasy of the novel's concluding section, strikes his wife in an attempt to dissipate this parallel reality. This alternate world, however, does not disappear when Marsha lapses into unconsciousness. Jack, initially confused by this turn of events, quickly realizes that his wife is not the Communist fantasy's author:

> McFeyffe was visibly growing. As they watched, he ceased to be a squat, heavyset little man with a potbelly and pug nose. He became tall. He became magnificent. A godlike nobility descended over him. His arms were gigantic pillars of muscle. His chest was massive. His eyes flashed righteous fire. His square, morally inflexible jaw was set in a stern and just line as he gazed severely around the room.[71]

McFeyffe joined the Communist Party during the Great Depression because, as he tells Jack, he was "just hungry and out of work and tired of taking it on the chin."[72] McFeyffe's cowardly scapegoating of Marsha to hide his true political leanings transforms his deification into the novel's most lacerating parody of McCarthy's larger-than-life, holier-than-thou arrogance. It also emphasizes McFeyffe's hypocrisy. Marsha, whom McFeyffe previously condemned as a conformist fellow traveler, is "more of a menace to Party discipline" than subversives like McFeyffe because she is part of the "cult of individualism. The idealist with his own law, his own ethics. Refusing to accept authority. It undermines society. It topples the whole structure. Nothing lasting can be built on it."[73] McFeyffe identifies the fundamental conflict between individualism and collectivism that had become, by the novel's 1957 publication, the predominant formulation of the Cold War's opposing American-Soviet ideologies. Dick, however, exposes both philosophies as fraudulent methods of socially enforced conformism that play upon the fear of difference. McFeyffe is imprisoned by this system as much as he seeks to ensnare Marsha in it because he cannot reveal his Communist proclivities without destroying his reputation, his career, and his life.

This uncomfortable truth leads to *Eye in the Sky*'s pessimistic conclusion. Once the proton beam's effects subside, Jack awakens in his primary reality. He unsuccessfully attempts to convince Colonel T. E. Edwards, his former employer, that McFeyffe is a Communist agent. McFeyffe, however, has not attended leftist meetings or rallies, so he is not a proven security risk. Jack knows that McFeyffe is a Communist, but cannot convince Edwards of this fact because Jack's suspicions do not constitute proof. Jack also knows that Marsha is no Communist, but cannot convince Edwards of this fact because McFeyffe's selective interpretation of the evidence against Marsha raises enough doubt to condemn her in the novel's historically accurate (and irrational) primary reality. The reader now recognizes that *Eye in the Sky*'s consensual world is no more or less real than McFeyffe's Communist fantasy, while McFeyffe's paranoid worldview infects the consensual world just as Tlön ideologically intrudes into Borges's primary reality in "Tlön, Uqbar, Orbis Tertius." The political imperatives of McFeyffe's fantasy operate more subtly in *Eye in the Sky*'s real world than Tlön does in Borges's short story, revealing Jack's paranoid primary reality to be just as treacherous as McFeyffe's Communist fantasy.

Jack decides to leave the defense industry altogether (to avoid McFeyffe's red-baiting) by partnering with Bill Laws, the Bevatron's African American tour guide, in a business that manufactures high-fidelity stereo equipment. This choice leaves McFeyffe in his high-ranking position with access to defense secrets that he can use against the United States, while Jack and Marsha begin a new, more financially uncertain life. The unfairness of this arrangement becomes even more evident when Edwards defends McFeyffe because the man is a Catholic war veteran. Jack's response notes the pitiful ironies that confront him: "I'm trying to say that a man can be all those things and still be a dangerous subversive. And a woman can sign peace petitions and subscribe to *In Fact*, yet love the very dirt this country is made of."[74] Jack, however, cannot escape the binary ideology that leads to the novel's fundamental conflict. He recognizes that dissenting from the political, social, and economic principles of America's anti-Communist social order threatens the status quo, but, rather than transcending this ideological dualism, Jack's entrepreneurial efforts risk reaffirming it.

Jake Jakaitis objects to the protagonist's selfish decision: "So the extent of Hamilton's moral opposition to authority is compromise . . . . *Eye in the Sky*'s resolution resolves little more than Hamilton's middle-class guilt."[75] Believing that *Eye in the Sky*, like many of Dick's early novels, "seeks a strategy of containment, a symbolic resolution to social conflict . . . through narrative,"[76] Jakaitis includes the novel in a group of Dick's early works that "reveals the inadequacy of Dick's imaginary interventions to excise an irrefutable Real that denies resolution of those social contradictions."[77] Dick, however, does not attempt (nor is he required to provide) an easy resolution to Jack's difficult circumstances. The novel refuses to transform Jack into a purified warrior for civil liberties who respects all people (including Communists) regardless of their beliefs. The complications and contradictions of McCarthyism—especially the fallacy that any person accused of Communist sympathies automatically represents the characteristically American values of free expression, rugged individualism, and resistance to authority—preclude such a conclusion. Jakaitis may long for a humanist happy ending, but Dick knows that this conclusion would endorse the binary discourse that he wishes to avoid because this discourse allowed McCarthyism's red-baiting accusers *and* its innocent victims to demonize each other as unpatriotic Americans.

Peter Fitting, in his careful reading of *Eye in the Sky*, finds more complexity in its resolution. Jack's retreat from missile research to stereo manufacturing

> is perhaps an idealistic solution, a nostalgic flight from the harsh reality of capitalism towards an earlier, pre-capitalist mode of production, [but] it is also a *practical* solution, typical of those many novels of Dick's where the problem of reality is resolved pragmatically . . . through action—more specifically, in a character's turning to manual and/or artisanal work.[78]

Jack cannot triumph over the governmental system that contains him because, whether in McFeyffe's Communist fantasy or in the consensual world of Jack's primary reality, an individual's actions are limited by the social, cultural, political, and economic boundaries mandated by the Cold War's dualistic ideology. Neither Jack nor McFeyffe creates these constraints, but both men perpetuate the binary discourse that characterizes *Eye in the Sky*'s Cold War narrative. McFeyffe's red-baiting tactics actively consolidate this discourse, while Jack's passive resignation capitulates to the Red Scare's unfortunate political fearmongering.

Like so many Americans of the McCarthy era, Jack remains beholden to its primary terminology: treason, subversion, anti-Americanism, and oppression. Jack believes that he defends true American ideals by resisting McFeyffe, but ultimately fails to reject the dualistic ideology that McFeyffe employs. This resolution is depressing, even upsetting (since Dick's readers, like Jakaitis, may passionately desire that Jack actively confront McCarthyism's excesses), but it does not artistically compromise Dick's novel. Rather,

Eye in the Sky's political subtext reflects the hysterical anti-Communism that characterized 1950s America to acknowledge McCarthyism's influence over even the thoughtful people who opposed McCarthy's tactics. If the novel has a message, it is that sociopolitical movements like the Red Scare cannot be easily or completely resisted. They instead alter the terms of debate so comprehensively that even subaltern oppositional movements, no matter how philosophically and politically sophisticated, must adopt their era's primary lexicon. Fitting recognizes the final irony of Dick's novel:

> Once the hallucinatory experience of the illusory realities has ended, Jack and the others return to "real" (i.e., consensual) reality, where his dismissal as a security risk . . . is maintained and reaffirmed. Jack is thus the first victim of his own belief in American pluralism. In this re-enactment of the witch-hunts of the 1950s . . . a group of extremists attempts to impose their construction of reality on others, *and they succeed.* . . . In this way *Eye* shows that pluralism is itself an ideology.[79]

This disheartening imposition illustrates that pluralism itself may constrain, as much as it liberates, political discourse. Jack must accept the distasteful paranoia that besets his consensual reality as much as it characterizes McFeyffe's Communist fantasy. Dick muddies the novel's ideological waters so effectively that, despite Jack's resistance to McFeyffe's anti-Communist tyranny, Jack affirms its basic program by endorsing McFeyffe's discursive, divisive, and binary logic.

A glorious humanist defeat of McCarthyism's fearful paranoia is, therefore, impossible in *Eye in the Sky*. The novel's resolution, in which people of good conscience try to save themselves (but not their society), speaks to the dispiriting compromises McCarthyism forced upon its victims. Dick's melancholy denouement honestly acknowledges democratic humanism's imperfect and fragmentary survival in a politically hostile world. *Eye in the Sky* demonstrates the perils of the Cold War's dualistic ideology by depicting multiple realities that cannot transcend the ideological restrictions of McCarthyist mistrust. This unpleasant conclusion may provide Dick's reader with an authentic view of McCarthyism's complex reality, but *Eye in the Sky* can neither resist nor demystify the cynical ambiguities of the McCarthy era. Nor should it try.

Defending Humanism

The binary Us versus Them ideology that *Eye in the Sky* sketches so precisely (and parodies so relentlessly) forces Dick's reader to wonder if the novel's sensitivity to Cold War discourse is anomalous. Even a brief review of Dick's earlier short stories, however, dissipates this suspicion. "The Defenders" is particularly notable for examining the Cold War tensions provoked by the nuclear arms race. This story also underscores the complicated humanism of Dick's fifties fiction by subverting the common SF trope of artificially intelligent mechanisms that terrorize, attack, and slaughter their human creators. Several Dick stories portray machines as dangerous threats to human identity and survival, but "The Defenders" is significant not only for imaginatively dramatizing human fears about technological proliferation, but also for accepting the inevitability of technology's growing role in human life. Dick's achievement in this story resonates with M. Keith Booker's assessment of 1950s science fiction's talent for deconstructing old binaries: "Among other things, the erosion of stable polar oppositions in the 1950s can be taken as a sign of incipient postmodernism."[80]

"The Defenders," beyond its postmodern implications, suggests that machines can deliver humanity from its own venality. The story's artificially intelligent robots become humanity's protectors rather than its oppressors. Fragmenting the division between humanity and mechanism makes "The Defenders" one of Dick's most important and impressive early works. The story includes a marvelous postmodern twist to the standard SF plot about future apocalypse when the story's human characters discover, much to their chagrin, that reality is so flexible that they cannot trust historical accounts assuring them that nuclear catastrophe has driven humanity underground.

Kingsley Amis characterizes "The Defenders" as a satire of the clichéd SF story about technology escaping human control:

> There is here and there even a complacency about man's ability to keep his creations under physical control, and in some places I detect a tendency to regard electronic behaviour as "better," because more rational and predictable, than human. This idea is delightfully burlesqued in a story by Philip K. Dick, "The Defenders," in which the human race is living underground while the robots fight the war on the surface.[81]

Considering the murderous potential of robots/androids in Dick's other stories and novels (especially "Second Variety" [1953] and *Do Androids Dream of Electric Sheep?*), Dick's reversal in "The Defenders" is even more important than Amis acknowledges. In Dick's tale, the leadies were originally designed to fight a nuclear war between the United States and the Soviet Union, but they end the conflict after humanity retreats to subterranean cities to avoid radiation poisoning. Once underground, humanity continues manufacturing leadies for the war effort, unaware that their mechanical creations have restored the terrestrial surface to pristine condition. Don Taylor, the story's protagonist, discovers this truth when he accompanies an American expedition to the surface to monitor the war's progress. The leadies have duped humanity into believing that the conflict still rages by producing televised images of nuclear devastation in a futuristic film studio. The leadies, consequently, have taken their programming to protect humanity to its logical limit: They preserve the entire human species, not simply the government that constructs them.

Dick demonstrates the idiocy of the arms race's Cold War Manicheanism by depicting technology as an agent of human salvation, not destruction. This development may seem odd for Dick, a man whose technological ambivalence is best summarized by his statement that

> [t]he ultimate in paranoia is not when everyone is against you but when everything is against you. Instead of "My boss is plotting against me," it would be "My boss's phone is plotting against me." Objects sometimes seem to possess a will of their own anyhow, to the normal mind; they don't do what they're supposed to do, they get in the way, they show an unnatural resistance to change.[82]

"The Defenders" diverges from Dick's usual fictional portrait of technological anxiety to recount a story of benevolent robots in the tradition of Isaac Asimov, whose famous Three Laws of Robotics virtually created this SF subgenre. Asimov's first law states: "A robot may not injure a human being or, through inaction, allow a human being to come to harm,"[83] which capably describes the leadies' behavior in "The Defenders." This story willingly bucks the pervasive pessimism of Dick's other android tales, to say nothing of the depressing tenor of many other SF robot stories, novels, and films of the 1950s.

Dick illustrates the sick irrationality of the Cold War's dualistic ideology when Taylor considers the history of the Soviet-American atomic conflict:

> Human beings had invented war, invented and manufactured the weapons, even invented the players, the fighters, the actors of the war. But they themselves could not venture forth, could not wage it themselves. . . . They were under the surface, in the deep shelters that had been carefully planned and built, even as the first bombs began to fall.
>
>   It was a brilliant idea and the only idea that could have worked. Up above, on the ruined, blasted surface of what had once been a living planet, the leady crawled and scurried and fought Man's war. And undersurface, in the depths of the planet, human beings toiled endlessly to produce weapons to continue the fight, month by month, year by year.[84]

The sheer nonsense of this arrangement, when combined with the passage's overconfident pride in humanity's genius for fighting a proxy war, requires little commentary, since Taylor's thoughts lampoon themselves. Taylor's reflection that "[n]obody *wanted* to live this way, but it was necessary"[85] also illustrates just how unpleasant and unnecessary are the dark, constrained, and pointless lives that human beings lead in "The Defenders." Dick's story is a nightmare extrapolation of military aggression, cultural ennui, and ideological insanity. "The Defenders," in other words, accomplishes in its opening pages what other Dick stories take their entire course to portray.

Dick reverses the normal state of affairs, in which humanity technologically controls the world, to infantilize the story's human characters. The leadies become the planet's caretakers, as well as humanity's stewards, by paternalistically enduring humanity's immature aggressiveness, which, in "The Defenders," resembles childish squabbling more than fearful warmongering. The leadies' parental status forces them to deceive their subterranean creators by perpetuating an enormous hoax designed to save humanity from itself. This hoax depends upon skillfully manipulating electronic media to highlight the ability of propaganda to transform human beings from rational people who think for themselves into childish receivers of official ideology. The human species, in Dick's terrible apocalyptic future, is powerless. The leadies form a mechanical elite that controls the world by intentionally blurring the boundary between reality and fiction.

The leadies create false newspaper articles about nuclear devastation, false military reports about the war's progress, and false television images of the scarred surface to reinforce the perception that the war condemns humanity to its imperfect subterranean existence. The leadies script an alternate world not only to confirm humanity's worst fears about nuclear conflict, but also to illustrate the war's gruesome horrors. "The Defenders," indeed, is Dick's earliest fictional elaboration of electronic media's ability to refashion human consciousness so completely that separating reality from fiction becomes impossible.[86]

The inability to distinguish reality from fantasy connects Dick's story to "Tlön, Uqbar, Orbis Tertius," but with far different results. After Taylor's expedition reaches the surface, the leadies seal all access ports to the underground world. Taylor and his teammates must spend their lives on the surface while the leadies' plan for unifying humanity goes forward. The robots, therefore, determine humanity's political fate rather than allowing the story's human characters to choose their own future. Borges's story, by contrast, sees humanity submit to Tlön's more orderly example because Tlön's "inhuman laws. . . entrance the minds of men."[87] Tlön, of course, is the fictional creation of a small group of men, whereas the new world that the leadies hope to create is the fictional creation of living machines.

Dick's attitude toward the leadies' new world, moreover, is deeply ambivalent. He employs the language of corporate capitalism to illustrate how naive the leadies' technological salvation of humanity is. The leady who reveals the war's true outcome invokes the terminology of property management to explain the robots' intentions:

We are caretakers, watching over the whole world. The owners have left for a time, and we must see that the cities are kept clean, that decay is prevented, that everything is kept oiled and in running condition. The gardens, the streets, the water mains, everything must be maintained as it was eight years ago, so that when the owners return, they will not be displeased. We want to be sure that they will be completely satisfied.[88]

This capitalist manifesto destroys the Cold War's competing political ideologies by conceiving human relationships in purely institutional terms. The robots do not wish to supplant humanity, but rather to radically change its worldview so that people—not machines—become the productive owners of an improved planet.[89]

This discourse reflects the nineteenth and twentieth centuries' dominant popular conception of American history, which John F. Kasson defines as "a steadily progressive record in which increased knowledge, technological development, and political liberty marched hand in hand. The course of technology was also bringing in sight a world civilization of reduced labor and enriched leisure, health and longevity, abundance, peace, and human brotherhood."[90] The leadies' project of global unification evokes this vision of perfection, although its reality depends upon political deceit, propaganda, and oppression. This engineered future represents the culmination of twentieth-century optimism about technology's ability to create a peaceful and prosperous world that human beings have long imagined, but never achieved.

The story's happy ending demonstrates the strange, fragmented, and postmodern humanism that characterizes "The Defenders." Russian soldiers who have occupied a nearby American village approach Taylor's group. Despite the mutual distrust shared by both expeditions, the leadies hope that the two groups will work together to reclaim the surface's empty cities for the human beings who will eventually emerge from their underground settlements. Soviet-American hostility quickly disappears once the Russian and American leaders reconcile. "The Defenders," indeed, concludes with extraordinary optimism:

> "It has taken thousands of generations to achieve," the A-class leady concluded. "Hundreds of centuries of bloodshed and destruction. But each war was a step toward uniting mankind. And now the end is in sight: a world without war. But even that is only the beginning of a new stage of history."
>
> "The conquest of space," breathed Colonel Borodoy.
>
> "The meaning of life," Moss added.
>
> "Eliminating hunger and poverty," said Taylor.
>
> The leady opened the door of the ship. "All that and more. How much more? We cannot foresee it any more than the first men who formed a tribe could foresee this day. But it will be unimaginably great."
>
> The door closed and the ship took off toward their new home.[91]

This utopian grandiosity laughably contrasts the story's otherwise grim tone. Amis correctly states that "The Defenders" parodies the tendency to regard technology as superior to humanity because Dick's leadies suppress human difference and diversity to achieve political unification.

Dick, therefore, satirizes the belief in uninterrupted progress that typified American democratic capitalism *and* Soviet Communism during the Cold War. Both ideologies promised to liberate humanity from the chains of ignorance, poverty, and primitivism by stressing conformity to a single nationalist vision, to routinized mass labor, and to military conflict as an instrument of foreign policy. Dick combines these elements into a story that powerfully illustrates what Kasson calls "the overriding paradox of the age": "the coexistence of technological progress and social chaos."[92] By emphasizing American anxieties about technology's potential to not only extend but also curtail human freedom, "The Defenders" becomes an exemplary humanist text whose postmodern ambivalence about technology sets the stage for much of Dick's later fiction.

Far more than a witty alternate-world tale, "The Defenders" mercilessly ridicules the technological utopia's narrative, thematic, and symbolic conventions to demonstrate Dick's mastery of Cold War rhetoric. Dick's 1953 SF story intensifies the Cold War's most oppressive tendencies to a level of self-mocking absurdity rarely seen in other genres, or other SF authors, of the 1950s. Dick's final work of this decade, *Time Out of Joint*, is both the apotheosis of such absurdity and a compassionate character study of its protagonist's mental instability. Exploring its narrative richness, complexity, and importance also reveals additional connections between Dick's and Borges's fiction.

Timely Ideologies

Time Out of Joint was a significant development in Dick's authorial sophistication and career. Published in 1959 by J.B. Lippincott as "a novel of menace," it was Dick's first hardcover sale. SF publisher Ace Books had rejected the novel, which underscores *Time Out of Joint*'s generic indeterminacy as a realist novel with SF flourishes, a mainstream work with surreal touches, and a humanist deconstruction of Eisenhower-era America's bourgeois conventionality. The novel's remarkably observant late-fifties small-town American setting is so authentic that the novel's reality breakdown disturbs the reader more deeply than if Dick had begun *Time Out of Joint* in its putatively "real" setting, the year 1998, in which Earth's lunar colony fights a civil war with the mother planet by firing missiles at the terrestrial surface. The novel's protagonist, Ragle Gumm, comes to believe that a massive governmental conspiracy obfuscates *Time Out of Joint*'s central yet fantastic truth: that Ragle is the most important man on Earth, whose uncanny talent for predicting lunar missile strikes prevents humanity's extinction. Dick's complex novel elaborates Ragle's paranoia to stress how provisional, artificial, and false objective historical narratives can be.

Time Out of Joint's central figurative conceit is a Borgesian paradox of mammoth proportions. Ragle spends his days solving a newspaper puzzle/contest titled "Where Will the Little Green Man Be Next?" Ragle is astonishingly successful in this enterprise, having been crowned national champion for two consecutive years. His victory results from extraordinary mental effort, since Ragle spends every day calculating probabilities, developing statistical models, and enduring intellectual labor that does not qualify as "real work" in the conventional bourgeois town where he resides. Ragle lives with his sister, brother-in-law, and nephew in their house, experiencing feelings of personal worthlessness, illegitimate occupation, and implicit emasculation. The research Ragle performs keeps him at home rather than at an office or in another "productive" job, such as his brother-in-law Vic Nielson's work as a grocery-store clerk.

A startling series of incidents, including the novel's most famous scene of a soft-drink stand disappearing before Ragle's eyes, convinces Ragle that his bourgeois suburban existence is a sham. Escaping from what is referred to only as Old Town, Ragle enters the "real" world of 1998 and its totalitarian police state, only to realize that both Old Town and the newspaper contest were ruses concocted by the Earth's military to take advantage of his facility for predicting (with uncanny accuracy) the locations of lunar missile strikes. The massive responsibilities that accompany saving the planet from repeated missile attacks combine with Ragle's growing suspicions about the Earth government's illegitimacy to produce enough stress that, prior to the novel's opening, Ragle has experienced a "withdrawal psychosis . . . back to a period before the war. To his childhood. To the late 'fifties, when he was an infant."[93] When Ragle, before the novel begins, tries to defect to the lunar colonists' side of the war, Earth's military command not only creates Old Town, but also "reconstructs" (or brainwashes) sixteen hundred volunteers to become the town's residents so that Ragle's fantasy seems completely normal. The novel concludes with Ragle departing for Venus after joining the lunar rebellion (known as the Lunatic cause) to fight for his beliefs.

Time Out of Joint continues the theme of false ontology seen in *Eye in the Sky* and "The Defenders," but with an epistemological twist. When Ragle recognizes his true identity as Earth's savior, the world around him dismantles in favor of a more aggressive future where war becomes the focus of his life. Ragle's 1950s world has been constructed to dupe him into accepting a political fiction that contradicts the true state of affairs: Ragle, in Old Town, believes himself to be an unimportant man leading a small life, even though, in reality, he is the most important person alive. This identity crisis, in one of the novel's most postmodern effects, threatens to destroy the world. Ragle's epistemological ambivalence mirrors the ontological uncertainty of Old Town's fake reality, which the novel conceives in terms of stagecraft. Margo Nielson, Vic's wife and Ragle's ersatz sister, provides the clearest voice for this idea:

> A sense of the finiteness of the world around her. The streets and houses and shops and cars and people. Sixteen hundred people, standing in the center of a stage. Surrounded by props, by furniture to sit in, kitchens to cook in, cars to drive, food to fix. And then, behind the props, the flat, painted scenery. Painted houses set farther back. Painted people. Painted streets.[94]

The levels Margo perceives—with painted houses located behind the scenery, which itself sits behind the props—are emblematic of *Time Out of Joint's* ontological intricacy.

Old Town's 1950s world, with which Dick's contemporary readers were intimately familiar, obscures Ragle's dystopian 1998 reality even though this reality is more fantastic than the ruse itself. This narrative arrangement, for Dick's characters and readers, is a metaphor for the disorienting shifts of technology, social dynamics, and institutional politics that characterized the 1950s. It suggests not only that reality is unstable, but also that reality can be so completely manipulated by unseen agents that the idea of ontological certainty becomes hopelessly naive. Booker's analysis of this point is significant:

> There is nevertheless a clear implication that all "reality" is to a certain extent a fiction promulgated by the powers that be and that Gumm's situation is merely an exaggerated version of what we all experience every day. One lingering implication of the book is the possibility of infinitely nested realities: if the 1959 town is a simulation created by the 1998 external world, then that world itself might be a simulation created by still another world, and so on.[95]

This ontological maze is also an epistemological puzzle, since Ragle does not initially know who or what he is. This confusion destabilizes the boundaries of the novel's 1959 and 1998 worlds even more, creating the postmodern possibility that each realm is as delusory as the other.

'50s/"Fifties"

The intellectual richness of *Time Out of Joint*'s premise not only affords its reader the opportunity to reconsider the relationship among reality, fiction, insanity, and perception, but also makes it one of Dick's most analyzed novels. Yves Potin goes so far as to call *Time Out of Joint* "a strange novel that is today a landmark in the evolution of literature."[96] Kim Stanley Robinson pronounces the novel a notable success, in which Dick

> finally found a method . . . to publish a novel that is a direct representation of current American reality. For despite its final revelations, most of *Time Out of Joint* is set in the year 1959, even if it is an "illusory" 1959. Not surprisingly, it is a very convincing illusion. Much attention is given to the details of everyday life in this small town, and the life of its residents is fully achieved.[97]

A sense of suburban anomie pervades Ragle Gumm's life in Old Town, while the accumulation of fifties detail is impressive. Vic and Margo Nielson belong to the Book of the Month Club; their son Sammy watches *Gunsmoke* every week; *Reader's Digest* is as common a cultural outlet as the *New Yorker*; Alfred Kinsey's reports on American sexual behavior are in print; Ragle's neighbor Bill Black, an organization man in William Whyte's sense of the term, is a white-collar employee who believes in hard work and social conformity; rock-and-roll and television are supplanting older cultural forms like radio; Bill Black's disdain for television gives him a sense of cultural refinement; and Ragle is at one point compared to Charles Van Doren, the

Columbia University English instructor who became a central figure in the decade's notorious quiz-show scandals.

The invocation of Van Doren is one of many clues that *Time Out of Joint*'s peaceful Americana covers darker, more subversive realities. Marilyn Monroe is unknown; *Uncle Tom's Cabin* is a contemporary novel; the Tucker automobile is in mass production; and the international political situation is replete with anxieties about nuclear destruction, the Cold War, and economic uncertainty. As Margo thinks to herself, "[N]othing was perfect. In all the world. Certainly not in this day and age, with H-bombs and Russia and rising prices."[98] By mixing accurate period detail with events that diverge from actual 1950s history, Dick creates a prototypical postmodern situation that questions the veracity of its reader's received notions about the history of the 1950s even as the novel deploys that decade's most identifiable characteristics (and personalities) to establish its historical legitimacy.

Fredric Jameson reads this aspect of Dick's novel dialectically, identifying it as a form of "historicity," one of the most useful concepts elucidated in *Postmodernism, or, the Cultural Logic of Late Capitalism*:

> Historicity is, in fact, neither a representation of the past nor a representation of the future (although its various forms use such representations): it can first and foremost be defined as a perception of the present as history; that is, as a relationship to the present which somehow defamiliarizes it and allows us that distance from immediacy which is at length characterized as a historical perspective.[99]

For Jameson, therefore, the 1950s become "the fifties," a cultural construct that reifies

> the position of Eisenhower America in the world itself and is thereby to be read as a kind of distorted form of cognitive mapping, an unconscious and figurative projection of some more "realistic" account of our situation, as it has been described earlier: the hometown reality of the United States surrounded by the implacable menace of world communism (and, in this period to a much lesser degree, of Third World poverty).[100]

The details Dick includes in *Time Out of Joint* participate in a double reification. First, the nostalgia encoded in Old Town's small-town utopia reformulates the social, economic, and racial inequities of the time as negligible anxieties unimportant to, or at least mostly unnoticed by, the upwardly mobile, white, bourgeois society that Bill Black and Vic Nielson exemplify. Second, the more fluid world that Ragle inhabits—with objects that mysteriously disappear (the soft-drink stand) or artifacts that indicate a history different from the one Ragle remembers (the telephone book and magazine covers that he soon discovers)—becomes a simulacrum that reproduces the fifties as a pliable reconstructed memory whose character changes to fit Ragle's infantile vision of what the decade was. Jameson sees this development as unabashedly political, as "an experience of our present as past and as history"[101] that makes historical representation a cultural commodity that simultaneously fragments and consolidates capitalism's hegemony over the United States' knowledge of its own past. By simplifying and centralizing "the fifties" as a prosperous era, *Time Out of Joint* obscures contentious issues of race and class even as Ragle's progressive disillusionment with his world deconstructs this delusion.

Jameson, however, misses the novel's key ideological development. Peter Fitting, thankfully, does not: "In *Time* democracy is no longer even an issue: the military are [sic] in control. *Time* thus illustrates another aspect of ideology and reality construction: ideology's efforts to erase its own traces, as it were, to 'naturalize' its own historical and class-based origins."[102] This naturalizing tendency not only reflects the refusal of 1950s middle-class white society to recognize itself as a cultural construction, but also demonstrates the assumption that bourgeois American values—honesty, hard work, temperance, family, social advancement, cultural refinement[103]—are universal principles gladly celebrated by all rational, right-thinking people. This cultural arrogance was also cultural ignorance: The average 1950s American knew little about foreign societies (particularly Third World cultures), which allowed the United States to promote itself as a democratic exemplar, benefactor, and savior that could liberate nations endangered by Soviet domination so that they might join the "Free World."[104]

Old Town epitomizes America's ideological naturalization and cultural conservatism, as demonstrated by Vic Nielson's conversation with Liz, the Texas checker who works at his supermarket:

> "We're in for a bad business year," [Vic] said to Liz.
>
> "Oh what do you care?" Liz said. "You don't own the store; you just work here, like the rest of us. Means not so much work. . . . Anyhow I don't think there's going to be any depression; that's just Democratic talk. I'm so tired of those old Democrats trying to make out like the economy's going to bust down or something."
>
> "Aren't you a Democrat?" he asked. "From the South?"
>
> "Not any more. Not since I moved up here. This is a Republican state, so I'm a Republican."[105]

The utter simplicity of Liz's final remark, as well as her unproblematic acceptance of Eisenhower-style optimism ignores (if it ever recognized) the racial, gender, and class-based inequities criticized by 1950s social critics like Lewis Mumford, C. Wright Mills, and William Whyte. The fact that a bad business year could put Liz out of work seems not to occur to her, while her political affiliation is purely a matter of social conformity. No irony informs Liz's apathy, while no awareness of the outside world influences her thinking. Liz seems like an ideological blank slate, but, as Fitting notes, this transparency depends upon the totalizing nature of the upwardly mobile philosophy of social contentment that allowed the white middle class to appoint itself the central representative of America's national life during the 1950s.

Dick subverts this restrictive, stifling vision by slowly disintegrating Ragle's utopian 1959 fantasy, which allows the dystopian 1998 reality of interplanetary civil war to emerge. The political implications of one world effacing another connect *Time Out of Joint* to Borges's "Tlön, Uqbar, Orbis Tertius," although Dick's novel unfolds much differently than Borges's story. Ragle's world, unlike Borges's, is not invaded by another; objects and people instead disappear. *Time Out of Joint*'s most memorable scene finds Ragle paralyzed by fear after ordering beer at a soft-drink stand:

> The soft-drink stand fell into bits. Molecules. He saw the molecules, colorless, without qualities, that made it up. Then he saw through, into the space beyond it, he saw the hill behind, the trees and sky. He saw the soft-drink stand go out of existence, along with the counter man, the cash register, the big dispenser of orange drink, the taps for Coke and root beer, the ice-chests of bottles, the hot dog broiler, the jars of mustard, the shelves of cones, the row of heavy round metal lids under which were different ice creams. In its place was a slip of paper. He reached out his hand and took hold of the slip of paper. On it was printing, block letters.

SOFT-DRINK STAND[106]

Ragle compounds this bizarre event by placing the paper slip into a box with five others, meaning that the soft-drink stand's dissolution is the sixth such incident he has observed. These events, the reader eventually realizes, are not functions of the 1998 government's carefully maintained illusion, so they are more plausibly explained as the product of the mental illness (or psychosis) that causes Ragle to retreat to his childhood fantasy. Old Town may be the military's way of giving physical form to his delusion, but the stand's disappearance suggests that this fake city is as much a product of Ragle's mind as it is an example of governmental ingenuity. Dick's reader cannot be certain that the stand ever existed, although its precise description indicates that Ragle's desire to return to his childhood home becomes so powerful that his memory supplies details about Old Town that its designers overlook.

Ragle, however, is not the only character to undergo this unusual experience. Vic Nielson searches for a light cord in his darkened bathroom for several minutes before realizing that it does not exist. Vic's militarily imposed mental conditioning is not perfect, allowing memories of his actual 1998 life (as a brainwashed solider) to slip through his "cover" personality as a dull, bourgeois resident of Old Town. Vic, while listening to the radio with his son, Sammy, momentarily thinks that all radio stations went out of business years ago, but cannot account for this impression. Vic's unease becomes palpable when he subsequently describes the light cord incident to Ragle: "I think something's wrong. . . . I don't mean with you or with me or with any one person. I mean in general."[107] This idea becomes terrifyingly real when Vic, while riding a commuter bus, concentrates his attention on "[dislodging] the presence of the bus and passengers."[108] Much to his surprise, the vehicle and the people become transparent for a short time, verifying for Vic his suspicion that "we have a hodge-podge of leaks in our reality."[109] These leaks are never rationally explained in *Time Out of Joint*, but they indicate how deeply perception influences the human understanding of reality (Ragle's mental illness may explain his strange experiences, but why would Vic be affected?). The fact that Vic convinces himself that the bus is transparent underscores Old Town's and *Time Out of Joint*'s postmodern character.

These experiences can also be read as metaphors for the unpredictable nature of Cold War life. During the 1950s, political movements like McCarthyism and political events like the arms race escaped institutional control to take on lives of their own. The Red Scare redounded on the home front by inflecting suburban American ennui with a nameless, pervasive fear that eroded the individual's efficacy, agency, and self-determination. Impossibly large institutional forces began dominating American life to unhinge the average citizen's independence, liberty, and autonomy. In *Time Out of Joint*, Dick captures the paranoia and horror of daily American life by showing that Ragle and Vic can neither ignore nor explain the mysterious events unfolding around them.

Rewriting History

Objects that should not be there also begin to appear in Old Town. Ragle finds an old telephone book, as well as several magazines, at an abandoned lot that Margo wants the city to redevelop. The phone book lists exchanges and people unknown to Ragle, while one of the glossy magazines (similar to *Life* and *Look*) features photos of Marilyn Monroe, a woman unknown to the members of the Nielson household. These 1998 artifacts serve the same purpose in *Time Out of Joint* as *hrönir* do in "Tlön, Uqbar, Orbis Tertius": supposedly unreal objects whose actuality indicates the presence of an alternate world that slowly seeps into the characters' consensual reality. The textuality of these objects—the paper slips left after an object disappears, the phone book, the magazines—recalls the forged encyclopedia entries that allow Borges to discover Tlön. Just as Tlön is the product of a secret cabal of scholars, industrialists, and mystics whose work eventually dissipates Borges's reality in favor of Tlön's fiction, the books and magazines Ragle discovers have been planted by a secret group of Lunatic sympathizers who wish to dissipate Ragle's Old Town fantasy in favor of the civil war's harsh reality. These objects, in *Time Out of Joint* and in "Tlön, Uqbar, Orbis Tertius," expose their protagonists' ostensible reality as a collection of small, intimate details that form surprisingly tenuous worlds. After these details are set out of joint (to use Ragle's Shakespearean expression), the protagonist pursues the truth in a quest that exposes the existence of an alternate reality. This new world occludes the protagonist's original reality by highlighting political mendacity in a narrative development that is unavoidably postmodern: History gives way to fiction (or is revealed to be fiction) so that the protagonist can never be certain who or what to trust.

Despite their thematic similarity, an apparently wide gulf separates Borges's story from Dick's novel. Borges, as his story's narrator, watches Tlön's fictional existence *supplant* the real world, while Ragle watches Old Town's artificial character *dismantle* to reveal 1998's political warfare. Dick's plot reverses Borges's story to suggest that *Time Out of Joint* embraces a cynical reality that "Tlön, Uqbar, Orbis Tertius" rejects. Both protagonists, however, retire from their newfound worlds rather than live in them. Borges, the reader recalls, rejects the Tlönian realm in favor of translating Browne's *Urn Burial*, while Ragle travels to the Lunatic sympathizers' Venus base because he believes that political passivity will end Earth's civil war.

Ragle, indeed, remembers that, before the war, he was a successful industrialist who, after the war began, patriotically volunteered his missile-predicting services to Earth's government. After many years of predicting missile strikes, however, Ragle concludes that the lunar colonists' desire to explore space is a more enlightened goal than the Earth government's refusal to allocate resources to learn about the cosmos. The civil war, therefore, becomes a battle between expansion and containment, future and past, progress and stasis that Ragle formulates in philosophical terms:

> No migration had ever been like this. For any species, any race. From one planet to another. How could it be surpassed? They made now, in these ships, the final leap. Every variety of life made its migration, traveled on. It was a universal need, a universal experience. But these people had found the ultimate stage, and as far as they knew, no other species or race had found that.
>
> It had nothing to do with minerals, resources, scientific measurement. Nor even exploration and profit. Those were excuses. The actual reason lay outside their conscious minds. If he were required to, he could not formulate the need, even as he experienced it fully. No one could. An instinct, the most primitive drive, as well as the most noble and complex. It was both at once. . . . It's not a political question, or even an ethical one.[110]

Ragle emphasizes movement, activity, and instinct. His dissatisfaction with his stagnant life, as well as Ragle's desire to discover new, exotic, and fulfilling circumstances, drive the man's need to discover the truth about Old Town once he suspects that the city is not real. Ragle also realizes that migrating to Venus will deprive Earth of his protective talent: "Without Ragle Gumm the government at Denver would yield . . . . The threat of missile attacks would be enough. Public feeling against the Lunar colonists did not go that far; three years of fighting and suffering for both sides had made a difference."[111] Ragle formulates this political analysis in notably apolitical terms. He conceives migration between the planets as a biological imperative that overrides intellectual concerns, explanations, and rationalizations. Ragle exemplifies Peter Fitting's insight about ideology naturalizing its own historical origins when colonizing new worlds becomes, in Ragle's view, humanity's birthright. This migratory discourse not only obscures the civil war's political origins, but also allows Ragle to dismiss Vic's accusation that defecting to the wrong (meaning Lunatic) side is treason: "'In a civil war,' Ragle said, 'every side is wrong. It's hopeless to try to untangle it. Everyone is a victim.'"[112] Ragle disavows political partisanship's binary ideology before withdrawing to Venus in a narrative development that allows *Time Out of Joint* to resonate strongly with "Tlön, Uqbar, Orbis Tertius." Ragle's simplistic justification for joining the Lunatics reflects the harmonious history that Tlön represents to the people who embrace its comforting worldview. Ragle's choice to join the Lunatics, in fact, is an ideological decision as artificial as Old Town's false reality. Ragle embraces an ersatz history that promotes humanity's natural right to colonize space while overlooking the harsh political, cultural, and ethical consequences of asserting ownership claims over foreign locales. Ragle erases the traces of this new ideology (an interplanetary version of Manifest Destiny) by depicting it as a biological drive that the Lunatics cannot resist.

Dick's reader can scarcely believe this uncomplicated discourse—or the history that it invokes—in light of the intricacies of *Time Out of Joint*'s Old Town delusion (or the lunar colonists' willingness to destroy Earth cities to secure unfettered access to space travel). This discourse also recalls Borges's characterization of Tlön's emergence into the real world: "[A]lready a fictitious past occupies in our memories the place of another, a past of which we know nothing with certainty—not even that it is false."[113] As *Time Out of Joint* concludes, Dick's reader cannot be sure that Ragle's "real" past is any truer than the novel's Old Town fantasy. The 1998 section occupies only one-fifth of the novel, lacking Old Town's scope and detail. The possibility of infinitely nested realities suggested by Booker looms over *Time Out of Joint*'s conclusion, implying that Ragle, rather than progressing from Old Town's falsity to 1998's reality, trades one political fiction for another.

The inherent instability of the novel's pliable history, for Dick as much as for his reader, is both a postmodern and a humanist nightmare that stresses ideology's power to erase its own cultural, social, philosophical, and political roots. Retiring from this state of affairs seems more attractive than submitting to the militaristic ideology that circumscribes, pervades, and controls Ragle's life. As *Time Out of Joint* ends, he does not care about justifying his political decision to escape to Venus. Ragle instead removes himself from the conflict, hoping that his absence will end the war.

Ragle's Borgesian retreat from this new world also proposes a new reading of "Tlön, Uqbar, Orbis Tertius" that emphasizes the provisional nature of the world from which Borges narrates his story, whose reader initially presumes this world to be real in the sense that Borges, Bioy Casares, and the *Encyclopaedia Britannica* all verifiably exist (or existed at some point in time). Tlön, however, supplants them when it becomes terrifyingly, destructively real. *Time Out of Joint* destabilizes the boundary between fiction and reality to encourage the critical reader of Dick's and Borges's fiction to reconsider the authenticity of "Tlön's" initial narrative frame.

This frame's textuality is apparent. Borges populates this realm with artifacts and people from the reader's primary reality (including Borges himself) that unseat a comfortable relationship between reality and fantasy in the same way that Old Town melds 1950s artifacts with fictional characters to deconstruct the border between reality and fiction. No matter how concretely Borges's reader may perceive the opening of "Tlön, Uqbar, Orbis Tertius" as the narrative re-creation of Borges's actual world, the narrator's concluding dismay (that Tlön has disintegrated his world) retroactively constructs it as flexible. The fluid relationship between Old Town and Ragle Gumm's 1998 existence exposes Borges's primary reality as no more real, but no less fictional, than Tlön. The imaginative reconstruction of Borges's world causes "Tlön's" plot to fluctuate between equally unreal histories that, rather than coexisting or cohering, instead compete with one another for narrative primacy. This instability of worlds (found in both Borges's story and Dick's novel) makes secure resolution impossible. It is also archetypically postmodern.

Such instability also has far-reaching political implications. In *Time Out of Joint*, Old Town may not be a secondary projection of the primary reality of 1998's civil unrest, but may instead be a tertiary realm (in this reading, 1998 is a secondary projection of an unknown primary reality that neither Ragle nor the reader can access). In "Tlön, Uqbar, Orbis Tertius," Tlön at first resembles a tertiary projection of the secondary world of Borges's initial narrative frame, which combines made-up objects with elements of Borges's primary reality. Any discussion of narrative strata in *Time Out of Joint* and "Tlön, Uqbar, Orbis Tertius," however, presumes the existence of a fundamental, primary reality that neither Borges's nor Dick's fiction endorses.

The inability to define base reality makes identifying a single political ideology for Ragle Gumm or for "Tlön's" narrator difficult because all realities can disperse into nothingness once their authority is questioned. The external manipulation to which the protagonist's political worldview is subjected (by a centralized government in *Time Out of Joint* and by a secret conspiracy of intellectual elites in "Tlön") fictionally represents how false ideologies consolidate their own power and control the lives of whole populations by promoting the illusion of individual autonomy. These pessimistic alternate-world tales counsel suspicion about the accuracy of officially authorized histories by resisting unsophisticated invocations of patriotism, loyalty, and allegiance. Dick and Borges depict characters that cannot triumph over the political bureaucracies that circumscribe their lives, thereby acknowledging ideology's power to create fake worlds that their inhabitants cannot distinguish from reality.

Dick and Borges, therefore, use the alternate-world story's extrapolative potential to portray the ideological compromises that powerful political institutions force upon their constituents. Dick's 1950s fiction is particularly prominent for engaging the Cold War, the Red Scare, McCarthyism, and the arms race. His writing of this period recodes these events into SF tropes and postmodern conventions that offer a humanist response to the anxiety, fear, and paranoia that characterized 1950s America, just as the fabulism of "Tlön,

Uqbar, Orbis Tertius" allows Borges to highlight the danger that simplistic intellectual movements pose to understanding any society's complicated historical, cultural, philosophical, and political life. "Tlön's" narrator, "The Defenders's" Don Taylor, *Eye in the Sky*'s Jack Hamilton, and *Time Out of Joint*'s Ragle Gumm retire from the worlds they inhabit after recognizing their status as pawns in a political game rigged against them. Their resistance to this game is neither perfectly ideological nor ideologically perfect, but instead embodies the political oppression that Dick and Borges see as an inevitable consequence of twentieth-century life. Neither author celebrates the final victory of the individual over the state, but their characters' struggle to overcome repression, always just out of reach, is the only hope for preserving humanist values within the twentieth century's confusing, depressing, and postmodern political landscape.

Notes

1. The variant spelling of "prophecy" in Le Guin's title was, according to Dick himself, not her doing. In *Philip K. Dick: In His Own Words* (2nd ed., Long Beach: Fragments West/Valentine, 1988), Gregg Rickman's extensive collection of Dick's interviews, Dick says, "I tell you, the word 'prophesy' is spelled wrong in the headline. She didn't write the headline, somebody else did" (103). The truth of this claim is difficult to verify, but reasonable.

2. Ursula K. Le Guin, "Science Fiction as Prophesy," *New Republic*, October 30, 1976, 33.

3. Le Guin, "Science Fiction as Prophesy," 33.

4. An exception is J. Andrew Brown's fine essay "Edmundo Paz Soldán and His Precursors: Borges, Dick, and the SF Canon," published in the November 2007 issue of *Science Fiction Studies*. Brown traces how Soldán, the Bolivian author of such novels as *Sueños digitales* (*Digital Dreams*) and *El delirio de Turing* (*Turing's Delirium*), invokes both Borges and Dick as precursors of his own fiction. Brown intelligently discusses the positions of Ursula K. Le Guin, Jonathan Lethem, and Harold Bloom about how appropriate it is to include Dick in the literary canon, particularly when placing Dick in a lineage that includes Borges and Kafka. Le Guin and Lethem find Dick a worthy fictional successor to Borges and Kafka, while Bloom, in Brown's words, "dismisses the connection out of hand" (481).

The oversight that Le Guin notes in "Science Fiction as Prophesy," unfortunate as it may be, is not difficult to understand when we consider the differences between the two writers. Borges first came to prominence as a poet whose renown as a writer of South American literature and as an artisan of the Spanish language brought him popular and academic acclaim long before his death in 1986. A dabbler in leftist causes during his youth, Borges adopted right-wing political stances that often disturbed his admirers, imitators, and literary colleagues. Borges's family lived in Europe from 1914 to 1921, exposing him not only to the trauma of World War I, but also to the Eurocentric cultural tradition that led Borges to his most important literary enthusiasms: the French Symbolist poets, Schopenhauer, and detective stories (especially those of Edgar Allan Poe and G. K. Chesterton). Publicly opposing the Perón regime after returning to Argentina, Borges progressively lost his eyesight, but continued writing in shorter fictional and nonfictional forms: the essay, the review, the magazine and/or newspaper article, and, most famously, the short story.

By contrast, Dick's slowly building reputation rested (and still rests) upon his novels more than his short stories. Born in Chicago in 1928, Dick briefly lived in Colorado and Washington, D.C., but spent his youth in Berkeley, California, and, with the exception of a two-month 1972 stay in Vancouver, British Columbia, resided in California all his life. Traveling to Europe only once to attend an SF festival in Metz, France (at which he was the guest of honor), Dick had little direct experience with other cultures, rarely leaving California to experience the regional varieties of place, people, and philosophy in his own country. Dick's politics, formed in the sometimes openly radical atmosphere of Berkeley, were leftist insofar as he mistrusted authority and believed in the importance of dissenting from governmental intrusion into the private lives of domestic and foreign peoples, even at the cost of material comfort: opposing the Vietnam War by signing the "Writers and Editors War Tax Protest" that appeared in the February 1968 edition of *Ramparts* magazine, Dick refused to pay income tax, which led the Internal Revenue Service to seize his car in 1969 (Lawrence Sutin, *Divine Invasions: A Life of Philip K. Dick* [New York: Citadel-Carol, 1989], 160). Renouncing the short story in favor of the novel for both pecuniary and artistic reasons, Dick rarely wrote in short forms, although his essays (originally given as speeches) "The Android and the Human" and "Man, Android, and Machine" are significant contributions to the now extensive body of critical thought about human identity's precariousness in the face of advanced technology. Until his last few years, Dick made a modest income from writing, sometimes skating on the edge of poverty. Unlike Borges, Dick was not comfortable with bourgeois amenities and manners, continuing to wear old clothing even when royalties from film options and foreign editions of his fiction allowed him to afford newer items.

For more biographical information about Borges, consult Gene H. Bell-Villada's *Borges and His Fiction: A Guide to His Mind and Art* (Austin: University of Texas Press, 1999) for an illuminating examination of Borges's writing that nicely integrates biographical concerns with literary analysis, as well as James Woodall's *The Man in the Mirror of the Book: A Life of Jorge Luis Borges* (London: Hodder and Stoughton, 1996) and Marcos-Ricardo Barnatán's *Borges: Biografía Total* (Madrid: Temas de Hoy, 1995). Bruce Stiehm's "Borges: Cultural Iconoclast, Dissident Creator of Semantic Traps," *West Virginia University Philological Papers* 44 (1998–1999): 104–11, and Michael Holquist's "Jorge Luis Borges and the Metaphysical Mystery," in *Mystery and Suspense Writers: The Literature of Crime, Detection, and Espionage,* ed.

Robin W. Weeks (New York: Charles Scribner's Sons/Macmillan, 1998), also offer excellent biographical assessments of Borges's fiction.

5. Kim Stanley Robinson, *The Novels of Philip K. Dick*, Studies in Speculative Fiction, no. 9 (Ann Arbor: UMI Research, 1984), 39.

6. See Bruce Gillespie's "Mad, Mad Worlds: Seven Novels of Philip K. Dick," in *Philip K. Dick: Electric Shepherd*, ed. Bruce Gillespie (Melbourne: Norstrilia Press, 1975): 9–21, for Gillespie's criticisms of *The Man in the High Castle*'s multifocal narration, as well as Darko Suvin's "P.K. Dick's Opus: Artifice as Refuge and World View," *Science Fiction Studies* 2, no. 1 (1975): 8–22, for his objections to Dick's portrayal of Japanese occupation as kinder than Nazi fascism. Many analyses of *The Man in the High Castle* not only note problems or difficulties with the text, but also regard the novel as one of Dick's best works.

7. See John Rieder's "The Metafictive World of *The Man in the High Castle*: Hermeneutics, Ethics, and Political Ideology," *Science Fiction Studies* 15, no. 2 (1988): 214–25, and Carl D. Malmgren's "Philip Dick's *Man in the High Castle* and the Nature of Science-Fictional Worlds," *Bridges to Science Fiction*, ed. George E. Slusser, George R. Guffey, and Mark Rose (Carbondale: Southern Illinois University Press, 1980): 120–30, for their political readings of Dick's novel.

8. Slavoj Zizek, *The Sublime Object of Ideology* (London: Verso, 1989), 20–1. The emphasis is Zizek's.

9. Zizek, *Sublime Object*, 21. The emphasis is Zizek's.

10. Jorge Luis Borges, *Labyrinths: Selected Stories and Other Writings*, ed. Donald A. Yates and James E. Irby (New York: New Directions, 1964), 8.

11. Borges, *Labyrinths*, 8.

12. Borges, *Labyrinths*, 8. The emphasis is Borges's.

13. Borges, *Labyrinths*, 8–9.

14. Borges, *Labyrinths*, 9.

15. Borges, *Labyrinths*, 5.

16. James E. Irby, "Borges and the Idea of Utopia," in *Modern Critical Views: Jorge Luis Borges*, ed. Harold Bloom (New York: Chelsea House, 1986), 95.

17. Borges, *Labyrinths*, 9.

18. Bell-Villada, *Borges and His Fiction*, 52.

19. Bell-Villada, *Borges and His Fiction*, 48–49.

20. Borges, *Labyrinths*, 9.

21. Borges, *Labyrinths*, 13.

22. Borges, *Labyrinths*, 10.

23. Borges, *Labyrinths*, 10.

24. Borges, *Labyrinths*, 10.

25. Irby, "Borges and the Idea of Utopia," 95.

26. Borges, *Labyrinths*, 13.

27. Borges, *Labyrinths*, 13. The emphasis is Borges's.

28. Borges, *Labyrinths*, 14. The emphasis is Borges's.

29. Irby, "Borges and the Idea of Utopia," 96–7. The emphasis is mine.

30. Hayden White, "Historical Emplotment and the Problem of Truth," in *Probing the Limits of Representation: Nazism and the "Final Solution,"* ed. Saul Friedlander (Cambridge: Harvard University Press, 1992), 37.

31. White, "Historical Emplotment and the Problem of Truth," 37.

32. Borges, *Labyrinths*, 15.

33. Borges, *Labyrinths*, 15.

34. Borges, *Labyrinths*, 18.

35. Borges, *Labyrinths*, 18.

36. Borges, *Labyrinths*, 18.

37. Borges, *Labyrinths*, 15.

38. Borges, *Labyrinths*, 17.

39. Bell-Villada, *Borges and His Fiction*, 140.

40. Borges, *Labyrinths*, 18.

41. David Halberstam, *The Fifties* (New York: Fawcett, 1994), 799.

42. Gregg Rickman, *To the High Castle: Philip K. Dick: A Life 1928–1962* (Long Beach, CA: Fragments West/Valentine, 1989), 241.

43. Rickman, *To the High Castle*, 193.

44. Halberstam, *The Fifties*, 416.

45. Rickman, *To the High Castle*, 240–41.

46. Rickman quotes Kleo as saying "at some time during that year (1952) the FBI showed up at the door" (*To the High Castle*, 239), while Sutin writes that the visit happened when "one day in 1953 or 1954 FBI agents George Smith and George Scruggs knocked on the door" (*Divine Invasions*, 83). Rickman mysteriously uses a pseudonym, John Flatt, for Scruggs, who taught Dick to drive. Sutin specifically identifies Scruggs as Dick's driving instructor and, in a letter dated August 15, 1975, Dick makes a Freedom of Information Act request for his FBI files, confirming that Scruggs and Smith were the two agents who contacted him in the early fifties (although he does not mention the specific year of this contact).

47. Rickman, *To the High Castle*, 239–40; and Sutin, *Divine Invasions*, 83–84.

48. This dislike of governmental authority did not prevent Dick, twenty years later, from notifying the FBI of his suspicions that literary scholars Peter Fitting and Fredric Jameson were potential Marxist agents. Both men, along with a group of enthusiastic admirers, had visited Dick's Fullerton home in May 1974. Despite the increasingly bizarre permutations that Dick's 1970s correspondence with the FBI initiated (and the equally rancorous reaction it has produced within Dickian scholarship), these 1950s visits by FBI agents—with whom Dick was on cordial and, in the case of Special Agent George Scruggs (who taught Dick to drive), friendly terms—provoked a suspicion of government surveillance that haunted Dick all his life. The story of Dick's 1970s FBI correspondence has generated heated debate within Dickian scholarship as to its meaning in terms of his larger political views, his various reactions to being labeled a Marxist SF writer, and his personal veracity. Some critics see it as evidence of Dick's mental instability; some see it as a simple sellout to governmental authority; and some see it as a vicious attempt to destroy the

reputations of Fitting, Jameson, other leftist academic critics, and Polish SF author Stanislaw Lem (whom Dick erroneously suspected of stealing royalties from a Polish edition of Dick's 1969 novel *Ubik* that Lem himself had worked to publish). Other commentators ardently defend Dick's right to report potentially subversive individuals and groups to the proper authorities. For its part, the FBI did not take Dick seriously, brushing off his concerns with a short letter of thanks for contacting the FBI. Dick later regretted his action and openly blames himself for "[cooperating] fully with my oppressors" (Sutin, *Divine Invasions*, 217) in a 1979 *Exegesis* entry that recounts his questionable behavior of five years before.

Since this episode in Dick's life exceeds my ability to summarize it here, consult the following sources for fascinating, confusing, and often dispiriting accounts of how paranoia, mistrust, and the fear of authority influenced Dick's behavior: chapter 10 of Sutin's *Divine Invasions*; Robert M. Philmus's "The Two Faces of Philip K. Dick," *Science Fiction Studies* 18, no. 1 (1991): 91-103; Gregg Rickman's "Dick, Deception, and Dissociation: A Comment on 'The Two Faces of Philip K. Dick,'" in *On Philip K. Dick: 40 Articles from "Science-Fiction Studies,"* ed. R. D. Mullen et al. (Terre Haute, IN: SF-TH, 1992), 262–64; Jeet Heer's "Marxist Literary Critics Are Following Me!" *Lingua Franca* 11, no. 4 (2001): 26–31; Frank C. Bertrand's "How Jeet Heer Betrayed Philip K. Dick Admirers to Marxist Literary Critics," May 14, 2002, http://www.philipkdickfans .com/frank/jeetheer.htm; and Dick's FBI and CIA files (which can be obtained through Freedom of Information requests of both agencies). Heer's and Bertrand's judgments (of Dick and of Heer's judgments of Dick, respectively) are full of accusations and, in Bertrand's case, invective. Philmus witheringly criticizes Dick's act of informing on Fitting, Jameson, and Lem by noting the serious harm it could have caused to their reputations had the FBI chosen to investigate them. Rickman believes that Dick suffered from multiple personality disorder at this time of his life, while Sutin interprets Dick's actions as a concerted effort to establish his loyalty to the United States government in hopes of relieving the distress caused by his belief that the FBI was surveilling him.

I agree with Rickman that Dick's 1970s correspondence with the FBI is appalling, but I also find it an instructive example of how Dick himself fell prey to the Communist hysteria that he satirized in his 1950s fiction. Rickman is correct to note that Dick's mental condition in the early 1970s was often precarious (Dick attempted suicide during his 1972 stay in Vancouver), but beyond any clinical diagnosis of Dick's psyche, this incident illustrates just how long anti-Communist sentiment survived McCarthy's popularization of the need to inform on subversive individuals and organizations.

49. Rickman, *In His Own Words*, 123.

50. Halberstam, *The Fifties*, 9.

51. Lynn Boyd Hinds and Theodore Otto Windt Jr., *The Cold War as Rhetoric: The Beginnings, 1945–1950*, Praeger Series in Political Communication (New York: Praeger, 1991), 166–67.

52. Barton J. Bernstein and Allen J. Matusow, eds., *The Truman Administration: A Documentary History* (New York: Harper Colophon, 1966), 363.

53. Hinds and Windt, *The Cold War as Rhetoric*, 175.

54. See Hinds and Windt, *The Cold War as Rhetoric*, 42–44, for more thorough information about the first domestic Red Scare, as well as Richard M. Freeland's *The Truman Doctrine and the Origins of McCarthyism* (New York: Alfred A. Knopf, 1972) for a precise analysis of how American fears of domestic subversion by Communist agents receded during the Great Depression, only to reappear in the late 1940s and throughout the 1950s.

55. Hinds and Windt, *The Cold War as Rhetoric*, 176. Alonzo L. Hamby provides another significant perspective on the Loyalty Program in his mammoth, massively researched biography of Harry Truman, *Man of the People: A Life of Harry S. Truman* (New York: Oxford University Press, 1995). Hamby's analysis of the Loyalty Program is measured and careful:

> It was impossible to argue that under the new conditions of Cold War no security problem existed, however grossly exaggerated it might be in the mind of the right. Few sober observers believed that the federal bureaucracy was riddled with subversives. Yet, especially after USSR embassy clerk Igor Guzenko revealed a major spy ring in Canada, no one could deny that there was a Soviet espionage network operating in North America. (427)

Hamby also notes that Truman hated the idea of invading any person's privacy, but, in the charged political climate of the era, had no choice but to deal with the widespread perception of Communist subversion within the federal government by taking decisive measures: "Nevertheless, Truman put his signature on an executive order that not only continued the flaws of the World War II loyalty program, but institutionalized them in a fashion almost guaranteed to inconvenience and harass many more federal employees, while wasting the time and energy of countless administrators" (428).

Hamby also corrects what he believes to be myths about the Loyalty Program and about McCarthyism by pointing out that Truman's hatred of J. Edgar Hoover made the president suspicious of the FBI, even if "FBI agents appear to have done investigations more professionally than Civil Service Commission personnel" (429). Hamby does not cite a source for this contention, although it leads him to downplay the reputation of the 1950s as a time of rampant political hysteria:

> If the FBI did not abuse its power, the program still functioned in unhealthy ways. Numerous scholars, writing as if it launched a reign of terror through the entire federal bureaucracy, have probably overstated its impact. The statistics are slippery, but it appears that during Truman's presidency 400 to 1,200 employees were dismissed under its procedures and 1,000 to 6,000 resigned—out of a total of some 2.5 million government workers. Most people who appeared before loyalty boards were cleared. Inevitably, however, the program led to some injustices, some of them to individuals who had been guilty of nothing more than questionable judgment on tricky foreign policy questions. (429)

Hamby cites David Caute's book *The Great Fear* (New York: Simon and Schuster, 1978) as the source for this paragraph's statistics, but the reasoning is Hamby's alone.

His conclusion contradicts other Cold War scholars' characterization of the Loyalty Program's influence being disproportionate to the number of people actually affected by its rules. Some of Hamby's disagreement may proceed from his unmistakably favorable view of Truman, as well as from his consequent desire to absolve Truman of responsibility for contributing to McCarthyist paranoia. Hamby's overall evaluation of the Loyalty Program, however, substantially agrees with Hinds and Windt's: Truman contributed to the growing anti-Communist hysteria of the 1950s by approving the Loyalty Program out of political need as much as personal conviction. Truman, indeed, detested McCarthy's and Hoover's tactics, and was not shy about privately revealing his contempt. Hamby confirms this view by quoting George Elsey, an aide to presidential adviser Clark Clifford, who once wrote that Truman "wants to be sure & hold FBI down, afraid of 'Gestapo'" (429).

It seems clear that Truman was conflicted about both the Loyalty Program and the increasingly uncivil tenor of his times. Although Attorney General Tom Clark was a driving force behind the Loyalty Program, Hamby does not avoid assigning responsibility to Truman: "Ultimately, however, the buck stopped with Harry S. Truman, who discovered that it was far easier to create a loyalty program than to control it" (429). Hamby's book is an indispensable source for anyone interested in Truman's presidency and the political climate of the early 1950s.

56. Halberstam, *The Fifties*, 52–53.

57. Philip K. Dick, *Eye in the Sky* (1957; New York: A.A. Wyn, 1985), 4.

58. Dick, *Eye in the Sky*, 6–7. The emphasis is Dick's.

59. Dick, *Eye in the Sky*, 8.

60. John Lewis Gaddis, *The United States and the Origins of the Cold War, 1941–1947*, Contemporary American History Series (New York: Columbia University Press, 1972), 33.

61. Dick, *Eye in the Sky*, 8. The emphasis is Dick's.

62. Dick, *Eye in the Sky*, 8. The emphasis is Dick's.

63. Dick, *Eye in the Sky*, 14.

64. Dick, *Eye in the Sky*, 13.

65. Dick, *Eye in the Sky*, 214. The emphasis is Dick's

66. Dick, *Eye in the Sky*, 207.

67. Dick, *Eye in the Sky*, 215.

68. Dick, *Eye in the Sky*, 216.

69. Borges, *Labyrinths*, 17. The emphasis is Borges's.

70. These metaphorical issues also influence the novel's political stance. The fact that McFeyffe, the novel's red-baiting demagogue, is a secret Communist reflects Dick's understanding of Stalinism and McCarthyism as equally perilous forms of totalitarianism. Apart from the novel's firm autobiographical resonance, with the official attention given to Marsha's political curiosity reflecting the notice that Kleo received from the FBI, Dick sees himself as an antitotalitarian writer, but not as a true Marxist:

> In many ways I was an anti-capitalist, but that didn't make me a Marxist. I was very, very suspicious, terribly suspicious of totalitarian states, whether right or left wing. I would say

that the real enemy, the enemy which to me is the paradigm of evil, is the totalitarian state, and it can be religious, it can be left wing, it can be right wing. I was just horrified at what I saw during the Eisenhower period in this country, at what appeared to me to be a great movement toward a totalitarian state in the United States. A right wing totalitarian state. Where anybody who is a dissenter is labeled as a traitor. That is of course the mark of a totalitarian society, when any dissent is regarded as treason. . . . At that point, a really moral person, once he notices that trend, of the equating of dissent and treason, has a moral obligation to oppose the authorities. (Rickman, *In His Own Words*, 121–22)

By painting himself as a moderate who criticizes all forms of repressive political control, Dick implicitly equates McCarthyism, the primary movement toward a right-wing American totalitarian state during the Eisenhower fifties, with Marxism, Communism, and Stalinism. As Jake Jakaitis notes, "Not only are political and moral vision conflated here, so are Marxist and Communist sympathies" (Jakaitis, "Two Cases of Conscience: Loyalty and Race in *The Crack in Space* and *Counter-Clock World*," in *Philip K. Dick: Contemporary Critical Interpretations*, ed. Samuel J. Umland, Contributions to the Study of Science Fiction and Fantasy, no. 63 [Westport, CT: Greenwood, 1995], 172), which Jakaitis sees as a failure of Dick's political understanding of the distinctions between Marxist doctrine and Stalinist Communist practice. Since Dick both denies and affirms his status as a Marxist writer at different times, this criticism has some merit, but it also illustrates how Dick is not the purely objective moderate thinker that he claims to be (although Dick's analysis of McCarthyism's totalitarian nature is astute). *Eye in the Sky*'s moral dimension is best expressed through the horror Jack Hamilton experiences while inhabiting all four of the novel's alternate worlds, which implicates Dick in the American tendency to regard unattractive political movements as monolithic. Neither Communism nor McFeyffism/McCarthyism have much internal narrative variation in *Eye in the Sky*, but this fact also leads to the novel's principal equation of McCarthyism with Stalinism. The textuality of this correlation is yet another example of two competing ideologies writing one other in a dialectical process that exposes their similarities.

71. Dick, *Eye*, 229.

72. Dick, *Eye*, 230.

73. Dick, *Eye*, 231.

74. Dick, *Eye*, 236. The emphasis is Dick's.

75. Jakaitis, "Two Cases of Conscience," 180.

76. Jakaitis, "Two Cases of Conscience," 191.

77. Jakaitis, "Two Cases of Conscience," 191.

78. Peter Fitting, "Reality as Ideological Construct: A Reading of Five Novels by Philip K. Dick," *Science Fiction Studies* 10, no. 2 (1983): 223. The emphasis is Fitting's.

79. Fitting, "Reality as Ideological Construct," 223–24. The emphasis is Fitting's.

80. M. Keith Booker, *Monsters, Mushroom Clouds, and the Cold War: American Science Fiction and the Roots of Postmodernism, 1946–1964*, Contributions to the Study of Science Fiction and Fantasy, no. 95 (Westport, CT: Greenwood, 2001), 19.

81. Kingsley Amis, *New Maps of Hell: A Survey of Science Fiction* (New York: Harcourt, Brace, 1960), 72.

82. Philip K. Dick, *The Collected Stories of Philip K. Dick, Volume One: The Short, Happy Life of the Brown Oxford* (New York: Citadel-Kensington, 1987), 404. Dick originally wrote these ideas in a commentary about his 1953 short story "Colony" for *The Best of Philip K. Dick* anthology published in 1977. The emphasis is Dick's.

83. Isaac Asimov, *The Complete Robot* (Garden City, NY: Doubleday, 1982), 171. The Three Laws of Robotics were first openly stated in "Runaround," a story published in the March 1942 issue of *Astounding Science Fiction*. Asimov, however, attributed the laws as much to editor John W. Campbell as to himself. Asimov, who disliked what he considered the SF cliché of the berserker robot that destroys its human creators in *Frankenstein*-like fashion, self-consciously set out to write a different type of robot tale. His success produced numerous robot stories and novels now considered to be formative texts in American science fiction. As an avid reader of *Astounding* and the other SF pulps, Dick was aware of Asimov's Three Laws, although Dick never explicitly addresses them in his own stories.

84. Dick, *Collected Stories, Volume One*, 70–71.

85. Dick, *Collected Stories, Volume One*, 68. The emphasis is Dick's.

86. Other significant works in this regard are "The Mold of Yancy" (1955), *Time Out of Joint* (1959), *The Penultimate Truth* and *The Simulacra* (1964), *Do Androids Dream of Electric Sheep?* (1968), *Flow My Tears, the Policeman Said* (1974), and *Radio Free Albemuth* (1985). Dick expanded "The Defenders's" basic premise, then grafted it to a portion of "The Mold of Yancy" to form *The Penultimate Truth*'s narrative core. In this novel, the leadies serve human beings who live on plush, enormous estates on Earth's sparsely populated postatomic surface. These wealthy surface dwellers enjoy the fruits of the labor of the remainder of the human populace, which toils in underground factories (called tanks) to produce all the material goods consumed by those living above ground. A duplicitous media system similar to that of "The Defenders" informs the "tankers" that war still rages on the surface. This key alteration makes the novel's theme of technology supplanting human control markedly different from "The Defenders," since the novel's leadies do the bidding of their human masters in the same way that the short story's A-class leady envisions robots serving humanity once it emerges from underground cities to reclaim the surface. The novel deals with a feudal political system divided into geographical lower and upper classes. Despite its lukewarm reception by Dickian scholars, *The Penultimate Truth* remains one of Dick's most fascinating novels.

87. Borges, *Labyrinths*, 17.

88. Dick, *Collected Stories, Volume One*, 81.

89. The political context of "The Defenders" may therefore seem to be a repressive technological dystopia in which machines subvert human freedom. As a warning about the inherent dangers of technologizing warfare to the point where mechanisms no longer obey human commands, the story is a cautionary Cold War allegory that

underscores the foolishness of stockpiling armaments so destructive that they can annihilate the planet.

The story's true irony, however, is that technology becomes humanity's salvation. The leadies' judgment, indeed, *is* more rational and less dualistic than the humans', as Taylor and the others concede when an A-class leady explains: "'You created us,' the leady said, 'to pursue the war for you . . . . But before we could continue the war, it was necessary to analyze it to determine what its purpose was. We did this, and we found that it had no purpose, except, perhaps, in terms of human needs" (Dick, *Collected Stories, Volume One*, 80). These needs include purging the natural tension that, according to the leadies, builds up in every human culture, each of which passes through phases just as a child growing to maturity does. This tension leads to inevitable social conflicts, which, as the leady explains, provokes war: "It is necessary for this hatred within the culture to be directed outward, toward an external group, so that the culture itself may survive its crisis. War is the result. War, to a logical mind, is absurd. But in terms of human needs, it plays a vital role. And it will continue to until Man has grown up enough so that no hatred lies within him" (80).

This pseudo-Freudian, pseudo-Spenglerian explanation of war's origin infantilizes humanity as an immature society that requires care and discipline to survive its difficult adolescence. The leadies, in the story's greatest irony, hope to provide this discipline.

90. John F. Kasson, *Civilizing the Machine: Technology and Republican Values in America 1776–1900* (New York: Hill and Wang, 1976), 185.

91. Dick, *Collected Stories, Volume One*, 85.

92. Kasson, *Civilizing the Machine*, 186.

93. Philip K. Dick, *Time Out of Joint* (1959; New York: Vinage-Random, 2002), 240.

94. Dick, *Time Out of Joint*, 238. Peter Weir's 1998 film *The Truman Show*, screenplay by Andrew Niccol, resembles *Time Out of Joint* so closely that it seems directly inspired by Dick's premise even if the film does not credit the novel as source material. Truman Burbank (Jim Carrey) experiences a seemingly perfect suburban life until he notices several odd details—including klieg lights mysteriously falling from the sky and the inability to travel outside the confines of his island home of Seahaven—that make him suspect this life to be unreal. Truman is correct; his life is in fact the mother of all reality shows, a television program that has followed his every move from conception to adulthood. The program's creator, Christof (Ed Harris), has constructed Seahaven as the largest film set in history, populating it with actors who portray Truman's wife, best friend, neighbors, and colleagues. At least one woman from the real world has tried to communicate the truth to Truman, just as a minor character named Mrs. Keitelbein works to break Ragle free from his delusion in *Time Out of Joint*, while the film concludes with Truman walking out of the Seahaven set (and the only life he has ever known) for an uncertain future. Seahaven is a marvelous cinematic realization of Margo's theatrical description of Old Town's staginess, even preserving the painted backdrops that she intuitively

senses must exist, while *The Truman Show* applies Dick's 1950s premise to the late 1990s world of media saturation and global capitalism.

95. Booker, *Monsters*, 30.

96. Yves Potin, "Four Levels of Reality in Philip K. Dick's *Time Out of Joint*," trans. Heather McLean, *Extrapolation* 39, no. 2 (1998): 148.

97. Robinson, *The Novels of Philip K. Dick*, 22.

98. Dick, *Time Out of Joint*, 16.

99. Fredric Jameson, *Postmodernism, or, the Cultural Logic of Late Capitalism* (Durham, NC: Duke University Press, 1992), 284.

100. Jameson, *Postmodernism*, 283. Ragle in some measure becomes the symbol of these inequities. As Andrew P. Hoberek points out in his insightful essay about *Time Out of Joint*'s depiction of postwar occupational masculinity, Ragle has an "ambiguous relationship to the norms of postwar white-collar labor" ("The 'Work' of Science Fiction: Philip K. Dick and Occupational Masculinity in the Post–World War II United States," *Modern Fiction Studies* 43, no. 2 [1997]: 385). Ragle is the variable in this sedate world, an unknown factor that personifies the fear of not fitting in even as he fears the conformity that Bill Black represents. Ragle, indeed, views "fitting in" as a seductive opportunity to achieve solace through the more acceptably masculine role that conformity offers him. The novel's positioning of Ragle, therefore, means that he, in Jameson's words, "must thus be read according to a negative and a positive hermeneutic simultaneously" (Jameson, *Postmodernism*, 282). Ragle is also the perfect metaphor for Booker's two principal fears of the 1950s: "the fear of being different from everyone else and the fear of being the same as everyone else" (Booker, *Monsters*, 19). Finally, in Jameson words, Ragle symbolizes "all our fantasies of mind control and unconscious exploitation" (282), meaning that he upsets any possibility of social, historical, and mental stability.

101. Jameson, *Postmodernism*, 286.

102. Fitting, "Reality as Ideological Construct," 225.

103. As Booker notes, the works of High Modernism became canonized during the 1950s as the most sophisticated Western art in direct opposition not only to the proletarian works of Soviet-bloc authors, but also to popular American mass-cultural productions like rock-and-roll and television drama. See pages 20–23 of *Monsters, Mushroom Clouds, and the Cold War* for Booker's discussion of the Cold War implications of modernism's academic canonization.

104. Jameson and Hoberek are both aware of this tendency toward ideological naturalization, but neither analyzes it in detail. Jameson acknowledges America's cultural blindness to the Third World in chapter 9 of *Postmodernism* (devoted in large part to *Time Out of Joint*), but never states it as explicitly or as persuasively as Fitting.

105. Dick, *Time Out of Joint*, 9.

106. Dick, *Time Out of Joint*, 54–55.

107. Dick, *Time Out of Joint*, 61.

108. Dick, *Time Out of Joint*, 109.

109. Dick, *Time Out of Joint*, 108.
110. Dick, *Time Out of Joint*, 245.
111. Dick, *Time Out of Joint*, 253.
112. Dick, *Time Out of Joint*, 251.
113. Borges, *Labyrinths*, 18.

CHAPTER THREE

~

Divine Textualities: Calvino, Dick, and Authoring Creation

Science Fiction, Spirituality, and Meaning

The relationship between science fiction, spirituality, and religion has generated intense scholarly debate. Although the spiritual and religious character of many SF texts has provoked passionate disagreement among the genre's authors, readers, and critics, the many opinions about science fiction's relationship to religion can be organized into three general categories that indicate the intellectual complexity of this debate.

The first category holds that religion and spirituality have no place in a genre that purports to base its fictional premises on the empirically logical methods of science. Religion and science fiction, in this view, are antithetical because religion depends upon believing in transcendent states of being that defy rational explanation and empirical measurement.

The second category embraces religion and spirituality as germane to science fiction. SF stories, from this perspective, can offer inventive empirical explanations for religion's supernatural or metaphysical elements (a favorite theme of this type of SF tale depicts deities as technologically advanced beings whose sophisticated knowledge of the natural world allows them to appear magical to less developed societies). Religion and spirituality also appear in science fiction as psychological necessities for individual characters, nations, and planets. Religion, therefore, cannot be denied or excised simply because it proposes nonrational methods of comprehending the universe.

The third category mediates the extremes of the first two by permitting an uneasy alliance between science fiction and spirituality that nonetheless privileges reason over faith and empirical physicality over metaphysical transcendence.[1]

This debate's essential tension disputes two different approaches to understanding existence: Phenomena available to the physical senses, which can be experienced as part of verifiable human reality, compete with phenomena that, although unavailable to the physical senses, participate in a larger, empirically unverifiable world that circumscribes human reality. This dichotomy is not endemic to science fiction, having existed in the Western world at least since Aristotle discussed a scientific method that tests theories about the natural universe to offer secular explanations about physical existence that do not refer to divine or spiritual origins.

The importance of this debate within SF scholarship gains new valence when applied to Philip K. Dick's fiction, much of which bears an overtly spiritual cast. Whether in his early novels, in his remarkably pessimistic 1967 story "Faith of Our Fathers," or in what Kim Stanley Robinson calls "Dick's final trilogy"[2]—namely, his last three novels, VALIS (1981), The Divine Invasion (1981), and The Transmigration of Timothy Archer (1982)—Dick's fiction manifests a consistent fascination with religious and spiritual matters. Baptized as an Episcopalian in January 1964,[3] Dick remained in this church for the rest of his life (although he continued to espouse unorthodox views based upon his extensive reading of Buddhist, Christian, Gnostic, Hindu, and Jewish texts). Lawrence Sutin, Dick's primary biographer, also maintains that Dick "adhered to no single faith. The one tradition indubitably his was SF—which exalts 'What IF?' above all."[4] For Dick, science fiction was a crucible in which religious, spiritual, and transcendent ideas could be advanced, analyzed, rejected, embraced, and melded with SF tropes, conventions, and characters. By combining spiritual themes with SF settings, Dick's fiction becomes an illuminating example of postmodern syncretism (rather than a haphazard pastiche of sacred and profane elements) that produces sophisticated humanist literature.

Writing allows Dick to understand the transcendental significance of religious experience. Reading spiritual tracts is not enough for Dick, who must copy down his bizarre religious ideas to comprehend their meaning. The prime example of this textual impulse is the Exegesis, an eight-thousand-page spiritual journal that Dick maintained after experiencing a series of dreams, visions, and hallucinations during February and March 1974. Dick was so troubled by these unsettling events that, until his 1982 death, he wrote in the Exegesis every night in an attempt to determine these visions' origin by considering every possible explanation (including the possibility that he had suffered a mental breakdown). The spiritual conundrums that Dick confronts in the *Exegesis*, in fact, provide much of the basic narrative material for his final trilogy. By textualizing his religious experiences, Dick develops his own cosmogony. He also creates a unique postmodern perspective about the cosmic importance of writing that enhances the complex humanism of his life, art, and work.

This complicated confluence of science fiction, religion, and spirituality makes Dick's metaphysical fiction an important part of his authorial career. Several Dickian scholars have commented upon the author's spiritual fixations,[5] but few have noted that Dick's textual representation of spiritual and religious principles (particularly the creation of the universe) connects his writing with the fiction of Italo Calvino, a writer often mentioned in the same breath with Jorge Luis Borges, but who produced a singular body of work. Calvino's fiction combines numerous literary genres and modes: fantasy, fable, folklore, fairy tale, picaresque, science fiction, and Italian neorealism. Calvino's international reputation, since his death in 1985, has transcended Rosetta Di Pace-Jordan's judgment of him "as one of Italy's major twentieth-century writers."[6] Calvino's stature has grown because his delightful stories playfully manipulate, subvert, and interrogate the structural and thematic assumptions of fiction itself. Calvino's best-known works—*The Baron in the Trees* (*Il Barone Rampante*, 1957), *Cosmicomics* (*Cosmicomiche*, 1965), *t zero* (*Ti con Zero*, 1967), *Invisible Cities* (*La Citta Invisibili*, 1972), and especially *If on a winter's night a traveler* (*Si una notte d'inverno un viaggiatore*, 1979)—all propose intriguing hermeneutic puzzles that invite (and, in the case of *winter's night*, require) the reader to speculate upon a fictional story's origins, development, and existence as a textual object.

Even so, this connection between Calvino and Dick may seem precarious because most critics refuse to identify Calvino as an SF writer. More damning is the assertion by Kathryn Hume that "Calvino's stories lack [science fiction's] speculative interest in how humans would respond to technologically defined situations,"[7] an assessment that particularly applies to the three Calvino works—the short-story collections *Cosmicomics* and *t zero*, as well as the novel *If on a winter's night a traveler*—that shed light on four notable examples of Dick's religious fiction: *The Three Stigmata of Palmer Eldritch*, "Faith of Our Fathers," *VALIS*, and *The Divine Invasion*. Both authors' fascination with the production of textual meaning, however, demonstrates that Dick's spiritual fiction and Calvino's hermeneutical writing are closely related to one another.

Hume, when discussing *Cosmicomics* and *t zero*, offers the most direct objection to aligning Calvino with Dick, stating, "Among [Calvino's] apparent aims in these stories is the desire to challenge the adequacy of science to serve as our only interpreter of the phenomenal world. What makes this challenge unusual is its lack of theological impetus."[8] Calvino's fiction nonetheless sees textual interpretation as a reflexive process that resembles, without replicating, scriptural hermeneutics. His writing, in other words, is not only aware of its existence as a textual object, but also helps the reader to better comprehend the theological subtext of Dick's science fiction. Calvino and Dick, indeed, so enthusiastically probe the correspondences between the production of literary meaning and the creation of the universe that their writing about creation is among the twentieth century's most intriguing, nuanced, and significant fiction.

The Spirit of Scientific Fiction

Even a peremptory review of Calvino's and Dick's fiction exposes their contrasting styles. Calvino's light, airy, and exuberant writing is happier than Dick's pessimistic, gloomy, and claustrophobic fiction (although considerable wit and gallows humor pervade Dick's writing). Both authors' fascination with cosmological and theological issues, moreover, cannot obscure the differences between how Calvino and Dick conceptualize the relationship between science and spirituality.

This conflict is evident when comparing Calvino's *Cosmicomics* and *t zero* to Dick's *The Three Stigmata of Palmer Eldritch* and "Faith of Our Fathers." Calvino's short-story collections chronicle the adventures of Qwfwq, a being whose unpronounceable palindrome of a name indicates the impossible position that he occupies in the narratives woven around him. Qwfwq, indeed, is present at the moment of the solar system's physical birth, whose artful description in the story "At Daybreak" merits extensive quotation:

> We were peering into this darkness, crisscrossed with voices, when the change took place: the only real, great change I've ever happened to witness, and compared to it the rest is nothing. I mean this thing that began at the horizon, this vibration which didn't resemble those we then called sounds, or those now called the "hitting" vibrations, or any others; . . . all the darkness was suddenly dark in contrast with something else that wasn't darkness, namely light. . . . There was what we would later have called a source of light, that is, a mass that was becoming incandescent, separated from us by an enormous empty space, and it seemed to be trying out all the colors one by one, in iridescent fits and starts. . . . In the midst of the sky, between us and that incandescent mass, a couple of islands, brightly lighted and vague [were] letting out a kind of chirping noise.

So the better part was done: the heart of the nebula, contracting, had developed warmth and light, and now there was the Sun. All the rest went on revolving nearby, divided and clotted into various pieces, Mercury, Venus, the Earth, and others farther on, and whoever was on them, stayed where he was. And, above all, it was deathly hot.[9]

This excerpt's humorous wonderment juxtaposes the awe of cosmic creation with Qwfwq's jovial throwaway observations about the event's excessive temperature. The audacity of writing a first-person account of creation recedes when the sensuality of the moment, awash in tactile vibrations, chirping noises, and visual iridescence, overwhelms Qwfwq's narration. Other intelligences identified by Qwfwq as his family and friends ("Father and Mother, Granny Bb'b, some uncles and aunts who were visiting, Mr. Hnw, the one who later became a horse, and us little ones"[10]) not only witness the universe's creation, but also survive the massive energies of solar genesis.

Calvino, rather than undercutting this premise's absurdity, increases its ludicrousness by recounting, in the story "All at One Point," Qwfwq's life *before* the Big Bang:

Naturally, we were all there,—old *Qwfwq said*,—where else could we have been? Nobody knew then that there could be space. Or time either: what use did we have for time, packed in there like sardines?

I say "packed like sardines," using a literary image: in reality there wasn't even space to pack us into. Every point of each of us coincided with every point of each of the others in a single point, which was where we all were. In fact, we didn't even bother one another, except for personality differences, because when space doesn't exist, having somebody unpleasant like Mr. Pber^t Pber^d underfoot all the time is the most irritating thing.[11]

This passage's paradoxes challenge a purely scientific account of the universe's origin by emphasizing the fictional nature of Qwfwq's narration. Despite the reader's rational knowledge that nothing can exist prior to the universe, Qwfwq gamely recounts how he and his associates became conscious of their own personality flaws. Much of Calvino's comic effect arises from subverting a cosmic event (or, in this case, the prelude to a cosmic event) with humorous observations and incongruous psychological comments about human behavior. Melding the cosmic and the comic not only demonstrates how aptly Calvino titles his short-story anthology, but also underscores the importance of language in authoring the universe's genesis. Qwfwq knows that literary images only approximate actual events because the reality of cosmic birth is much different from Qwfwq's retroactive attempts to reconstruct it. His account of cosmic parturition defies scientific notions of the universe's actual genesis to produce literary metaphors that Calvino's reader must interpret.

The resulting narrative makes no pretense at rational objectivity. Qwfwq's wry humor and world-weariness dissipate the restrictions of time and space so that the origin of the universe becomes the adventurously funny first-person account of a practiced raconteur. The Qwfwq tales, consequently, do not represent, but merely resemble, a human perspective. John Earl Joseph expertly recognizes the literary-historical character of Calvino's narrator:

> Whatever kind of force or intelligence Qwfwq & co. represent in *Cosmicomics*, two things are clear: first, that they are undeniably superior to history in every conceivable sense; second, that while their understanding is beyond that experienced by humans, it is expressible in human terms, and their sensibilities are entirely human. They could not have come from the pen of someone bound by the deterministic view of man as object of history. The delightful, dancing prose of *Cosmicomics* is that of an author joyous at having this great weight lifted from him.[12]

This transhistorical exuberance carries over into the forms that Qwfwq adopts: a disembodied intelligence (whether mathematical formula or cosmic particle) in "At Daybreak" and "All at One Point," an amphibious creature in "The Aquatic Uncle," a dinosaur in "The Dinosaurs," and an unidentified (yet organic) observer of evolution in "The Origin of Birds." Calvino can reveal the universe's magnificence by ignoring or dissolving the limitations imposed by order, causal logic, and scientific detail. He proposes marvelous fantasies that witness processes of creation, cosmic development, and species evolution that, while based upon scientific events, exceed all rational explanation. Hume, as previously noted, describes Calvino's legacy in writing *Cosmicomics* and *t zero* as a challenge to strictly rational thinking: "Among his apparent aims in these stories is the desire to challenge the adequacy of science to serve as our only interpreter of the phenomenal world."[13]

The same may be said of Dick's 1960s fiction. Two of Dick's gloomiest works, *The Three Stigmata of Palmer Eldritch* and "Faith of Our Fathers," appropriate a common (even clichéd) SF subgenre, the alien-invasion tale, to meditate upon humanity's fallen nature. Scientific rationality, in these stories, gives way to ontological depression and spiritual ennui. *Palmer Eldritch* depicts a barely livable, miserably hot Earth in which the oceans evaporate, the humidity becomes intolerably high, and people must wear massive amounts of sunblock if they wish to safely travel outdoors. Circumstances are worse, however, for the off-world colonists whom Earth's government has forcibly relocated to Mars, Venus, and Ganymede to live in hovels that barely sustain their human residents. Most colonists are committed users, if not addicts, of Can-D, a narcotic that "translates" them into a group-mind experience in which the colonists inhabit the perfectly shaped bodies of two dolls: Perky Pat and her boyfriend, Walt. This delusion has a physical antecedent: a miniaturized, Barbie-doll-like "layout" replicates whatever scene the colonists wish to experience (a day at the beach, a romantic evening, or a relaxing drive). By arranging the layout into the desired scene before ingesting Can-D, a colonist's consciousness transfers to the Perky Pat or the Walt doll to enjoy, all too briefly, a beautiful illusion that is Dick's prescient fictional forerunner of virtual reality.

Complicating matters is a competing narcotic named Chew-Z that soon appears in the colonies to challenge Can-D's primacy as the off-world drug of choice. Chew-Z originates in the Proximus star system, having been brought to Earth and Mars by industrialist Palmer Eldritch after his decade-long sojourn on this alien system's central planet. Eldritch claims that Chew-Z, rather than temporarily translating its user into an inconstant world of false perfection, instead creates its own fully real paradise, in which Eldritch becomes the creator, legislator, and overseer of a new world. "God," Eldritch arrogantly proclaims in the novel's most famous line, "promises eternal life. I can do better; *I can deliver it.*"[14]

This deliverance is ambivalent. The novel's two protagonists, Leo Bulero and Barney Mayerson, discover after ingesting Chew-Z that Eldritch is an extraterrestrial creature that manipulates the alternate realities through which they, like all Chew-Z users, move. They cannot escape Eldritch's influence to rediscover their primary reality because Eldritch can impersonate anyone he wishes. Bulero and Mayerson, therefore, can never determine for certain what is real and what is not. The novel concludes with a ship carrying Eldritch, in the person of Bulero, toward Earth to bring his "gift" to all humanity.

The stark nature of *Palmer Eldritch*'s setting, characters, and themes contrasts the jaunty tone of *Cosmicomics* and *t zero*. "Faith of Our Fathers" is an even greater departure. In this unremittingly pessimistic story, which Eugene Warren calls "[one] of Dick's most shocking novellas,"[15] protagonist Tung Chien, a minor functionary working in the Hanoi division of the totalitarian society created by the Absolute Benefactor (and leader) of the People's Republic of China, sees reality crumble around him after ingesting an antihallucinogen. Chien, much to his horror, discovers that the Absolute Benefactor is neither the Asian man that Chien sees on television nor the Caucasian man that Chien sees at a stag party held at the leader's private villa. The Benefactor, instead, is a destructive extraterrestrial creature bent on draining life from every human being with whom he comes into contact. Chien attends the stag party after receiving an antihallucinogen from Tanya Lee, member of an underground organization that wishes to expose the Benefactor's true identity. Chien comes to believe that the Benefactor is the creator of the universe. This truth, captured in Chien's unnerving realization that "God was death, it was one force, one hunter, one cannibal thing,"[16] is not the story's final horror. "Faith of Our Fathers" concludes with Chien recognizing that he will soon die from a wound (given to him by the Benefactor) that refuses to stop bleeding.

This development leaves the reader, like Chien himself, bereft of all hope. Warren says that the story "succinctly carries the dark side of Dick's vision of life to its ultimate extreme end,"[17] while Karl Wessel describes it "as Maoism turned metaphysical nightmare."[18] These assessments, no matter how astute, cannot capture the story's oppressive atmosphere. Rather than Calvino's joyful wonderment, Dick's reader encounters rampant paranoia. "Faith of Our Fathers" may narrate the mystery of creation, just as *Palmer Eldritch* may illustrate a secular path to transcendence (through addiction to an extraterrestrial narcotic), but neither story accepts science as an adequate "interpreter of the phenomenal world,"[19] to return to Hume's phrase. Dick's vision, like Calvino's, transcends scientific discourse to endorse metaphysical perspectives.

Cosmicomics and *t zero*, however, are not explicitly religious texts, as Hume acknowledges in her fine assessment of Calvino's short-story anthologies:

> What makes this challenge [the challenge to science's adequacy as an interpreter of nature] unusual is its lack of theological impetus. The inability of science to see the evidence of God's handiwork through its microscope is not an issue. Calvino accepts the Godless universe. He delights in forcing very ordinary forms of "human" consciousness to face the full scientific complexity of this universe. He raises questions about meaning in life and death, and offers answers that owe nothing to religious doctrine.[20]

Qwfwq, more accurately, never considers that creation has a divine purpose or that it originates from a transcendent source. His tales confine themselves to physical events whose scientific explanation makes religious description unnecessary. The separation between science and religion, in fact, finds unproblematic expression in Calvino's scientific fantasies.

Calvino's Qwfwq stories, therefore, do not document cosmological theory, but rather employ scientific principles to imaginatively synthesize science, fantasy, fiction, and fable. Hume notes that Calvino combines "imaginative and scientific modes of perception"[21] to augment objective rationality with metaphysical fantasy. *Cosmicomics* and *t zero*, therefore, like *The Three Stigmata of Palmer Eldritch* and "Faith of Our Fathers," textually consolidate spirituality, metaphysics, and scriptural writing to advance humanist values and postmodern principles.

Narrating Creation

Calvino's audacity in writing first-person accounts of cosmological, planetary, and biological creation is potentially blasphemous, for he usurps a role that in Buddhism, Christianity, Hinduism, Islam, and Judaism is normally reserved for prophets or for people touched by the divine. Calvino does not recount the Qwfwq tales directly (for how could he, not having been present during the events recorded in these tales?), but instead creates a fictional narrator to offer firsthand accounts of cosmic happenings. This simple act requires Calvino's reader to begin a hermeneutical quest that probes, doubts, and explores the narrator's reliability. Assessing Qwfwq's trustworthiness involves many questions: Who or what is Qwfwq? How can he be present before creation? How does he survive the massive energies of the Big Bang? Why does he choose to tell these tales in the first place? Why has he waited so long to recount them?

One literary answer is obvious: Qwfwq is a narrative device that Calvino employs to retell the story of creation from a secular vantage point. Calvino gives his reader the ultimate insider's view by writing the universe's perspective of its own genesis. This outlook is not a god's-eye view because the cosmological origin recounted by Qwfwq is a fanciful version of the Big Bang rather than a religious creation myth. By escaping the restrictions of both scientific accuracy and narrative mimesis, the Qwfwq tales become inventive, humorous, and colorful descriptions of how the universe's first moments must have unfolded.

Another answer provides spiritual and hermeneutical complications. Qwfwq, within the confines of the stories he narrates, becomes the author of all creation. He is not only the fundamental witness to, but also the primary voice of, cosmic birth, planetary parturition, and biological evolution. Qwfwq may not be a divine creature, but he conflates metaphysical and scientific perspectives into one narrative viewpoint that percolates with spiritual overtones even as it transcends history. Although Qwfwq is not the universe's creator, he is also not a simple cosmic particle. Qwfwq speaks words that generate worlds, meaning that this textual process, written in pages for future human generations to read, makes Qwfwq a scriptural author, as well.

Palmer Eldritch occupies a similar role in the novel bearing his name. Eldritch tells Leo Bulero as much when explaining the alternate world that they both inhabit after Bulero first ingests Chew-Z:

> "But," Eldritch said, "you didn't construct this—establishment, here; I did and it's mine. I created . . . this landscape—" He gestured with his stick. "Every damn thing you see, including your body."
>
> "My body?" Leo examined himself. It was his regular, familiar body, known to him intimately; it was his, not Eldritch's.
>
> "I willed you to emerge here exactly as you are in our universe," Eldritch said. "You see, that's the point that appealed to Hepburn-Gilbert [Secretary General of the United Nations], who of course is a Buddhist. You can reincarnate in any form you wish, or that's wished for you, as in this situation."[22]

Eldritch is the deity of a universe that springs from his intentional act of creation, as he reveals when saying of the gluck, a hideous creature that wishes to devour Bulero, "I made it out of a portion of myself."[23] Eldritch even allows Bulero to fashion objects by "[projecting] a fraction of your essence; it'll take material form on its own. What you supply is the logos."[24] When Bulero creates a King James Bible to protect himself, Eldritch states the situation as baldly as possible: "This is my domain. . . . We don't want to scare people away; religion has become a touchy subject."[25] The spiritual and mystical nuances of Eldritch's deification are clear. He links the universe that Chew-Z allows him to produce to Buddhist reincarnation, to an essential human logos whose roots in Judaism and Christianity stretch as far back as Zoroastrianism, and to the unwelcome King James Bible. Eldritch, indeed, inscribes a new world directly onto Bulero's consciousness. Leo initially rejects Eldritch's vision as a drug-induced sham, but seeing Eldritch's three "stigmata"—steel teeth, artificial eyes, and mechanical arm—appear on all the people around him (including Leo himself, in the novel's final scene) extends Eldritch's control onto everything the creature touches.

A hermeneutical reading of Dick's novel becomes possible because any attempt to interpret Eldritch in purely secular terms, as nothing more than an alien creature that employs narcotics to trap people into artificially induced hallucinations, becomes unstable when Barney Mayerson, a Bulero employee who has also been exposed to the "ersatz universe"[26] of Eldritch's Chew-Z, realizes that "[o]nce you've taken Chew-Z you're delivered over. . . . It's the condition of slavery. Like the Fall. And the temptation is similar."[27] This spiritual interpretation indicates that Eldritch's supposed alternate world has so permeated the novel's objective reality that no person, including the reader, can be certain that Eldritch's universe is not authentic. The fact that

Palmer Eldritch's first scene sees Mayerson waking "to find himself in an unfamiliar bedroom in an unfamiliar conapt [condominium-apartment] building"[28] with his head "unnaturally aching,"[29] with no explanation ever offered for this amnesia, suggests, in light of the novel's conclusion, that the entire story occurs within Eldritch's alternative reality. This ontological instability results from Eldritch inscribing his own apotheosis onto all human beings, whether they live on Earth or in its colonies. The scriptural implications are disheartening: All interpretations lead to Eldritch, the human being/ extraterrestrial creature/deity, meaning that all exegetical efforts spin through a profusion of constructed universes that trap each human being in a private, individualized hell.

David Golumbia recognizes the hermeneutical challenge posed by Dick in *Palmer Eldtritch*:

> The pursuit of Absolute Reality is most often conceived as an anti-establishment quest, to break through the arbitrary structures of reality imposed from without; this is the dynamic that licenses the general ideological interpretation of Dick, in which artificial or otherwise unacceptable considerations are imposed on the perceiving subject's ability to understand and perceive the "actual," read "material," structures of the world.
>
> But in . . . *Three Stigmata* we have the inklings of a different way to read Dick, in which it isn't the falsity, or the deceptiveness, of the ideologically-imposed Reality, but the very attempt to *posit* such a reality that is called into question. . . . In this respect it is wrong to locate the ideological critique in *Three Stigmata* only with a general critique of capitalism or even of imperialism; rather it is critical of univocal—that is, Realist—readings of the world.[30]

The final irony is that Eldritch attempts to impose just this type of univocal reading on the novel's characters. The reader's hermeneutical attempt to distinguish the novel's "true" reality from Eldritch's false worlds highlights the scriptural and spiritual maze that Dick creates. The written text—Dick's novel *The Three Stigmata of Palmer Eldritch*—interrogates the boundaries between science, spirituality, divinity, and authentic reality. Eldritch himself becomes a narrative device by which to enter this textual game, an entity that authors his own spiritual revolution through the secular application of an alien narcotic.

The Authors of Creation

Qwfwq is neither as menacing nor as megalomaniacal as Eldritch, but Qwfwq's metaphysical properties create hermeneutical challenges for

Calvino's reader. Nearly all the Qwfwq tales found in *Cosmicomics* and *t zero* begin with specific narrative markers that interrupt declarative sentences: in "The Distance of the Moon": "How well I know!—*old Qwfwq cried,*—the rest of you can't remember, but I can";[31] in "At Daybreak": "Pitch-dark it was,—*old Qwfwq confirmed,*—I was only a child, I can barely remember it";[32] in "Crystals": "It could have been different, I know,—*Qwfwq remarked,*—you're telling me";[33] and, most directly, in "Games Without End": "I was only a child, but I was already aware of it,—*Qwfwq narrated,*—I was acquainted with all the hydrogen atoms."[34] These markers not only emphasize Qwfwq's textual existence, but also remind the reader that, although Qwfwq verbalizes his tales, Calvino's audience cannot physically hear Qwfwq's voice; rather, it reads his words.

The differences between speaking and writing—or between listening and reading—become significant in light of Calvino's and Dick's spiritual, scriptural, and reflexive fiction. Paul Ricoeur differentiates between dialogue (verbal language) and discourse (written language) to underscore how much each depends upon the other:

> What counts for the present discussion is that the polysemy of words calls forth as its counterpart the selective role of contexts in determining the current value of words in a given message, addressed by a specific speaker to a hearer in a particular situation. Sensitivity to context is the necessary complement and the unavoidable counterpart of polysemy.
>
> But the use of contexts in turn brings into play an activity of discernment which takes place in a concrete exchange of messages between interlocutors and whose model is the language game of question and answer. This activity of discernment is properly called interpretation. It consists in recognizing which relatively univocal message the speaker has constructed upon the polysemic base of the common lexicon.[35]

Dialogue and discourse mutually reinforce one another in this analysis. Ricouer implies that writing's dialogical qualities and speech's discursive traits are inevitable components of polysemy. Context, in this formulation, functions as the selective and self-limiting referee of any message's value. Ricoeur believes speech to be a type of linguistic information exchange between apparently equal interlocutors, an egalitarian view of interpretation that has important consequences for Calvino's and Dick's metaphysical fiction. The author, no longer a privileged dispenser of information, participates in a linguistic game where speech and writing become complementary methods of communicating knowledge. Writing is not a comprehensive system, but rather a limited province within the larger territory of language.

Ricoeur's fertile conceptualization of hermeneutics sees speech as less practiced and more immediate than writing. Since speech and writing buttress one another, however, the act of interpretation is more dialectical than it might initially seem. *Cosmicomics* and *t zero* revel in the spoken word's immediacy, which Calvino beautifully captures in the Qwfwq tales. Calvino also unearths writing's dialogical character and speech's discursive nature by transcribing Qwfwq's tall tales of cosmic, planetary, and biological genesis into textual form. Qwfwq may speak, but writing down the unrehearsed immediacy of his dialogue allows the reader to "hear" it. Calvino's artistry even allows the audience to temporarily forget that it is reading fiction.

No matter how unpracticed and natural Qwfwq's dialogue may appear, Qwfwq's inability to exist in any rationally scientific account of cosmogenesis marks him as a divine, or at least metaphysical, creature. The textual reproduction of Qwfwq's words and worlds, therefore, is scriptural insofar as it transforms stories based on secular, scientific phenomena into spiritual documents without specific religious overtones. Qwfwq's role as the narrator/author of whole worlds links him to Palmer Eldritch's similarly complicated metaphysical status, meaning that Qwfwq's stories occupy a literary borderland between science and spirituality, just as *The Three Stigmata of Palmer Eldritch* does.

If, as Ricouer implies, writing becomes a dialectical process of give-and-take rather than a one-way information exchange between active authors and passive readers, then interpretation becomes far more than the reader's attempt to ascertain a text's meaning. Writing is also not simply the author's method of transmitting meaning to docile readers, but instead becomes a dialogic process that resembles speech even while differing markedly from spoken discourse. This formulation calls to mind the *différance* that Jacques Derrida explores in his writing about deconstruction by questioning two fundamental assumptions about the nature of writing: first, that writing is more refined (and therefore purer) than speech, and, second, that writing represents the highest achievement of Western culture. Derrida instead focuses upon how developing "all the means of conserving the spoken language, of making it function without the presence of the speaking subject"[36] makes writing a restrictive medium:

> This development, coupled with that of anthropology and the history of writing, teaches us that phonetic writing, the medium of the great metaphysical, scientific, technical, and economic adventure of the West, is limited in space and time and limits itself even as it is in the process of imposing its laws upon the cultural areas that had escaped it.[37]

Derrida recognizes how writing depends upon speech even as writing erases the need for its subjects to speak. He disrupts the dichotomy between speaking and writing to suggest that writing is a hollow substitute that cannot capture the immediacy of spoken discourse.

Derrida's concept of *différance*, therefore, refers to the mutual deference between speech and writing. Each informs, influences, and reacts to the other in a complex tangle of symbolization and signification:

> Between being and mind, things and feelings, there would be a relationship of translation or natural signification; between mind and logos, a relationship of conventional symbolization. And the *first* convention, which would relate immediately to the order of natural and universal signification, would be produced as spoken language. Written language would establish the conventions, interlinking other conventions with them.[38]

Writing and speech produce *and* establish one another, just as Qwfwq's speaking voice produces and establishes the written tales that Calvino transcribes (or, following Derrida's terminology, translates) in *Cosmicomics* and *t zero*. The reader, while seeing Qwfwq's words, also hears Qwfwq's voice.

This simultaneous process emphasizes the difficulty of defining Qwfwq's tales as either written or spoken texts. Their generic permeability (as both secular *and* spiritual texts) is notable because Qwfwq neither acknowledges nor intimates divine, spiritual, or metaphysical agents. Calvino's Qwfwq stories are simultaneously secular *and* transcendent tales that evoke spiritual ideas without directly referencing religion.

Dick's fiction, as "Faith of Our Fathers" demonstrates, has many religious implications. The story's spiritual subtext, in a horrifying turn, frankly acknowledges the evil that underscores religious thinking. Dick's short story, like Calvino's Qwfwq tales, posits a corporeal creator with metaphysical properties. The Absolute Benefactor, as protagonist Tung Chien discovers, is both a physical creature and a transcendent being. Even after taking the antihallucinogen provided by Tanya Lee, Chien cannot see the Benefactor directly:

> Yet if he turned his head, caught it out of a sidelong glance, he could determine its boundaries.
>
> It was terrible; it blasted him with its awareness. As it moved it drained the life from each person in turn; it ate the people who had assembled, passed on, ate again, ate more with an endless appetite. It hated; he felt its hate. It loathed; he felt its loathing for everyone present—in fact he shared its loathing. . . . I know who you are, Tung Chien thought to himself. . . . You go

anywhere, appear any time, devour anything; you engineer life and then guzzle it, and you enjoy that.

He thought, You are God.[39]

The Absolute Benefactor, now unmasked, taunts Chien by revealing its cannibalistic intentions: "I founded everything. . . . I founded it all. As if they were blades of grass. . . . As you live on, unable to stop, I will torment you. . . . I will deprive you, item by item, of everything you possess or want. And then when you are crushed to death I will unfold a mystery"[40] that offers no comfort to the beleaguered Chien: "The dead shall live, the living die. I kill what lives; I save what has died. And I will tell you this: *there are things worse than I.* But you won't meet them because by then I will have killed you."[41] This terrible vision of divinity, steeped in pain and cruelty, magnifies, to hopeless proportions, the Gnostic conception of a supreme deity who creates imperfect worlds for its personal consumption. Neither Chien nor the reader finds solace from the horror that "Faith of Our Fathers" presents about the spiritual foundation of human life.

The Absolute Benefactor's metaphysical pronouncements about cosmogenesis, like Qwfwq's, become textually inscribed. Dick's reader tries to answer the story's many unresolved questions, such as determining the Benefactor's true identity ("non-terrestrial" is as much as Chien tells Tanya),[42] wondering how the torment of human beings gives the Benefactor strength, and asking why the Benefactor creates such a cruel and unforgiving universe. This final idea conflicts with twentieth-century Christian, Jewish, Islamic, and Buddhist ideas of God as a merciful, loving patriarch who promises everlasting salvation to the faithful. The fact that Chien requires antihallucinogenic drugs to recognize the awful truth about the Benefactor's metaphysical reality, shrouded as it is by multiple layers of illusion, inscribes secular rationalism into a spiritually minded story. The Benefactor's revelation about its true nature, moreover, cannot be trusted because, like a nightmarish trickster god, the Benefactor may create another delusion to further confuse Chien, thereby forestalling resistance to the Benefactor's insidious plans. Any attempt to interpret "Faith of Our Fathers" one way or the other—as a text based upon scientific principles or upon religious doctrine—fails in its exegetical task because Dick's story fuses the two into a transgeneric examination of how scientific and spiritual thought intermingle.

In Dick's fiction, just as in Calvino's, the textual becomes scriptural when metaphysical ideas invest apparently secular stories with implicit (Qwfwq's tales) or explicit ("Faith of Our Fathers") spiritual resonances. This interchange forces the reader to question rigid divisions between secularism and spirituality, and then deconstruct these binary oppositions. The differences between Calvino's and Dick's individual approach to spirituality may not disappear, but both writers are more complicated than an oppositional, either-or reading acknowledges.

Deconstructing the Textual Universe

Calvino and Dick unseat the binary opposition between secular and spiritual fiction in different ways. They merge material and transcendent perspectives into complicated renderings of spirituality's place within a scientifically rational universe. Calvino's Qwfwq tales and Dick's science fiction achieve similar goals, but Calvino probes physical and metaphysical issues to reach much sunnier resolutions than Dick. Each Qwfwq tale explores a different aspect of the physical universe (creation, evolution, new life, death) from the fantastical, transhistorical, and transgenerical perspective of its witty nonhuman narrator. Qwfwq's seemingly omniscient vantage point might suggest a divine or spiritual origin, but his enthusiasm for new discoveries grounds Qwfwq in scientifically secular contexts. The opening of "The Origin of Birds" most clearly communicates this phenomenon:

> In those days we weren't expecting any more surprises,—*Qwfwq narrated*,—by then it was clear how things were going to proceed. Those who existed, existed; we had to work things out for ourselves: some would go farther, some would remain where they were, and some wouldn't manage to survive. The choice had to be made from a limited number of possibilities.[43]

Birds, much to Qwfwq's surprise, arise. He cannot control evolution, meaning that Qwfwq is simply one of many existing intelligences. His secular observations, moreover, call his divinity into doubt.

The spiritual traces of Qwfwq's insights and the scriptural affinities of their written form, however, are unmistakable. Qwfwq, like Palmer Eldritch and the Absolute Benefactor, inscribes creation onto a material text that mediates his speech into readable format. Qwfwq's tales are not forgotten once he tells them, but preserved by printed discourse. Qwfwq, unlike Eldritch and the Benefactor, does not masquerade as a deity even though his presence at the instant of creation transcends human limitations. Qwfwq, therefore, possesses scriptural authority that Calvino's readers must interpret, analyze, and evaluate to determine exactly what Qwfwq may be. He is neither a godlike creator nor the solely physical transcriber of creation's events. He instead participates in two realms—physical and metaphysical, temporal and spiritual, secular and religious—to transcend dualistic conceptualizations of the universe.

This plurality underscores another difference between Dick's overtly spiritual fiction and Calvino's implicitly metaphysical writing. Qwfwq's tales are optimistic scientific fables told by a metaphysical narrator, while Dick's stories begin as secular tales that slowly reveal the everyday world's pessimistic spiritual foundation. Dick's fiction, in other words, consciously reveals its spiritual content and religious phenomena; Calvino's short-story anthologies do not.

The Qwfwq tales, however, have spiritual implications. Calvino undermines Qwfwq's spirituality even as he inscribes it within the text of *Cosmicomics* and *t zero*. Qwfwq's existence as the narrator/creator of new textual worlds also preserves one of Calvino's most perplexing ambiguities: Qwfwq both is and is not present in the stories that he narrates. Qwfwq may only be a narrative voice created by Calvino, but Qwfwq observes, interprets, and recounts the birth of the universe as if he were the author of these events. This literary conceit challenges readers who accompany Qwfwq on his thrilling intellectual journeys through the first moments of creation to indulge metaphysical thoughts that cannot be confined to material forms, even though material objects (specifically, the books *Cosmicomics* and *t zero*) allow Qwfwq to communicate with his readers. This paradox deconstructs space and time to produce the airy and hallucinatory tone that makes Qwfwq's stories such enjoyable reading experiences. The liberating sense that Calvino's readers are unbound by the constraints of material reality is one of the author's great artistic accomplishments in writing *Cosmicomics* and *t zero*. Both books deconstruct the physical basis of reality by imagining a realm that, while based upon human experience, is more pliable than its readers' quotidian lives. Calvino's short-story anthologies, as such, embrace metaphysical concerns without directly mentioning divine or religious themes.

Dick's overtly spiritual fiction also questions the strict separation between empiricism and spirituality. Although neither *Palmer Eldritch* nor "Faith of Our Fathers" is as cheerful as Calvino's Qwfwq stories, Dick's writing frequently breaches the boundary between science and spirituality. Dick's extraordinary 1966 self-evaluation of "Faith of Our Fathers," written before the story appeared in Harlan Ellison's acclaimed 1967 anthology *Dangerous Visions*, nicely summarizes the complexities of textual spirituality and metaphysical fiction:

> I don't advocate any of the ideas in "Faith of Our Fathers"; I don't, for example, claim that the Iron Curtain countries will win the cold war—or morally ought

to. One theme in the story, however, seems compelling to me, in view of recent experiments with hallucinogenic drugs: the theological experience, which
so many who have taken LSD have reported. This appears to me to be a true
new frontier; to a certain extent the religious experience can now be scientifically studied . . . and, what is more, may be viewed as part hallucination but
containing other, real components. God, as a topic in science fiction, when
it appeared at all, used to be treated polemically, as in [C. S. Lewis's novel]
Out of the Silent Planet. But I prefer to treat it as intellectually exciting. What
if, through psychedelic drugs, the religious experience becomes commonplace
in the life of intellectuals? The old atheism, which seemed to many of us—
including me—valid in terms of our experiences, or rather lack of experiences,
would have to step momentarily aside. Science fiction, always probing what is
about to be thought, become, must eventually tackle without preconceptions
a future neo-mystical society in which theology constitutes as major a force as
in the medieval period. This is not necessarily a backward step, because now
these beliefs can be tested—forced to put up or shut up. I, myself, have no
real beliefs about God; only my experience that He is present . . . subjectively,
of course; but the inner realm is real, too. And in a science fiction story one
projects what has been a personal inner experience into a milieu; it becomes
socially shared, hence discussable.[44]

Dick evokes a fluid interchange among ontology, epistemology, theology,
science, mysticism, metaphysics, experimental drugs, and public explorations
of private spirituality. His notion that inner realms have their own realities
and that God's presence is vaguely subjective find textual expression in
Dick's spiritually themed SF stories. He combines secularism with spirituality, subjectivity with objectivity, and reality with imagination to expand the
borders of science fiction to include—if not to encompass—divine, metaphysical, and transcendent subjects. Dick, like Calvino, projects personal
inner experiences into socially shared fiction that reconfigures the complex
relationship between science and spirituality from fractious opposition to
collegial congress.

Paradise Explained

Dick's vision of the scientific universe's spiritual character, however, does
not merely oscillate between unremitting horror and unattainable divinity.
His 1981 novel *The Divine Invasion* merges Gnostic and Jewish themes into
a story that recounts how the godhead's wounded, amnesiac male avatar re-
unites with its female half to defeat the evil of Belial (Satan) on a future Earth
whose political power is delicately balanced between the religious Christian-
Islamic Church and the secular Scientific Legate (successor to the Soviet

Union's Communist Party), which have joined "into one mega-apparatus, with two chiefs-of-state, as in ancient Sparta."⁴⁵ The novel's future world exacerbates tensions between scientific and religious perspectives, although the Church and the Legate manifest equally unrestrained appetites for political domination. *The Divine Invasion* recasts the story of the Second Coming to distinguish Dick's metaphysical fiction from Calvino's Qwfwq tales by reversing Calvino's primary metaphor of the secular protagonist as metaphysical agency. Dick's novel instead secularizes its metaphysical/religious protagonist—the Savior (who, although never identified as Jesus Christ, is clearly Christlike)—by awarding him a thoroughly physical existence (and a verifiably empirical presence) in the human world. Qwfwq never achieves full physicality in *Cosmicomics* and *t zero*, remaining an ambiguous creature (as much narrative device as physical presence). Dick's novel, consequently, more directly incorporates religious themes than do Calvino's Qwfwq tales.

The Divine Invasion's savior is immaculately conceived on a planet in the CY30-CY30B star system to a human colonist, Rybys Rommey. The planet's local deity, named Yah, not only impregnates Rybys, but also gives her multiple sclerosis so that she may safely travel to Earth, which forbids human colonists such as Rybys (who have been forcibly relocated off-world) from returning. Rybys, in short, is the prodigal mother of humanity's messiah. *The Divine Invasion*'s savior, named Emmanuel, receives injuries during an airborne shuttle accident that not only kills Rybys, but also damages Emmanuel's brain. The resulting amnesia is so severe that Emmanuel cannot recall his fundamental identity as the person who will fight, and ultimately defeat, Belial. The prophet Elijah, assuming the form of Elias Tate, becomes Emmanuel's ward. Elias, as the novel opens, takes the ten-year-old Emmanuel to school, where the boy meets an equally strange girl named Zina who soon reveals herself to be Hagia Sophia, the living embodiment of Wisdom, as well as the godhead's female aspect. Emmanuel and Zina, after discovering their divine purpose, defeat Belial before *The Divine Invasion* concludes in a complicated, life-affirming, and emotionally moving resolution.

Two notable elements of *The Divine Invasion* link this book with its predecessor, Dick's 1981 novel *VALIS*, and with Calvino's inventive 1979 novel *If on a winter's night a traveler* to illustrate how fruitfully science fiction can combine scientific empiricism, spiritual longing, secular reason, and religious fervor: (1) Dick invents a device called the holoscope that graphically demonstrates how hermeneutical thinking helps preserve humanist principles in the novel's fallen world, and (2) Dick emphasizes how male-female romance helps successfully resolve the book's metaphysical mysteries. *The Divine Invasion*, while not a naively optimistic rendering of the relationship between faith and science, proposes a happier combination of these two phenomena than much of the rest of Dick's writing.

F. Scott Walters identifies a crucial strategy by which Dick's penultimate novel fuses the spiritual with the secular: "In *The Divine Invasion* Dick can present mythical Demiurges and Sophias as literalized, actual beings, a process that is a strength of fantasy and SF: it literalizes metaphors."[46] For Dick, literalizing the Gnostic belief in a demiurge that is ignorant and self-deluded (and, in Emmanuel's case, debilitated) gives pungent materiality to Douglas A. Mackey's notion that Gnosticism conceives the universe as "one vast snare for the senses, causing man to forget his inner spiritual reality."[47] Elias Tate, avatar of the prophet Elijah, knows this sensual trap all too well: "The law stipulated that Manny could not go to a regular school because of his [brain-damaged] condition; there was nothing Elias Tate could do about that. He could not get around the government ruling because this was Earth and the zone of evil lay over everything. Elias could feel it and, probably, the boy could feel it, too."[48] This evil is Belial's presence on Earth, in which the entire planet—including the joint political authority of the Christian-Islamic Church and the Scientific Legate—becomes a terrible illusion that traps humanity in a world of sin, suffering, and privation.

These passages recall the metaphysical pessimism of *Palmer Eldritch* and "Faith of Our Fathers," although *The Divine Invasion* is far more hopeful than its forerunners. Emmanuel's task is not simply to defeat Belial, but, in Walters's cogent summary, "to effect what amounts to a 're-write' of the 'book' of the universe."[49] This transformative project finds its most remark-able symbol in the holoscope, an electronic device that not only takes all the Judeo-Christian scriptures as its text, but that also illustrates the human mind's hermeneutical capacity:

> After dinner [Emmanuel] spent some time with the holoscope, studying Elias's most precious possession: the Bible expressed as layers at different depths within the hologram, each layer according to age. The total structure of Scrip-ture formed, then, a three-dimensional cosmos that could be viewed from any angle and its contents read. According to the tilt of the axis of observation, differing messages could be extracted. Thus Scripture yielded up an infinitude of knowledge that ceaselessly changed. It became a wondrous work of art, beautiful to the eye, and incredible in its pulsations of color. Throughout it red and gold pulsed, with strands of blue.[50]

Interpretation, thanks to the holoscope, cannot remain static, but constantly changes. The holoscope, as a metaphor for the hermeneutical process, allows its user to experience infinite interpretations of scripture that shift according to its viewer's perspective. The holoscope's pliable holographic reproduction of the Bible suggests that individuals can not only recognize, but also understand scripture by applying their own intelligence to biblical texts without relying upon orthodox interpretations. In *The Divine Invasion*, the Gnostic insight that *gnosis* (knowledge) allows its user to pierce the phenomenal world's illusory existence to uncover the underlying pneumal core of human spiritual life is a key narrative, thematic, and symbolic element. Such knowledge becomes, through the holoscope, the technologically sophisticated affirmation of the human mind's ability to analyze, to comprehend, and to explain the universe's physical and metaphysical aspects. Epistemology and ontology blend into an unexpectedly startling evocation of the close ties between spiritual and scientific discourse.

The holoscope also celebrates human intelligence. The holoscope's capacity for revision turns discourse into dialogue, meaning that the holoscope's human user/reader/observer helps create a living universe. This creativity, so unorthodox in its possibilities, poses a threat to temporal authority:

> If you learned how you could gradually tilt the temporal axis, the axis of true depth, until successive layers were superimposed and a vertical message—a new message—could be read out. In this way you entered into a dialogue with Scripture; it became alive. It became a sentient organism that was never twice the same. The Christian-Islamic Church, of course, wanted both the Bible and the Koran frozen forever. If Scripture escaped out from under the church its monopoly departed.[51]

This independent dialogue challenges religious authority while consolidating the spiritual focus of the holoscope's user. Scriptural texts transform into free-floating visual information unencumbered by the linearity of a printed page, "translated," as Roger J. Stilling notes, "into a vibrant multidimensional state that much more closely approximates the immaterial existence of information in the mind."[52] Stilling successfully argues that *The Divine Invasion*'s holoscope is a metaphor for the mind of the novel's reader. The reading mind, in Dick's novel, not only analyzes texts, but also evaluates visual images to underscore the comprehensiveness of the hermeneutical process. The living, sentient, holographic scripture never repeats itself, which engages the reader in a textual-visual dialogue that mutates unpredictably from moment to moment. This brand of mutual authorship, in which the holoscope allows its user to create scripture anew, illustrates *The Divine Invasion*'s kinetic depiction of visionary states, metaphysical fiction, and spiritual life.

Stilling's sense of textual translation, moreover, recalls Derrida's sense of linguistic translation to describe the relationship between writing and speaking (or between discourse and dialogue) that Dick's metaphysical fiction repeatedly enacts. The Bible, in Dick's formulation, becomes a nexus (or matrix) of authorial and interpretive possibilities that the holoscope reconfigures into nonlinear visual representations of Christianity's holy book. *The Divine Invasion's* postmodern theological innovation allows the Bible to inspire infinite interpretations, which gives fictional life to Derrida's argument that all acts of writing, which are inherently uncertain, alter humanity's understanding of God's place in history:

> To write is not only to know that the Book does not exist and that forever there are books, against which the meaning of a world not conceived by an absolute subject is shattered, before it has even become a unique meaning; nor is it only to know that the non-written and the non-read cannot be relegated to the status of having no basis by the obliging negativity of some dialectic, making us deplore the absence of the Book from under the burden of "too many texts!" It is not only to have lost the theological certainty of seeing every page bind itself into the unique text of the truth, the "book of reason" as the journal in which accounts (*rationes*) and experiences consigned for Memory was formerly called, the genealogical anthology, the Book of Reason this time, the infinite manuscript read by a God who, in a more or less deferred way, is said to have given us use of his pen.[53]

The paradoxes Derrida observes—a Book that becomes many books, an infinite manuscript with finite dimensions, a transcendent God whose mystical writing affects the temporal realm—draw out the perplexities of *The Divine Invasion's* Gnostic evocation of the fall, salvation, and redemption of humanity by a fragile, debilitated, and imperfect savior who still manages to defeat Belial's evil. Scripture, in Dick's holoscope, becomes both material and spiritual, both physical and metaphysical, to alter its user's perception of the relationship between authors and readers. The Bible's author is an undefinable and unlocatable God, who, being simultaneously present and absent in scripture, also symbolizes the literary author—whether Dick or Calvino—who remains physically present during a text's creation, but then disappears so that readers may enjoy the text's contents. *The Divine Invasion's* storyline, therefore, is more overtly scriptural than either *Cosmicomics* or *t zero*. Dick's novel fuses Gnostic and Jewish themes, combines spiritual motifs with a fairy tale's breezy tone, and encourages its reader to think deeply about the plot's mystical ramifications.

Much the same can be said of Calvino's Qwfwq stories. Qwfwq may more indirectly visualize textual worlds than Dick's holoscope, but Qwfwq's loose, freewheeling, and informal narration multiplies the interpretive possibilities inherent in *Cosmicomics* and *t zero*. Qwfwq transcends the strictures of scientific objectivity to portray the evolving universe in precise, humorous, and wonder-filled prose. This unique narrative voice creates images, vistas, and worlds that genuinely surprise the audience even though readers can predict what will happen: Matter will coalesce into star systems, planets will form, life will evolve, the dinosaurs will become extinct, and Qwfwq's era will pass into the dim memory of history. Qwfwq converses with *Cosmicomics*'s and *t zero*'s reader to transform these tales into discursive dialogues. Calvino's and Dick's audiences, therefore, become their partners in generating textual universes. Qwfwq and the holoscope give Calvino's and Dick's readers access to creation's beauty, joy, and wonder, which, despite the metaphysical, spiritual, and transcendent significance that creation implies, finally rests upon one foundation: the romantic entanglement of men and women.

The Book of Love

Calvino and Dick ground their metaphysical concerns within recognizable human relationships to make spiritual and cosmological issues relevant to their readers. Calvino's Qwfwq stories and Dick's *The Divine Invasion*, beyond their status as entertainment, demonstrate how interpreting fiction alters the reader's understanding of the physical universe. Dick portrays the universe as an information hologram that cannot be properly understood until its inhabitants become good enough readers (meaning people who develop sufficiently sophisticated analytical and exegetical abilities) to recognize the authentic world that remains hidden within the all-encompassing sensory illusion that is daily life. *The Divine Invasion* literalizes this Gnostic quest by presenting two significant romances: Emmanuel and Zina are the novel's primary couple, while Herbert Asher, Emmanuel's foster father, becomes involved with Linda Fox, a popular singer who also serves as Asher's metaphysical protector. These relationships parallel the romantic (and often sexual) entanglements of Qwfwq and his contemporaries in *Cosmicomics* and *t zero*.

Calvino and Dick embody love as a feminine force that makes the universe possible. Calvino's "All at One Point" gives the reader an image of Mrs. Ph(i)NK$_0$, who comforts Qwfwq and his cramped associates before the Big Bang, when they occupy a single spatial point:

> We got along so well all together, so well that something extraordinary was bound to happen. It was enough for her to say, at a certain moment: "Oh, if I

only had some room, how I'd like to make some noodles for you boys!" And in that moment we all thought of the space that her round arms would occupy, moving backward and forward with the rolling pin over the dough . . . and at the same time we thought of it, this space was inevitably being formed, at the same time that Mrs. Ph(i)NK$_0$ was uttering those words: " . . . ah, what noodles, boys!" the point that contained her and all of us was expanding in a halo of distance in light-years and light-centuries and billions of light-millennia, and we were being hurled to the four corners of the universe.[54]

Female compassion gives birth to space and time, making life possible by nurturing the universe into existence. Kathryn Hume shrewdly observes that "this feminized creation myth . . . makes the scientist in us wonder at the inconceivability of the big bang."[55] Calvino, however, pursues a more emotional fictional project: cosmic romance. Qwfwq narrates the universe's creation by recalling pleasant memories of male-female interaction. Qwfwq's relationship with Mrs. Ph(i)NK$_0$, although far from sexual, demonstrates how foundational masculine and feminine principles are to Calvino's cosmogony. The pre-universe described by Qwfwq is not an androgynous point, but rather a sexually divided space that anticipates the biological differences that arise after Mrs. Ph(i)NK$_0$'s generosity creates the universe.

Sexual love and competition also drive many of Calvino's cosmic tales, including "The Distance of the Moon," in which Qwfwq unrequitedly loves the married Mrs. Vhd Vhd; "Without Colors," in which Qwfwq falls for Ayl's beauty after the universe's first rays of light reveal her presence; "The Aquatic Uncle," in which Qwfwq's vertebrate lover Lll chooses to marry Qwfwq's less evolved fish uncle; and, especially, "Mitosis," where Qwfwq experiences the intense love and sexual unity of a single cell before it is overtaken by the chaotic fragmentation of division.

Love and sex, in these Qwfwq tales, symbolize secular processes of cosmic and biological creation that become overtly spiritual in Dick's *The Divine Invasion*. Even so, love functions as the fulcrum upon which Emmanuel's conversations with Zina hinge in Dick's novel. Patricia S. Warrick sees this development as the key difference between *The Divine Invasion* and its immediate predecessor, *VALIS*: "*The Divine Invasion* dramatizes another kind of quest—the quest of love. . . . Its mode is very different from that of *Valis*. It is nonchronological. Its purpose is not to portray the process of ratiocination as *Valis* did, but rather to portray a transformation accomplished by love and wisdom. Consequently, this novel uses metaphor as a dramatic device."[56] *VALIS* does not exclude love, but this earlier novel depicts *caritas*, the love of friendship that leads its protagonist, Horselover Fat, to despair over the suicides of two close female friends, rather than *eros*, or sexual desire. *The Divine Invasion* demonstrates that sexual and emotional intimacy must overcome Belial's evil to heal the wounded godhead by integrating its male (Emmanuel) and female (Zina) aspects.[57] This theme transforms *The Divine Invasion* into a unique text with significant scriptural and humanist implications.

Walters reads Emmanuel's and Zina's roles in *The Divine Invasion* as explicitly authorial in nature: "The Creator-Author and the Wise Editor . . . are needed to make the fictional world authentically whole."[58] A small but humorous exchange that Emmanuel and Zina share near the novel's center certifies Walters's reading. Ten years after the accident that deprives Emmanuel of his mother and his memory, the boy lectures Herb Asher about the relationship between God and the universe. This sermon neatly describes an author's relationship to his or her text:

> The Creator would not be the Creator if there were no universe, and the universe would cease to be if the Creator did not sustain it. The Creator does not exist prior to the universe in time; he does not exist in time at all. God creates the universe constantly; he is *with* it, not above or behind it. This is impossible to understand for you [Herb] because you are a created thing and exist in time.[59]

Emmanuel identifies how Creator and universe, or author and text, mutually sustain one another in a process that recalls Qwfwq's interpenetration by all other objects in "All at One Point." After he finishes, a droll comment by Zina spoofs the dialogic nature of Emmanuel's disquisition: "'Emmanuel,' the girl Zina said, 'you are ponderous.'"[60]

Zina is correct. The male god ruminates so sententiously about cosmic matters that Zina must puncture his sermon by disclosing the existence of a world that she has constructed: the paradisiacal Commonwealth with its beautiful Palm Tree Garden, where beauty and joy predominate. Emmanuel believes the Commonwealth to be a too-perfect rendering of reality (which, for Emmanuel, has degenerated into suffering and strife due to Belial's presence). Emmanuel, who reveals himself to be the Old Testament's Yahweh, firmly endorses the notion that justice demands an eye for an eye. Zina, however, reproaches Emmanuel for his vengeful ways before informing him, "Belial is in a cage at the Washington, D.C. zoo. . . . In my realm. As an example of extraterrestrial life—a deplorable example."[61]

These conflicting worldviews generate *The Divine Invasion*'s most surreal plot development. Emmanuel and Zina decide to contest Herb Asher's life in Job-like fashion by creating an alternate reality—alternate even to Zina's

Commonwealth—where Herb receives the opportunity to love singer Linda Fox even after discovering that Linda, far from the fantasy woman he imagines her to be, is a flawed human being. When Herb accepts Linda's imperfections, Emmanuel recognizes Zina as "the *Shekhina*, the immanent Presence who never left the world"[62]—namely, the female side of God. Emmanuel then heals his wounded mind, recalls his true identity as humanity's Savior, and integrates his divided halves into a unified whole.

Belial, however, escapes his cage, assumes the form of a goatlike creature, and commandeers Herb's flying transport *while still in the alternate reality created for Herb by Emmanuel and Zina*. Belial transforms Linda Fox into a goatlike creature, then tries to absorb her life force in an effort to become human. Linda, however, kills Belial by revealing herself to be Zina's avatar in this alternate world. Linda also functions as Herb's spiritual protector, his "Beside-Helper,"[63] by developing a loving sexual relationship with him. The novel concludes within Herb's alternate reality as Linda and Herb watch Belial's remains being collected after his (Belial's) defeat. This emotionally moving and life-affirming resolution notably contrasts the ambivalent conclusions of Dick's earlier metaphysical works *The Three Stigmata of Palmer Eldritch* and "Faith of Our Fathers":

> But to [Herb's] surprise he saw not the carcass of a wizened goat-thing; instead he saw what looked like the remains of a great luminous kite that had crashed and lay in ruins all across the roof.
>
> Somberly, he and Linda gazed at it as it lay broken everywhere, vast and lovely and destroyed. In pieces, like damaged light.
>
> "This is how he was once," Linda said. "Originally. Before he fell. This was his original shape . . . ."
>
> Herb Asher said, "He was very beautiful."
>
> "He was the morning star," Linda said. "The brightest star in the heavens. And now nothing remains of him but this."
>
> "How he has fallen," Herb Asher said.
>
> "And everything else with him," she said. . . .
>
> Above them the city machine worked, gathering up the remains of Belial. Gathering together the broken fragments of what had once been light.[64]

This scene accentuates the spiritual and secular triumph of good over evil by providing a scriptural victory that not only fuses the godhead's male and female elements together, but also heals the fractured universe by merging significant dichotomies: text/image, reality/illusion, memory/amnesia, and science/spirituality. The sanitation hovercraft, a product of science, gathers the remains of Belial, a spiritual and metaphysical being, for disposal after

Belial loses the battle between good and evil. In these paragraphs, Dick masterfully integrates the novel's emotional, spiritual, and secular themes into an autumnal finale.

Belial's original form also recalls the light of creation present in Calvino's "At Daybreak." Calvino's and Dick's fictional universes cannot endorse rigid boundaries between secular science and immaterial spirituality, but instead intermingle these elements to connect the act of literary creation to transcendental events. Calvino and Dick textually come to terms with the mysteries of cosmic existence by consolidating science, literature, and spirituality. Their success in the intellectually provocative metaphysical fiction of *Cosmicomics*, *t zero*, and *The Divine Invasion* testifies to the compatibility of spiritual themes and science fiction.

Reflexive Divinity

Calvino's and Dick's metaphysical fiction upsets conventional relationships between authors and readers by transforming the modernist model of active author and passive reader into a fluid interchange between each agent that allows greater freedom of interpretation. The modernist model assumes a hierarchical, even parental, relationship between author and reader not shared by Calvino's and Dick's postmodern fiction. Modernist authors write texts to entertain, to inform, and/or to instruct their readers, not to collaborate in a project of shared literary creation. The modernist author generally expects readers to interpret a text in the same manner that a child obeys a parent's commands: silently and without objection. The reader's tendency to misunderstand or to ignore these expectations becomes significant only if it produces incorrect responses, readings, and interpretations.

This model's exegetical pattern allows power to flow from the author to readers who must unravel, locate, and understand that author's meaning. This relationship does not resemble a conversation so much as a lecture, erecting a barrier between reality and fiction, or, in Brian McHale's words, a heterocosm that makes readers aware "of the *otherness* of the fictional world, its separation from the real world of experience."[65] The world constructed by a work of fiction, in other words, is never "real" in the same tactile sense as daily life because it need not reproduce the mundane world in every detail. This ontological separation sustains the dichotomy between reality and fantasy that Dick's and Calvino's metaphysical fiction disrupts. Calvino's inventive 1979 novel *If on a winter's night a traveler* and Dick's bizarre 1981 spiritual masterpiece *VALIS* so insistently dismantle the boundary between real and fictional worlds that they are two of the most reflexive novels written during the second half of the twentieth century. VALIS and *If on a winter's night a traveler*, indeed, develop the theme of interpretive indeterminacy so powerfully that their spiritual implications become as provocative as they are unexpected.

Both novels defy concise summary. Warrick's comment about the relationship between VALIS and *The Divine Invasion* productively describes the relationship between VALIS and *If on a winter's night a traveler*: "To briefly summarize the novels . . . seems almost dishonest intellectually, suggesting, as it does, that easy comprehension is possible. Not so. The two novels are an intricate and complex maze barring any but the most determined from penetrating to the secret at the center."[66] VALIS and *winter's night* are so fruitful that both novels have become objects of significant scholarship.[67] Their reflexive narratives are important innovations in the SF genre's ability to incorporate spiritual and scriptural themes into its secular, humanist, and postmodern subject matter.

Warrick's summary of VALIS is a useful, if incomplete, starting point to discuss these novels:

> *Valis* portrays an anguished mind (Horselover Fat's mind) that has encountered God in a theophany. He then attempts, through reason and the intellectual process, to understand his theophany and the nature of God. After failing, Fat abandons the use of reason to build a theoretical construct explaining God's nature. In the second half of the novel, he sets out in search of the Savior. His quest succeeds briefly, but the Savior is accidentally killed. As the novel ends, he is still searching to understand his theophany.[68]

Fat believes that a divine presence has contacted him, although his friends Kevin and David, as well as the novel's narrator, a character named "Phil Dick," question this possibility. Their doubt, however, recedes after "Phil," Kevin, and David meet a two-year-old girl named Sophia who claims to be the Savior. Sophia's death reignites Fat's quest to find a new, living avatar of the Savior in Micronesia.

This astounding plot's spiritual richness and fragmented narration are unusual, even for Dick (the author). The novel's greatest surprise appears in its opening chapter, when "Phil Dick" (the narrator) says, "I am Horselover Fat, and I am writing this in the third person to gain much-needed objectivity."[69] Fat, therefore, reveals himself to be a projection of "Phil Dick's" tortured mind ("Philip" means "lover of horses" in Greek, while "Dick" is German for "fat"). This schizophrenic persona helps "Phil" accept the theophany mentioned by Warrick, which so psychologically unsettles "Phil's" mind that a new personality (Fat) emerges. "Phil" speaks of (and to) Fat as a friend throughout *VALIS*, while the novel develops Fat's character so artfully that the reader may forget that Fat is part of "Phil Dick's" mind (and that "Phil Dick," the narrator, should not be mistaken for Philip K. Dick, the author). Even so, a triple conflation—of Fat the fictional character with the narrator "Phil Dick," of the narrator "Phil Dick" with the author Philip K. Dick, and, consequently, of Fat the fictional character with the author Philip K. Dick—certainly occurs, especially after Sophia heals "Phil's" wounded mind to integrate Fat's and "Phil's" disparate psyches. Fat, after this seemingly miraculous development, disappears from *VALIS* until Sophia dies, only reappearing when "Phil" the narrator's mind once again splinters. The novel concludes with "Phil" watching television, privately wondering if he has received divine guidance from a commercial.

VALIS's postmodern narrative, particularly the manner by which Fat (the character), "Phil" (the narrator), and Philip K. Dick (the author) merge and separate, calls into question which agent controls, writes, and reads the novel. *VALIS*'s reader, therefore, occupies a much more uncertain position than normal. Walters also notes that the pink beam of light that transmits information directly into Fat's brain during his theophany is not simply the novel's primary symbol of divine intervention, but also a phenomenon that "[fragments] his personality even further, into the analogs of Kevin and David."[70] The fact that the first letters of the names Phil, Kevin, and David compose the acronym PKD certainly supports Walters's point. The distinction between *VALIS*'s internal fiction and the reader's external reality erodes, implicating the novel's reader even more deeply within Fat's/"Phil's"/Dick's tripartite personality. These complicated personas emphasize a reflexive and recursive reading process that transforms *VALIS* into a postmodern novel that merges spiritual, secular, metaphysical, and material concerns.

The autobiographical source of Fat's strange experiences further diminishes the barrier between fiction and reality in *VALIS*. Dick, from February to March 1974, experienced a monthlong series of visions, hallucinations, and dreams that perplexed him for the remainder of his life. Dick's tireless quest to explore their meaning led him to write his eight-thousand-page spiritual journal, the *Exegesis*, in which he considers every possible explanation about the provenance of the 2-3-74 visions (as Dick came to call them). The *Exegesis* exposes how fearlessly Dick entertained even personally embarrassing theories, including the possibilities that he had been touched by the divine, that he had been contacted by an extraterrestrial force masquerading as a divine presence, and that financial pressures (exacerbated by the birth of his son Christopher in 1973 and Dick's fears that the IRS would imprison him for not paying income taxes) drove him to despair. Dick's theological musings in the *Exegesis* lead him to construct an independent cosmogony that he interpolates into *VALIS* as Horselover Fat's own spiritual journal, titled *Tractates Cryptica Scriptura*. These textual interpolations explain Fat's metaphysical quest for spiritual answers to the theophany he has experienced, but that *VALIS*'s reader cannot verify. The looping nature of the *Tractates* passages, which replicate *Exegesis* entries, not only makes distinguishing Horselover Fat (the character), "Phil Dick" (the narrator), and Philip K. Dick (the author) even more difficult, but also indicates the extent of the novel's textual reflexivity. *VALIS*, as Christopher Palmer recognizes, "retreats into textuality"[71] to create a narrative "unthreatened by comparison to events in prevailing reality."[72]

Fat's cosmogony is among the novel's most fascinating aspects: "Fat later developed a theory that the universe is made out of information,"[73] "Phil" informs the reader. The relevant *Tractates* entry expands upon this notion: "The universe is information and we are stationary in it, not three-dimensional and not in space or time. The information fed to us we hypostatize into the phenomenal world."[74] The universe, therefore, becomes an information-rich hologram encompassing three-dimensional reality that Fat reads and interprets. To Fat, space and time are illusory, meaning that only a monumental act of hermeneutical (or exegetical) interpretation can reveal this truth. The universe-as-information-hologram theory in *VALIS* presages *The Divine Invasion*'s holoscope by textually synthesizing numerous phenomena: science, Gnostic spirituality, cybernetic information theory, Christian and pre-Christian history, schizophrenia, religious sectarianism, and SF tropes and symbols.

VALIS employs Fat's madness to mediate multiple narrative strands that never cohere into a unified whole. By driving the modernist conventions of the unreliable narrator past all fictional boundaries, *VALIS* pushes its reader into ambiguous territory where Horeselover Fat's, "Phil Dick's," and Philip K. Dick's personalities unpredictably converge, mingle, and separate. The novel's postmodern narrative also never loses sight of the humanist principles of compassion, charity, and love for one's fellow human beings.

Even more intriguing is how closely *VALIS* connects with Calvino's *If on a winter's night a traveler*, an equally puzzling novel whose disrupted narration confuses reality with fiction. *Winter's night* erases the boundary between fact and fantasy by snaring its reader in an ontological mystery from the first line: "You are about to begin reading Italo Calvino's new novel, *If on a winter's night a traveler*. Relax. Concentrate. Dispel every other thought."[75] Who, the reader asks, tells this story: Italo Calvino the author or an unknown narrator who directly addresses the reader to create intimacy but not identification? Immediately mentioning the novel's title and author upsets the conventional author-reader relationship, even if Calvino's presence within the text is elusive. The narrator, after all, never reveals his identity, yet employs second-person voice to create the impression that Calvino speaks directly to the reader. This strategy also transforms the reader into "the Reader," who plays the role of a character within *If on a winter's night a traveler*'s complicated plot.

Winter's night is a textual detective story that tracks the male Reader, who, after purchasing a copy of *If on a winter's night a traveler*, discovers that the novel's first sixteen-page signature accidentally repeats throughout the book. Only the first chapter, therefore, is available to him. The Reader returns his copy to the bookstore to find that he has not encountered the initial pages of *winter's night* after all, but has instead read the opening chapter of a novel titled *Outside the town of Malbork*, by Polish novelist Tazio Bazakbal, because the bindery has mistakenly mixed it with *winter's night*. The perplexed Reader then meets Ludmilla, the female Other Reader, who joins his effort to acquire the full Bazakbal novel. This desire initiates *If on a winter's night a traveler*'s complex double narrative: numbered chapters that narrate Ludmilla's and the Reader's encounters with ten incipits (the opening chapters of ten different novels) alternate with the text of these incipits. The Reader-Ludmilla plot interpolates the incipits into its frame narrative just as *VALIS* incorporates Horselover Fat's *Tractates* into its storyline.

Winter's night is syncretic because its ten incipits come from ten different fictional genres, including the spy thriller, the adventure novel, and magic realism. This generic pastiche forces Ludmilla and the Reader to navigate a discontinuous series of unrelated fictions, although the Reader is not simply an adaptable, disembodied, floating narrative voice that engages in unrestrained postmodern bricolage. As Teresa de Lauretis writes, "To call him a postmodern reader . . . is not quite correct. It would be better said that 'you' is the Reader of a postmodern text—and a Reader of postmodern texts against his will."[76] Since the numbered chapters' frame story (the story of the Reader's and Ludmilla's quest to find the complete text of *If on a winter's night a traveler*) connects the incipits to one another, the Reader becomes the character that keeps the novel's plot moving. His ambiguous status recalls Horselover Fat's/"Phil Dick's"/Philip K. Dick's hybridity in *VALIS*. By simultaneously occupying the roles of character, audience, narrator, and/or author, the Reader and Fat/"Phil"/Dick range more freely over their narrative spaces than conventional fictional characters.

VALIS and *winter's night*, as a result, are not traditional novels. Both bring their strangely spiritual plots to optimistic conclusions. *VALIS*, for instance, ends when "Phil Dick" (the narrator) speaks by phone to Horselover Fat, who thinks that he has located the Savior in Micronesia. "Phil," however, reveals that his own spiritual quest is far less adventurous than Fat's: "My search kept me at home; I sat before the TV set in my living room. I sat; I waited; I watched; I kept myself awake. As we had been told, originally, long ago, to do; I kept my commission."[77] "Phil," in other words, remains open to the possibilities of goodness and redemption, even if they emanate from VALIS, the titular Vast Active Living Intelligence System of satellites that connects Earth to Albemuth (the star system that, "Phil" learns during the course of the novel, was humanity's first home). Albemuth's noncorporeal inhabitants wish to save humanity, whose progenitors traveled to Earth from Albemuth millennia ago but became trapped in Earth's toxic biosphere after adopting human form.

The Albemuthians constructed the VALIS satellite system to communicate the truth of this existence to their fallen human cousins. "Phil's" commission assures him that human beings can surmount the pain of material existence if they remain patient because time itself is a delusion that true knowledge of self (*gnosis*) will dissipate. Neither "Phil's" nor Fat's quest has succeeded when *VALIS* concludes (primarily because the schizophrenic splitting of "Phil's" mind generates Fat's persona), but Phil is content to wait for salvation. This incomplete resolution implies that a path out of *VALIS*'s textual maze exists, although both "Phil" and *VALIS*'s reader may never find it.

Winter's night concludes just as ambivalently in its twelfth numbered chapter:

> Now you are man and wife, Reader and Reader. A great double bed receives your parallel readings.
>   Ludmilla closes her book, turns off her light, puts her head back against the pillow, and says, "Turn off your light, too. Aren't you tired of reading?"
>   And you say, "Just a moment, I've almost finished *If on a winter's night a traveler* by Italo Calvino."[78]

The two protagonists, now joined in marriage, pursue parallel tracks. The Reader's comment to Ludmilla illustrates that *winter's night* has returned to the novel's starting point, meaning that its textual ambiguities may never cease. The novel's circular plot, in other words, becomes a postmodern narrative that threatens to endlessly repeat itself. *If on a winter's night a traveler*, like *VALIS*, transcends strict generic, thematic, and symbolic boundaries not only to call its own premise into doubt, but also to implicate its reader in a textual game that never resolves itself into a firm denouement.

This textual self-consciousness allows Calvino's reader to recognize him- or herself as the novel's primary interpreter. Mariolina Salvatori notes how voyeuristic *If on a winter's night a traveler*'s reader is:

> Although we are set up to be voyeurs, we can redirect the glance to ourselves; by becoming voyeurs of ourselves *as* voyeurs we may come to the conclusion that we need to erase the ironic distance—the stance of superiority—that separates us from the [Reader] as we recognize in his shortcomings and prejudices our own, and in this moment of reflexivity we may achieve critical self-consciousness.[79]

Calvino foregrounds such self-consciousness in chapter 7, when the narrator addresses "the Other Reader": "What are you like, Other Reader? It is time for this book in the second person to address itself no longer to a general male you, perhaps brother and double of a hypocrite I, but directly to you who appeared already in the second chapter as the Third Person necessary for the novel to be a novel."[80] Dick (the author), as previously seen, acknowledges the self-consciousness of *VALIS* by observing, in chapter 1, "I am Horselover Fat, and I am writing this in the third person to gain much-needed objectivity."[81] Both passages turn the reader from a passive observer into an active participant in the text's evolving narrative, thereby subverting the conventional relationship between active authors and passive readers. *VALIS* and *winter's night* synthesize fiction, reality, literary genres, and narrative voices into more intricate interpretive experiences for their readers.

Both novels are eminently aware of their existence as fiction, making readers conscious of their own status as literary consumers who participate in stories that disintegrate the barrier between fiction and reality. *VALIS* and *winter's night* also promise to perpetually renew themselves because their stories never end. "Phil" still waits for divine enlightenment as *VALIS* concludes, while the Reader has not finished *If on a winter's night a traveler* when Calvino's novel stops. By pushing their readers beyond all dichotomies of fiction and reality, Calvino and Dick suggest, in quintessentially postmodern fashion, that all such categories are insufficient.

Calvino and Dick also stress the humanist values of individuality, creative self-fulfillment, and personal enlightenment. The Reader, Horselover Fat, and "Phil Dick" embody these values even if, as flawed individuals, they cannot resolve the contradictory emotions (love, hope, doubt, and despair) that characterize *VALIS* and *winter's night*. Each novel's ambiguities, fractured narration, and ambivalent plot enhance its postmodern approach to questions of transcendence, spirituality, and salvation. Calvino and Dick offer few final answers to these queries, leaving their readers to ponder the cosmic and comic mysteries that fascinate both authors.

Conclusion

Calvino's and Dick's metaphysical fiction falls under many rubrics: science fiction, fantasy, fable, fairy tale, spirituality, empiricism, and scriptural writing. Although they were literary contemporaries, Calvino and Dick had little, if any, direct influence upon one another. Their fictional affinities, particularly their thematic interest in spiritual, cosmic, and hermeneutic subject matter, reveal two unique minds willing to confront the complexities of creation. Calvino's and Dick's fascination with how human beings invest their lives with meaning produces boldly imaginative writing that examines the intricate relationships between reality and fiction. Despite these common concerns, one man's fiction could never be mistaken for the other's. Dick's writing is more overtly spiritual and more pessimistic than Calvino's fiction, which explores the physical universe's scientific operation more rigorously (and more whimsically) than Dick's.

Both authors, however, acknowledge that transcendent worlds, realms, and beings may exist. Calvino's and Dick's metaphysical fiction, as a result, inflects their readers' quotidian lives with wonder, horror, and sublime feeling. Each author challenges empirical explanations of human existence by writing fiction that stimulates, exceeds, and unseats conventional viewpoints. Calvino and Dick also stress how significant interpretation is to understanding their cosmic texts. Such interpretation cannot always succeed, and frequently falls short of satisfactory understanding. Calvino's and Dick's reflexive fiction, however, offers their readers new perspectives about the relationships among fiction, reality, science, and spirit to demonstrate how congenial science fiction and spiritual writing can be. Calvino and Dick are, therefore, literary cousins even if, in life, they were unaware of their shared ancestry.

Notes

1. The contentious place of religion and spirituality within science fiction can be seen in even a cursory review of the scholarly literature devoted to this topic. Douglas A. Mackey declares that "[a]ll science fiction is a metaphor for transcendence" (112) in "Science Fiction and Gnosticism" (*Missouri Review* 7, no. 2 [1984]), his persuasively argued essay about the Gnostic themes to be found in the work of Philip K. Dick, Olaf Stapledon, David Lindsay, and J. G. Ballard. Robert Hunt is more circumspect in

"Visionary States and the Search for Transcendence in Science Fiction" (in *Bridges to Science Fiction*, ed. George E. Slusser, George R. Guffey, and Mark Rose [Carbondale: Southern Illinois University Press, 1980]), writing that "[r]ecent criticism of science fiction has tended to subsume all religion under the vague category 'myth.' Both in the criticism and in the literature itself, the wellspring of religion—the individual's religious experience—is often ignored or treated in the most cheap and obvious manner" (64). Even so, Hunt not only believes science fiction to be well suited "to the depiction of visionary states and the religious revelations they bring or seem to bring" (64), but also includes Dick in a small group of SF writers who effectively combine spiritual and SF themes into intriguingly suggestive fiction.

Adam J. Frisch and Joseph Martos are even more enthusiastic supporters of combining science fiction and spirituality. In their fascinating essay "Religious Imagination and Imagined Religion" (in *The Transcendent Adventure: Studies in Science Fiction/Fantasy*, ed. Robert Reilly, Contributions to the Study of Science Fiction and Fantasy, no. 12 [Westport, CT: Greenwood, 1985]), Frisch and Martos identify three basic features of religious imagination (fundamentalizing, ultimatizing, and moralizing) that unambiguously acknowledge religion's significance to science fiction:

> Writers of speculative fiction since Mary Shelley have explored many aspects of religion, and, in doing so, they themselves have exhibited some of the fundamental features of religious consciousness. Perhaps this is because there is a universality about religious consciousness that transcends differences between both religions and individuals. Perhaps it is because writers of fiction naturally portray imagined realities along the lines of familiar realities, religion being no exception. (11)

Frisch and Martos then examine SF works as diverse as Shelley's *Frankenstein*, James Blish's *A Case of Conscience*, and Gene Roddenberry's *Star Trek* television series to highlight their religious and spiritual themes. William A. Quinn, in "Science Fiction's Harrowing of the Heavens" (in *Transcendent Adventure*, ed. Reilly), is less sanguine about the success of spiritual science fiction: "The genre's occasional fusion of science and religion remains tense and intermittent at best. The vast majority of sf writers do seem either opposed or oblivious to most religious concerns" (37). Quinn analyzes the theological rigor of several SF authors, including Blish, Marion Zimmer Bradley, Arthur C. Clarke, C. S. Lewis, and Roger Zelazny, by discussing their depictions of extraterrestrials as contemporary manifestations of the medieval debate about the place of non-Christians in a Christian universe.

While Quinn's observation about the religious skepticism of some SF writers has merit, particularly in regards to Isaac Asimov, Quinn also ignores SF authors of spiritual science fiction, especially Walter M. Miller Jr. and Philip K. Dick. Darko Suvin agrees with Quinn by stating, in *Metamorphoses of Science Fiction* (New Haven, CT: Yale University Press, 1979), "It is intrinsically or by definition impossible for SF to acknowledge any metaphysical agency, in the literal sense of an agency going beyond *physis* (nature). Whenever it does so, it is not SF, but a metaphysical or (to translate the Greek into Latin) a supernatural fantasy-tale" (emphasis Suvin's; 66).

This assertion seems unnecessarily restrictive, although it is consistent with Suvin's larger argument that science fiction depends upon cognitive logic (by which he means scientific rationality).

Istvan Csicsery-Ronay Jr. finds an intriguing middle ground between these divergent perspectives when analyzing the explicitly spiritual writing that Dick produced toward the end of his life: "*Valis* and the *Exegesis* are symptoms of a new development, the frequent collapse of the distance between SF and religion" ("Pilgrims in Pandemonium: Philip K. Dick and the Critics," in *On Philip K. Dick: 40 Articles from Science-Fiction Studies*, ed. R. D. Mullen et al. [Terre Haute, IN: SF-TH, 1992], xviii). Csicsery-Ronay, writing in 1992, notes that including religion in science fiction during the 1960s, 1970s, and 1980s became far less problematic than it had been during the 1940s and 1950s, causing him to acknowledge Dick's special place in the tradition of mystical science fiction. This observation is more satisfying, since any thoughtful depiction of extraterrestrial societies (or future human societies) must take into account their notions of creation, morality, mortality, and social organization, which, broadly speaking, are four important aspects of religious thought. Since scientific thinking has not erased religion's role in the twenty-first-century Western world (indeed, religious fundamentalism remains a powerful social, economic, and political force), the reductive conclusion (implicit or otherwise) of some SF writers that a technologically advanced culture naturally embraces secular rationalism ignores the significance of religion in shaping the human search for meaning. Science and spirituality can indeed accommodate one another, as Joseph Campbell's work on religion, mythology, and science (particularly *The Inner Reaches of Outer Space: Metaphor as Myth and as Religion* [New York: A. van der Marck Editions, 1986]) has demonstrated.

Two mass-media examples of science fiction also offer provocative meditations about spirituality within secular scientific contexts. J. Michael Straczynski's television series *Babylon 5* (1994–1999) depicts three extraterrestrial societies that combine spiritual concerns with science and technology. Minbari society features a specific religious caste whose members unapologetically utilize advanced technology. Narn society pays homage to a great spiritual-historical text known as the *Book of G'Quan* that allows the Narn to survive the occupation of their home world by an invading species known as the Centauri. The terse, wise, and prophetic pronouncements of the series's Vorlon characters indicate the profound spiritual wisdom of a culture that, as one of the galaxy's oldest species, possesses remarkably advanced technology. The Vorlons, during their rare appearances, also resemble angelic creatures of light.

Rick Berman and Michael Piller's television series *Star Trek: Deep Space Nine* (1993–2001) centers upon an extraterrestrial society known as the Bajora, whose mystical religion not only allows its members to resist the brutal alien occupation of their planet for more than fifty years, but also claims the series protagonist, Benjamin Sisko (Avery Brooks)—a human representative of the secular and scientifically advanced United Federation of Planets—as the emissary of their timeless deities, known as the Prophets. The fact that both series appeared in the early 1990s (*Deep Space Nine* premiered in January 1993, while *Babylon 5* began its series run in January 1994 after broadcasting a two-hour pilot film in February 1993) demonstrates that spirituality in science fiction has an important, but underappreciated, place. The transcendence Mackey believes science fiction communicates through symbol and metaphor has been significant to the genre for decades (even if some SF authors attempt to demystify and/or discredit it by offering rational and scientific explanations for religious beliefs and events). Philip K. Dick saw little conflict between science and religion in his fiction, especially in his final trilogy of novels: *VALIS* (1981; New York: Vintage-Random, 1991), *The Divine Invasion* (1981; New York: Vintage-Random, 1991), and *The Transmigration of Timothy Archer* (1982; New York: Vintage-Random, 1991).

2. Kim Stanley Robinson, *The Novels of Philip K. Dick*, Studies in Speculative Fiction No. 9 (Ann Arbor: UMI Research, 1984), 111. David G. Hartwell, an editor who worked with Dick at Simon and Schuster, noted during a 1993 convention devoted to Dick in Cambridge, Massachusetts, that *The Transmigration of Timothy Archer* was not intended to be the final book of the *VALIS* trilogy:

> [Dick] told me the story of Bishop Timothy Archer and I said I would publish that, but the *real* contract, the center of attention, was *The Owl in Daylight*. *The Owl in Daylight* was to be the third book of the VALIS trilogy. And that was going to be his transcendental masterpiece. [. . .] In all of my conversations with Phil, [*Timothy Archer*] was clearly not the third book of the VALIS trilogy. It was in some people's best interests when he died to call the VALIS trilogy complete . . . thematically complete. I don't mind. ("The Religious Visions of Philip K. Dick." *New York Review of Science Fiction* 7, no. 5 [January 1995]: 13)

Dick does not mention the possibility that *The Owl in Daylight* would become the third *VALIS* book in his extensive conversation about this proposed novel with Gwen Lee in *What If Our World Is Their Heaven? The Final Conversations of Philip K. Dick* (Woodstock, NY: Overlook, 2000), although he specifically relates *The Transmigration of Timothy Archer* to *VALIS* in his discussion about this final novel with Gregg Rickman in *Philip K. Dick: In His Own Words* (2nd ed.; Long Beach, CA: Fragments West/Valentine, 1988): "This book (*Timothy Archer*) will be an analysis of religious mania. In a way it's a reaction to *VALIS*. It's another viewpoint on the religious mania in *VALIS*. But it's a much more negative viewpoint, much much more hostile than the viewpoint that I as a character had in *VALIS* toward Horselover Fat" (203).

Russell Galen, Dick's agent from 1978 until the author's 1982 death (as well as *VALIS*'s dedicatee) recalls circumstances differently in an e-mail response to questions about this discrepancy:

> I remember Phil speaking all the time about the so-called "Valis Trilogy," which was really a trilogy only in his mind, and that it consisted of *VALIS*, *The Divine Invasion*, and *Timothy Archer*.

I don't remember much at all about *Owl*, since, of course, it never became a novel and my memories of it are thus not as deeply rooted as they would be if there'd ever been a full manuscript to read. . . . I also don't remember if it had what you might call "Valis-related themes" or is in some direct way directed to the Valis theme current in Phil's later work. My memory is that it had no connection with *VALIS* of any kind and that at the time he wrote the *Owl* proposal Phil thought of Valis as a theme he had now completed dealing with, but I wouldn't swear to that memory. What I would swear to is that all his references to the so-called "Valis Trilogy" were to *VALIS*, *The Divine Invasion*, and *Timothy Archer*.

Galen also mentions that David Hartwell is a "smart man and if I had to pick which of us was the more reliable witness, I would pick him." It seems clear that Dick had the notion of a trilogy in mind; less clear is which novel he intended as the third *VALIS* book. It is also possible that, given Dick's propensity for espousing contradictory statements, he told Hartwell one story while telling Galen another. I agree, however, with F. Scott Walters that *VALIS*, *The Divine Invasion*, and *The Transmigration of Timothy Archer* compose an "'elastic' or loose unit" ("The Final Trilogy of Philip K. Dick," *Extrapolation* 38, no. 3 [1997]: 222) and with Jay Kinney that they are "a trilogy of sorts" ("The Mysterious Revelations of Philip K. Dick," *Gnosis* 1 [1985]: 8). As Galen indicates, Dick himself thought of the books as a trilogy, even if no one else did. Based on Dick's comments to Gwen Lee about *The Owl in Daylight*, it would certainly have had spiritual, religious, and metaphysical ramifications, but nothing that specifically links it to *VALIS*. Since Dick died before writing the novel, his readers will never know for certain.

3. Lawrence Sutin, *Divine Invasions: A Life of Philip K. Dick* (New York: Citadel-Carol, 1989), 128. Pages 126–28 chronicle Dick's conversion to Episcopalianism, as well as his growing fascination with the doctrines of the Episcopal Mass, the ritual of Eucharistic transubstantiation, and Gnosticism in general.

4. Sutin, *Divine Invasions*, 233.

5. A partial list of the extensive scholarly analyses of Dick's spiritual/religious fiction follows: Andrew Butler, "Science Fiction as Postmodernism: The Case of Philip K. Dick," in *Impossibility Fiction: Alternativity—Extrapolation—Speculation*, ed. Derek Littlewood and Peter Stockwell (Amsterdam: Rodopi, 1996), 45–56; Lorenzo DiTommaso, "Gnosticism and Dualism in the Early Fiction of Philip K. Dick," *Science Fiction Studies* 28, no. 1 (2001): 49–65; Frisch and Martos, "Religious Imagination and Imagined Religion"; Robert Galbreath, "Salvation-Knowledge: Ironic Gnosticism in *Valis* and *The Flight to Lucifer*," in *Science Fiction Dialogues*, ed. Gary Wolfe (Chicago: Academy Chicago, 1982), 115–32; David Golumbia, "Resisting 'the World': Philip K. Dick, Cultural Studies, and Metaphysical Realism," *Science Fiction Studies* 23 (1996): 83–100; Hartwell, "The Religious Visions of Philip K. Dick"; Hunt, "Visionary States and the Search for Transcendence in Science Fiction"; Mackey, "Science Fiction and Gnosticism"; Christopher Palmer, "Postmodernism and the Birth of the Author in Philip K. Dick's *Valis*," *Science Fiction Studies* 18 (1991): 330–42; Georg Schmid, "The Apocryphal Judaic Traditions as Historical Repertoire: An Analysis of *The Divine Invasion* by Philip K. Dick," *Degrés* 51 (1987):

f/1–f/11; David Seed, "Mediated Realities in the Works of Philip K. Dick," in *Narrative Turns and Minor Genres in Postmodernism*, ed. Theo D'haen and Hans Bartens, Postmodernism Studies 11 (Amsterdam: Rodopi, 1995); Roger J. Stilling, "Mystical Healing: Reading Philip K. Dick's *VALIS* and *The Divine Invasion* as Metapsychoanalytic Novels," *South Atlantic Review* 56, no. 2 (1991): 91–106; Walters, "The Final Trilogy of Philip K. Dick"; and Patricia S. Warrick, "Philip K. Dick's Answers to Eternal Riddles," in *The Transcendent Adventure: Studies in Science Fiction/Fantasy*, ed. Robert Reilly, Contributions to the Study of Science Fiction and Fantasy, no. 12 (Westport, CT: Greenwood, 1985), 107–26.

   6. Rosetta Di Pace-Jordan, "Italo Calvino's Legacy: The Constant and Consistent Vision," *World Literature Today* 66, no. 3 (1992): 468.

   7. Kathryn Hume, "Science and Imagination in Calvino's *Cosmicomics*," *Mosaic* 15, no. 4 (1982): 47.

   8. Hume, "Science and Imagination in Calvino's *Cosmicomics*," 47.

   9. Italo Calvino, *Cosmicomics*, trans. William Weaver (1965; San Diego: Harvest–Harcourt Brace, 1968), 26.

   10. Calvino, *Cosmicomics*, 19.

   11. Calvino, *Cosmicomics*, 43.

   12. John Earl Joseph, "Man, History, Subject, Object: Calvino in Crisis," *Review of Contemporary Fiction* 6, no. 2 (1986): 29.

   13. Hume, "Science and Imagination in Calvino's *Cosmicomics*," 47.

   14. Philip K. Dick, *The Three Stigmata of Palmer Eldritch* (1964; New York: Vintage-Random, 1991), 86. The emphasis is Dick's.

   15. Eugene Warren, "The Search for Absolutes," *Philip K. Dick*, ed. Martin Harry Greenberg and Joseph D. Olander, Writers of the 21st Century Series (New York: Taplinger, 1983), 182.

   16. Philip K. Dick, *The Collected Stories of Philip K. Dick, Volume Five: The Eye of the Sibyl* (1987; New York: Citadel-Carol, 1992), 218.

   17. Warren, "The Search for Absolutes," 182.

   18. Karl Wessel, "Worlds of Chance and Counterfeit: Dick, Lem, and the Preestablished Cacophony," in *Philip K. Dick: Contemporary Critical Interpretations*, ed. Samuel J. Umland, Contributions to the Study of Science Fiction and Fantasy, no. 63 (Westport: Greenwood, 1995), 43.

   19. Hume, "Science and Imagination in Calvino's *Cosmicomics*," 47.

   20. Hume, "Science and Imagination in Calvino's *Cosmicomics*," 47.

   21. Hume, "Science and Imagination in Calvino's *Cosmicomics*," 48.

   22. Dick, *Palmer Eldritch*, 88.

   23. Dick, *Palmer Eldritch*, 88.

   24. Dick, *Palmer Eldritch*, 88.

   25. Dick, *Palmer Eldritch*, 89.

   26. Dick, *Palmer Eldritch*, 94.

   27. Dick, *Palmer Eldritch*, 187.

   28. Dick, *Palmer Eldritch*, 3.

29. Dick, *Palmer Eldritch*, 3.

30. Golumbia, "Resisting 'The World,'" 93. The emphasis is Golumbia's. This article's excellent argument owes much to the writing of Hilary Putnam, whom Golumbia identifies as an anti-Realist who disagrees with the philosophical Realist belief that "truth consists in some kind of correspondence between the objects in the world and the words of a language" (84). Golumbia believes that Putnam characterizes Metaphysical Realism as a threefold doctrine in the same sense that philosopher Hartry Field does: "[T]he world consists of a fixed totality of mind-independent objects, . . . there is exactly one true and complete description of the way the world is," and "truth involves some sort of correspondence" (84). This formulation of Metaphysical Realism differs from the more common conceptualization of metaphysics as a field of study and/or experience that transcends the physical world, so the two should not be confused.

31. Calvino, *Cosmicomics*, 3. The emphasis is Calvino's.

32. Calvino, *Cosmicomics*, 19. The emphasis is Calvino's.

33. Italo Calvino, *t zero*, trans. William Weaver (1967; New York: Harvest–Harcourt Brace, 1969), 28.

34. Calvino, *Cosmicomics*, 63. The emphasis is Calvino's.

35. Paul Ricoeur, "The Task of Hermeneutics," in *Heidegger and Modern Philosophy: Critical Essays*, ed. Michael Murray (New Haven, CT: Yale University Press, 1978), 142.

36. Jacques Derrida, *Of Grammatology*, trans. Gayatri Chakravorty Spivak (1967; Baltimore: Johns Hopkins University Press, 1976), 10.

37. Derrida, *Of Grammatology*, 10.

38. Derrida, *Of Grammatology*, 11. The emphasis is Derrida's.

39. Dick, *Collected Stories, Volume Five*, 217–18.

40. Dick, *Collected Stories, Volume Five*, 219.

41. Dick, *Collected Stories, Volume Five*, 219.

42. Dick, *Collected Stories, Volume Five*, 220.

43. Calvino, *t zero*, 15.

44. Dick, *Collected Stories, Volume Five*, 391.

45. Dick, *Divine Invasion*, 11.

46. Walters, "Final Trilogy of Philip K. Dick," 228.

47. Mackey," Science Fiction and Gnosticism," 112.

48. Dick, *Divine Invasion*, 7.

49. Walters, "Final Trilogy of Philip K. Dick," 229.

50. Dick, *Divine Invasion*, 69–70.

51. Dick, *Divine Invasion*, 71.

52. Stilling, "Mystical Healing," 98.

53. Jacques Derrida, *Writing and Difference*, trans. Alan Bass (1967; Chicago: University of Chicago Press, 1978), 10.

54. Calvino, *Cosmicomics*, 46–47.

55. Hume, "Science and Imagination in Calvino's *Cosmicomics*," 52.

56. Warrick, "Philip K. Dick's Answers to Eternal Riddles," 113.

57. In addition to the articles already cited in this chapter by Douglas A. Mackey ("Science Fiction and Gnosticism"), Roger J. Stilling ("Mystical Healing"), F. Scott Walters ("The Final Trilogy of Philip K. Dick"), and Patricia S. Warrick ("Philip K. Dick's Answers to Eternal Riddles"), consult the ninth chapter of Kim Stanley Robinson's *The Novels of Philip K. Dick*, as well as Georg Schmid's excellent article "The Apocryphal Judaic Traditions as Historical Repertoire," for illuminating discussions (and disagreements) about love in Dick's penultimate novel.

58. Walters, "Final Trilogy of Philip K. Dick," 229.

59. Dick, *Divine Invasion*, 133. The emphasis is Dick's.

60. Dick, *Divine Invasion*, 133.

61. Dick, *Divine Invasion*, 148.

62. Dick, *Divine Invasion*, 199. The emphasis is Dick's.

63. Dick, *Divine Invasion*, 231.

64. Dick, *Divine Invasion*, 237–38.

65. Brian McHale, *Postmodernist Fiction* (New York: Methuen, 1987), 27. The emphasis is McHale's.

66. Warrick, "Philip K. Dick's Answers to Eternal Riddles," 110–11.

67. For additional critical investigations of *If on a winter's night a traveler*, consult the following sources: Wiley Feinstein, "The Doctrinal Core of *If on a winter's night a traveler*" in *Calvino Revisited*, ed. Franco Ricci, University of Toronto Italian Studies 2 (Ottawa: Dovehouse Editions, 1989), 147–55; Geoffrey Green, "Ghosts and Shadows: Reading and Writing in Italo Calvino's *If on a winter's night a traveler*," *Review of Contemporary Fiction* 6, no. 2 (1986): 101–105; Francesco Guardiani, "Optimism without Illusions," *Review of Contemporary Fiction* 6, no. 2 (1986): 54–61; Kathryn Hume, "Calvino's Framed Narratives: Writers, Readers, and Reality," *Review of Contemporary Fiction* 6, no. 2 (1986): 71–80; Teresa de Lauretis, "Reading the (Post)Modern Text: *If on a winter's night a traveler*" in *Calvino Revisited*, ed. Ricci; Carl D. Malmgren, "Romancing the Reader: Calvino's *If on a winter's night a traveler*," *Review of Contemporary Fiction* 6, no. 2 (1986): 106–15; Warren F. Motte Jr., "Calvino's Combinatorics," *Review of Contemporary Fiction* 6, no. 2 (1986): 81–87; Marshall C. Olds, "Another Book, Another Author: Calvino, Flaubert, Mallarmé," *Review of Contemporary Fiction* 6, no. 2 (1986): 117–23; and Ian Rankin, "The Role of the Reader in Italo Calvino's *If on a winter's night a traveler*," *Review of Contemporary Fiction* 6, no. 2 (1986): 124–29. For *VALIS*, see all the sources listed in n. 57, as well as Butler, "Science Fiction as Postmodernism"; Neil Easterbrook, "Dianoia/Paranoia: Dick's Double 'Impostor,'" in *Philip K. Dick: Contemporary Critical Interpretations*, ed. Samuel J. Umland, Contributions to the Study of Science Fiction and Fantasy, no. 63 (Westport, CT: Greenwood, 1995), 19–41; Carl Freedman, "Towards a Theory of Paranoia: The Science Fiction of Philip K. Dick," *Science Fiction Studies* 11 (1984): 15–24; Palmer, "Postmodernism and the Birth of the Author in Philip K. Dick's *Valis*"; Samuel J. Umland, "To Flee from Dionysus: *Enthousiasmos* from 'Upon the Dull Earth' to *VALIS*," in *Philip K. Dick*, ed. Umland; and chaps. 10 and 11 of Sutin's *Divine Invasions*.

68. Warrick, "Philip K. Dick's Answers to Eternal Riddles," 110.

69. Dick, *VALIS*, 11.

70. Walters, "Final Trilogy of Philip K. Dick," 225.

71. Palmer, "Postmodernism and the Birth of the Author in Philip K. Dick's *Valis*," 334.

72. Palmer, "Postmodernism and the Birth of the Author in Philip K. Dick's *Valis*," 335.

73. Dick, *VALIS*, 22.

74. Dick, *VALIS*, 230.

75. Italo Calvino, *If on a winter's night a traveler*, trans. William Weaver (1979; New York: Harvest–Harcourt Brace, 1981), 3.

76. de Lauretis, "Reading the (Post)Modern Text," 133.

77. Dick, *VALIS*, 228.

78. Calvino, *winter's night*, 260.

79. Mariolina Salvatori, "Italo Calvino's *If on a winter's night a traveler*: Writer's Authority, Reader's Autonomy," *Contemporary Literature* 27, no. 2 (1986): 196. The emphasis is Salvatori's.

80. Calvino, *winter's night*, 141.

81. Dick, *VALIS*, 11.

CHAPTER FOUR

~

Time, Love, and Narcosis:
The Importance of
Now Wait for Last Year

As its story unfolds, *Now Wait for Last Year* synthesizes Philip K. Dick's favorite themes, characters, and plots of the 1960s. This novel, first published in 1966, was one of eleven that Dick wrote during 1963 and 1964 in what biographer Lawrence Sutin calls "an amphetamine-fueled writing streak that was torrid even by Phil's standards."[1] This two-year burst of creativity, accentuated by Dick's drug use, coincides with the breakdown of his third marriage, to Anne Williams Rubenstein. Dick's furious fictional output during this personally traumatic but professionally triumphant period was briefly interrupted when, in September 1963, he won the Hugo Award for his 1962 novel *The Man in the High Castle*. Dick, however, had little time to enjoy his laurels. He wrote intensively not only to provide his large family (including his four daughters) with a decent income, but also to respond to the political, personal, economic, and social tensions of the early 1960s. American involvement in Vietnam, President John F. Kennedy's assassination, the paltry income he received from writing SF novels, and marital difficulties all contributed to Dick's prolific writing of these years, which produced two of his most admired works: *The Three Stigmata of Palmer Eldritch* and *Dr. Bloodmoney*.[2]

Now Wait for Last Year does not normally appear on lists of Dick's best books, even though he wrote it during what is arguably his most creative period (1962–1968). This six-year stretch saw Dick finish several of his most fondly remembered novels: *The Man in the High Castle* (1962), *The Three Stigmata of Palmer Eldritch* (1964), *Martian Time-Slip* (1964), *The Simulacra* (1964), *Dr. Bloodmoney* (1965), and *Do Androids Dream of Electric Sheep?*

(1968). This period also lays claim to some of Dick's worst-received fiction, including *The Penultimate Truth* (1964), *The Crack in Space* (1966), and *The Zap Gun* (1967). Commentators, if they notice *Now Wait for Last Year* at all, typically describe it as an intriguing novel with bizarre ideas, passable characters, and perplexing storylines that, like many pulp SF potboilers of its era, falls short of being great literature. Such, however, may be expected of a book written at the blinding pace that Dick maintained during 1963 and 1964. The uneven quality of his 1960s novels, at least for scholars Kim Stanley Robinson, Patricia Warrick, and Istvan Csicsery-Ronay Jr., results from Dick's authorial speed, which disallowed the careful composition process that typifies (or that literary scholars generally believe typifies) artistically relevant literature.[3]

The haphazard movement of Dick's plots, his sometimes clumsy prose, and his occasionally predictable themes, characters, and plots mean that any reader possessed of what Jonathan Culler calls "literary competence"[4] may find Dick's fiction unimpressive. This perspective, however, does not explain *Now Wait for Last Year*'s philosophical, political, and emotional complexity. Although Dick's critics might expect *Now Wait for Last Year* to succumb to the defects that mar some of his other 1960s fiction, the novel resists the arbitrary, everything-plus-the-kitchen-sink mentality of pulp science fiction at its most breathless.

Now Wait for Last Year, indeed, is not only one of Dick's best books, but also a splendid 1960s novel that melds themes crucial to Dick's oeuvre: extraterrestrial invasion, time travel, drug abuse, political repression, war, and an unhappy marriage. *Now Wait for Last Year*'s narrative complexity and raw emotional power, therefore, are emblematic aspects of Dick's postmodern humanism that allow him to explore the nature of love and the meaning of sacrifice in a future America bereft of democratic values. The novel's temporal paradoxes become metaphors for the inherent contradictions of American life during the 1960s, including the destruction of political idealism by the exigencies of war, the emotional compromises forced upon people of good conscience by events outside their control, and, finally, the advent of feminism in a patriarchal culture. *Now Wait for Last Year*'s tragicomic tone, in one of its greatest achievements, allows Dick to perceptively examine the ambiguities of mid-century American politics and the mysteries of midsixties sexual relationships.

Postmodern Style, Humanist Fashion

Like many of Dick's 1950s characters, Dr. Eric Sweetscent, *Now Wait for Last Year*'s fancifully named protagonist, loses his already precarious hold on reality. For instance, Eric feels oppressed by time in the novel's opening passage:

> The apteryx-shaped building, so familiar to him, gave off its usual smoky gray light as Eric Sweetscent collapsed his wheel and managed to park in the tiny stall allocated him. Eight o'clock in the morning, he thought drearily. And already his employer, Mr. Virgil L. Ackerman, had opened TF&D Corporation's offices for business. Imagine a man whose mind is most sharp at eight a.m., Dr. Sweetscent mused. It runs against God's clear command. A fine world they're doling out to us; the war excuses any human aberration, even the old man's.[5]

This excerpt recalls Gregor Samsa's bleak surrender to the drudgery of office life in *The Metamorphosis*'s first chapter. Dick, in this short paragraph, initiates several of the novel's major themes by indicating how troubled his protagonist is. Eric's belief that the sharpness of Virgil Ackerman's mind at what, for Eric, is an unreasonably early hour, as well as the petty remark that Ackerman's mental acuity contravenes God's law, reveals Eric's defeatist attitude. He snidely dismisses the world around him because unseen authorities prosecute an unnamed war rather than building a better life for their citizens. Eric's passivity in the face of these events accentuates his world's repressive politics, while oppressive capitalism—represented by Eric's employer, the Tijuana Fur & Dye Corporation—seems capable of manipulating the most basic functions of human life: space (the barely adequate parking stall provided for Eric) and time (his hectic morning schedule).

Now Wait for Last Year's opening chapter, like the novel it introduces, chronicles the doubts and disaffections of a protagonist who cannot resolve the contradictory pressures that define his life. Eric Sweetscent's story, despite its large number of subplots, paradoxes, and narrative instabilities, never falls into narrative incoherence. *Now Wait for Last Year* is more fragmented than much of Dick's 1960s fiction, but nonetheless consolidates the author's humanist concerns about personal integrity, political liberty, economic independence, and individual agency into a postmodern novel whose bizarre future world challenges its reader's expectations at almost every turn.

Time travel is *Now Wait for Last Year*'s primary narrative device, as well as its major SF trope. Dick, however, challenges SF convention by making the novel's only "time machine" a drug, JJ-180 (also known as Frohedadrine), that moves its user backward and forward in time. JJ-180, Eric soon discovers, is also a weapon of war designed to addict its user after one dose. This addiction, in the novel's most tragic development, produces irreversible neurological damage. JJ-180, therefore, symbolizes the pervasive immorality of *Now Wait for Last Year*'s future society, in which corporations conspire with military forces to circumscribe human liberty in the name of security. The political oppression that results from the wartime invasion of Earth by extraterrestrials and the technological proliferation that attempts to repel this invasion produce complex emotional wounds in the novel's human characters—wounds that time, no matter how permeable, cannot heal.

Dick, indeed, puts these themes into play within *Now Wait for Last Year*'s first two pages. Immediately after arriving at work, Eric is stopped by a "highly repellent . . . robant"[6]—a robot servant—that demands payment for an expensive overdue bill incurred by Eric's wife, Kathy Sweetscent, who works at Tijuana Fur & Dye Corporation as an antique buyer for the firm's founder and president, Virgil Ackerman. Kathy has purchased a pre–World War II Lucky Strike cigarette package to add to Ackerman's collection of authentic American memorabilia. This object bespeaks not only Kathy's professional interest in the past, but also the novel's fascination with temporal dislocation. *Now Wait for Last Year*, by fracturing clear chronologies of plot, theme, and character, intensifies uncertainties about authentic human subjectivity into a remarkable story of social and sexual confusion. The disintegration of Eric and Kathy Sweetscent's marriage parallels the destruction of human liberty in one of Dick's most emotionally supple and politically mature novels.

Time Heals

Time travel becomes *Now Wait for Last Year*'s most perplexing narrative development by challenging its reader's linear perception of the world, by disrupting its reader's causal conception of daily life, and by unsettling its reader's comfortable understanding of human identity. The novel includes paradoxes that not only subvert consensual reality, but also dislocate its reader's sense of authentic human personality. By whipsawing Eric Sweetscent back and forth through time, Dick employs one of science fiction's best-known generic conventions to unveil Eric's complex character, to expose 2055 Earth's rampant political corruption, and to create contradictions that call the novel's narrative basis into question. The resulting ambiguity suggests that history is inconstant, or that the past can be revised without humanity's knowledge or consent. These disturbing possibilities further imply that human consciousness and identity are fluid, not unitary, constructions that submit to powerful historical, social, and political forces.

Such mutable history is evident in Jorge Luis Borges's "Tlön, Uqbar, Orbis Tertius" and Dick's own *Time Out of Joint*, but *Now Wait for Last Year* raises the narrative stakes by allowing Eric Sweetscent to shape history to his own ends. The novel's many plots and subplots, in fact, reinforce this possibility without certifying it. Eric, in the novel's major storyline, becomes personal physician to *Now Wait for Last Year*'s secondary protagonist, United Nations Secretary General Gino Molinari. Eric must keep the ailing dictator (who controls Earth's economy and military from his Cheyenne, Wyoming, headquarters) alive long enough for Molinari to extricate Earth from a devastating war between two extraterrestrial species: the inhabitants of the Lilistar Alpha Centaurus Empire, who long ago colonized Earth and Mars, and the reegs, a species that resembles large, six-foot-tall ants. After becoming "supreme elected leader of Terra's unified planetary culture, and the supreme commander of its armed forces in the war against the reegs,"[7] Molinari, a man known as "the Mole" who is a "mixture of Lincoln and Mussolini,"[8] signs a Pact of Peace with Lilistar to become allies with the species, which bills itself as "the dominant military power in the galaxy."[9]

The 'Starmen, as Lilistar's natives are known, infiltrate the United Nations' bureaucracy until they effectively conquer Earth. This de facto colonization of the planet does not win Lilistar's war with the reegs, but merely convinces the human population (of whom Eric is the primary representative) that freedom is now a relic of the past: "But these days their [the Terran population's] opinions were not being solicited by the Mole or by the government of Lilistar itself. In fact it was universally believed—openly noised about at bars as well as in the privacy of living rooms—that even the Mole's opinion was not being asked."[10]

Eric, an artificial-organ transplant surgeon, must stick close to Molinari in case the latter's many health problems overwhelm his ability to rule Earth. Eric, however, becomes capable of influencing the war's course when *Now Wait for Last Year*'s first important subplot materializes: Kathy Sweetscent, Eric's wife, surreptitiously addicts him to JJ-180 to force him to cure the neurological damage she suffers because of this drug. JJ-180's effect on Eric, however, is unusual. Most of the drug's users travel into the past, but Eric mysteriously travels into the future, including an alternate/parallel future where he learns that Earth and the reegs successfully cooperate to defeat Lilistar. This outcome inspires Eric, once he returns to his primary reality, to help Molinari resist Lilistar's occupation of Earth by brokering an alliance with the reegs.

Dick combines time travel, parallel realities, narcotics abuse, and extraterrestrial invasion in an intricately plotted novel. Time travel not only fractures *Now Wait for Last Year*'s storyline to underscore the book's postmodern ethos, but also accentuates its humanism by permitting Eric to fight for republican values that the novel's technologically sophisticated alien-invasion tale imperils. Time travel also offers Eric and Kathy Sweetscent tenuous control over their lives that fails to fully resolve Earth's political or the Sweetscents' personal problems. Kathy realizes this truth when she travels 120 years into the past, to the year 1935, in an attempt to alter Earth's future by mailing a transistor to her employer, Virgil Ackerman. Since Virgil is only a boy in 1935, Kathy's gift will guarantee Ackerman's wealth by giving him advanced technology well ahead of its time. Kathy, hoping that this action will also assure her own future affluence, signs her name to a note that briefly explains the transistor's importance:

> She had done it. Insured Virgil's economic future and therefore her own. This would make his career and hers forever.
>
> The hell with you, Eric Sweetscent, she said to herself. I don't ever have to marry you now; I've left you behind.
>
> And then she realized with dismay, I've still got to marry you in order to acquire the name. So that Virgil can identify me, later on in the future, in our own time. What she had done, then, came to exactly nothing.[11]

This futility, in which the better future offered by time travel remains illusory, stresses the historical rigidity that Kathy's experience symbolizes: History is an immutable, unchanging record of what has previously happened, and all attempts to rewrite it are doomed to failure.

Dick, however, does not drop the matter here. *Now Wait for Last Year* offers competing views of history and historical truth because individual characters respond differently to JJ-180, with Eric moving forward in time while Kathy goes backward. Kathy, who suffers neurological damage before traveling to 1935, cannot alter the past or change the future. History, therefore, becomes a static series of inevitable events that not only condemns Kathy to an unhappy marriage, but also forces Earth to endure occupation by a stronger colonial power (Lilistar) that develops JJ-180 as a weapon of war against its human allies as much as against its declared enemies, the reegs. This nightmare scenario, in perhaps *Now Wait for Last Year*'s largest challenge to humanism's survival in technologically and politically corrupt eras, acknowledges the depressing possibility that human life may simply be enthralled to forces beyond the individual's control.

Eric, however, encounters divergent historical outcomes when traveling to the future. JJ-180, therefore, is also an agent of historical change, making Eric's time jumps (one year, one decade, and one century ahead) *possible* futures that will not necessarily come to pass. This uncertainty does not endorse an historical duality that sets static, unchangeable, and pessimistic views of history against fluid, changeable, and optimistic ideas about a bright utopian future. Eric, in fact, cannot distinguish the true course of forthcoming events after returning to 2055 Tijuana (the home of TF&D Corporation) from the future. Eric brings back the formula for an antidote to JJ-180, but cannot feel happy about this accomplishment:

> The click of heels against the pavement, the rushing forward into life; that's gone and only a slopping, dragging sound is left behind. The most horrid sound in the world, that of the *once-was*: alive in the past, perishing in the present, a corpse made of dust in the future. Nothing changes in Tijuana and yet nothing lives out its normal span. Time moves forward too fast here and also not at all.[12]

The hope that Eric experiences during his journey to the future, where he learns that resistance to colonial occupation is possible and that Kathy's brain damage (although irreversible) can be treated, is not enough to ensure a brighter tomorrow. Eric is left with a depressing paradox: History will change as it moves forward, but will not necessarily progress toward a better future. *Now Wait for Last Year* may take Eric from 2055 to 2155, back to 2056 and, finally, home to 2055 in the novel's final seventy-five pages, but this mind-tripping voyage cannot dispel the ennui that Eric feels encroaching upon him.

This melancholy tone underscores the ambiguous postmodern relationship between past and present that characterizes *Now Wait for Last Year*. Eric Sweetscent cannot be certain of his place in time because events occur so quickly that his perception of them becomes a historicizing process. As Fredric Jameson explains, historicizing events results from "a perception of the present as history, that is, as a relationship to the present which somehow defamiliarizes it and allows us that distance from immediacy which is at length characterized as a historical perspective."[13] Jameson, in fact, assigns the term "historicity" to the anxieties about incomplete memory, inadequate history, and fractured human identity that postmodern fiction exemplifies.

Now Wait for Last Year extends these anxieties by projecting them into a future world whose inhabitants struggle with the consequences of colonial occupation. Time travel becomes a method of destabilizing Lilistar's imperial ambitions, but the novel's temporal gymnastics do not follow standard SF conventions. No character who travels back in time (including Kathy) prevents Lilistar's occupation of Earth, while no character who travels forward in time (including Eric) gains sufficient political or technological expertise to defeat the 'Starmen upon returning to the present. The novel instead reveals tangled alternate histories, parallel realities, and possible futures that defy concise or logical summary. Dick does not fashion a consistent timeline (for if he did, Kathy's transistor might well change Virgil Ackerman's future so that he never founds the Tijuana Fur & Dye Corporation and never employs Eric, thereby subverting the novel's narrative premise), but rather questions the possibility of viewing history as a coherent set of comprehensible events.

Parallel realities in *Now Wait for Last Year* symbolize the unstable historical chronology Eric experiences. He ingests JJ-180 to travel forward in time, where he hopes to find an antidote to the drug's neurological damage, but arrives in 2155, exactly one century ahead, to discover that humanity and the reegs peacefully coexist. Eric initially mistakes this development as a sign that Lilistar has been conquered and that Earth has been occupied by the reegs. Taubman, an employee of JJ-180's manufacturer, the Hazeltine Corporation, soon reveals the truth to Eric: "Gino Molinari . . . signed the Era of Common Understanding Protocols with the reegs and then the reegs and the 'Starmen started fighting and Molinari brought us in, on the reeg side, because of the protocols, and we won."[14] Eric soon realizes that he has entered an alternate future with its own history, or, as Willy K, a telepathic inhabitant of Betelgeuse who also works at Hazeltine, puts it, "Dr. Sweetscent comes from a universe in which a pact exists between Terra and Lilistar. And that in his year, 2055, a war is being fought in which they are slowly but steadily losing. Clearly this is not our past but another past entirely."[15] Taubman then recognizes how significant Eric's access to parallel universes is: "This must be why so few time travelers have shown up here . . . . They're scattered through all the different possible futures."[16] History, in *Now Wait for Last Year*, becomes a palimpsest capable of infinite revision, implying that Eric can change his own history.

Molinari, however, has reached the same conclusion. Willy K confirms that the Mole "has already discovered this rank of parallel universes and has made use of it for his immediate political advantage"[17] to develop an ingenious plan: Molinari has arranged for his counterparts in parallel universes to replace him should he die (of natural causes or assassination) so that Molinari can survive long enough to resist Lilistar. After learning of Molinari's scheme, Eric dryly observes that "[t]his rather enlarged the concept of political maneuvering."[18] Molinari, therefore, can perpetually rule Earth by consolidating his political power to subjugate time and, inevitably, history itself.

The ontological and epistemological consequences of these alternate realities are significant. Eric can never be certain that his historical memories are authentic, or even verifiable, because alternate possibilities always exist. Molinari's power to appropriate parallel temporal tracks allows him to rewrite history without end, calling into question the historical veracity of the world that opens the novel, that Eric perceives as real, and that readers accept as authentic. Reality in *Now Wait for Last Year* dismantles to the point that Eric cannot comfortably situate himself in relation to past, present, or future. This postmodern development dislocates *Now Wait for Last Year*'s ontological, epistemological, and historical verities so fully that it should deprive every character of agency. Dick, however, refuses this depressing conclusion. The novel's discourse about republican values, as a comparison of *Now Wait for Last Year*'s fictional history to the history of 1960s America will prove, salvages humanism for Dick's characters and readers.

Technology, Tyranny, and the Struggle for Freedom

Now Wait for Last Year's "inventive, intricate [plot]," as Ursula K. Le Guin has commented about several Dick novels, "move[s] on so easily and entertainingly that the reader, guided without effort through the maze, may put the book down believing that he's read a clever sci-fi thriller and nothing more."[19] *Now Wait for Last Year*, however, offers its reader more than clever thrills by chronicling how advanced technology diminishes the republican values of personal freedom, social liberty, and self-determination. The novel's 2055 setting incorporates issues and events relevant to 1960s America. Dick, indeed, uses *Now Wait for Last Year*'s SF context to examine colonialism, economic exploitation, and political oppression by comparing Earth's precarious position between Lilistar and the reegs to Vietnam's difficult place between American democracy and Soviet totalitarianism during the long struggle for control of that nation's government. By doing so, Dick emphasizes how technological change and market capitalism restrict human freedom.

Now Wait for Last Year, in other words, both challenges and reaffirms the fundamental tenets of American republicanism. John F. Kasson, in his influential 1976 study *Civilizing the Machine: Technology and Republican Values in America 1776–1900*, identifies republicanism as a sociopolitical system that requires its citizens, leaders, and institutions to behave ethically in order to reconcile the divergent interests of America's many communities and cultures. Republicanism, in Kasson's reading, promotes the social virtues of frugality and restraint while inhibiting the social vices of selfishness and luxury to advocate mutual responsibility between all citizens.[20] Kasson, in the course of his lucid analysis, honestly acknowledges the conflict between collective harmony and individual achievement that, to him, characterizes American history. Republicanism, in its quest to provide order, security, and liberty for America's citizens, restricts personal freedom while celebrating the doctrine of rugged individualism.

Dick was not only profoundly skeptical about twentieth-century American capitalism, but also decried the selfishness, profit mongering, and personal excess that, he believed, opposed social responsibility and justice. Dick's ideas, therefore, closely match Kasson's analysis. Eric Sweetscent, as a result, becomes Now Wait for Last Year's primary representative of republicanism's saving power by transforming himself from a man consumed by his failing marriage into a person willing to sacrifice his professional life, social standing, and personal freedom to resist Lilistar's occupation of Earth. He exemplifies the link between private and public virtue not only by deciding to remain with his brain-damaged wife rather than abandoning her to an ignominious death, but also by choosing to help Gino Molinari fight Lilistar rather than consigning Earth's political struggle to defeat. Eric's marital, political, and social fidelity concludes Now Wait for Last Year more optimistically than it begins, but his unenviable choices—particularly the pain that he experiences in the face of Kathy's deteriorating mental condition—prevent the novel from ending happily.

Technology proves to be the greatest threat to Eric's (and Earth's) republican ideals. Lilistar colonizes Earth during its supposedly noble war against the reegs by employing advanced technology to repress human freedom. Lilistar and its supreme representative on Earth, Minister Freneksy, rule the planet by proxy. They install sympathetic human beings in key positions within Molinari's administration while organizing a fearsome secret police squad that enforces Freneksy's political will. JJ-180, an agent of chemical warfare that Lilistar develops to poison the reegs and to control disloyal human beings, is the novel's most cynical symbol of foreign occupation.

JJ-180, however, equips Eric to resist Lilistar's occupation by shuttling him forward in time. While in the future, Eric not only recognizes that victory over Lilistar is possible, but also learns that Molinari, with Eric's assistance, will escape Lilistar's control, flee to Mars, and ally Earth with the reegs. The warships and pharmacological weapons that Earth has manufactured for Lilistar's militaristic campaign against the reegs not only become instruments that help liberate humanity from its long occupation, but that also endorse the republican values of freedom and democracy.

Now Wait for Last Year's ambivalent regard for technology, therefore, reproduces American republicanism's traditional technological suspicions. Kasson usefully summarizes these anxieties:

Could modern technology expand the possibilities for creative power and human liberty, free Americans from drudgery and deadening routine, and bring them into closer communication with one another and with nature? Or might technology instead blunt people's imaginations and ethical sensibilities, alienate them from their environment, and perhaps even serve as a new instrument of tyranny?[21]

Dick's novel perfectly realizes these fears. Aggressive political power in *Now Wait for Last Year* threatens liberty, encourages private vice (particularly hedonistic greed), and corrupts humanity, whose ethical sensibilities languish until Eric employs technology to aid Molinari's resistance movement. Only by pursuing social justice—whether by using his knowledge of the future to help defeat Lilistar's occupation or by helping rehabilitate his ailing wife—does Eric fulfill the republican values that the novel advocates. These values, however, challenge the uncomfortable realities of the decade in which *Now Wait for Last Year* was composed, especially American involvement in Vietnam.

Future War

The social, political, and economic turbulence of 1960s America was inextricably linked to the Vietnam War, which was one of the decade's most polarizing events. Dick opposed this conflict, not by attending protest rallies, but by signing *Ramparts* magazine's February 1968 "Writers and Editors War Tax Protest." Dick, like all the other signatories, refused to "pay the proposed 10% income tax surcharge or any war-designated tax increase" or "the 23% of our current income tax which is being used to finance the war in Vietnam."[22] Lawrence Sutin notes this action's psychological effects on Dick: "Phil's stance, which enabled him to influence public opinion without facing the psychological ordeal of leaving the house, nonetheless exacted high personal costs—an IRS seizure of his car in 1969, as well as an intense, lingering fear"[23] that the government would arrest him.

Dick's refusal to involve himself in direct political action characterizes Eric Sweetscent as *Now Wait for Last Year* begins. Dick's sensitivity to Vietnam-era America's civic anxiety, paranoia, and sadness appears early in the novel, when Eric confronts the difficulties of military conflict with the reegs:

What hadn't the war changed? And who had ever thought, when the Pact of Peace was signed with the ally, Lilistar, that things would go so badly? Because according to Lilistar and its Minister Freneksy, this was the dominant military power in the galaxy; its enemy, the reegs, was inferior militarily and in every other way and the war would undoubtedly be a short one.

War itself was bad enough, Eric ruminated, but there was nothing quite like a losing war to make one stop and think, to try—futilely—to second-guess one's past decisions—such as the Pact of Peace, to name one example, and an example which currently might have occurred to quite a number of Terrans, had they been asked. But these days their opinions were not being solicited by the Mole or by the government of Lilistar itself. In fact it was universally believed—openly noised about at bars as well as in the privacy of living rooms—that even the Mole's opinion was not being asked.[24]

This passage, written in 1964, presciently summarizes the growing dismay expressed by many Americans at the time of the novel's 1966 publication toward their nation's ability to win a military conflict in Southeast Asia that was increasingly called a quagmire. The public's inability to influence governmental policy concerning the Vietnam conflict not only sparked numerous protests, rallies, and riots, but also cemented the decade's reputation as one of angry activism. Earth, a planet full of political malaise and social ennui, symbolizes the United States of the early sixties.

While Eric Sweetscent's growing political consciousness may parallel the American public's increased awareness of governmental policies toward Vietnam, Earth does not merely represent the United States. Earth, much like Vietnam, becomes a pawn in the military struggle between two contending political powers, initially making the reegs Now Wait for Last Year's clearest symbol of Vietnam's northern Communist government, the Vietcong. The official story perpetuated by Freneksy, that the reegs are primitive people whose aggressiveness must be checked by military action, closely matches the propaganda President Lyndon Johnson's administration produced after August 1964's Gulf of Tonkin incident prompted Congress to authorize full-scale military action against the Vietcong. Freneksy's assurances about the war's brevity parallel Johnson's repeated assertions that the conflict in Vietnam would quickly conclude. The reegs are an insect species whose hivelike social organization values collectivism over individualism in Dick's fictional evocation of American beliefs about Communism that, Johnson claimed, threatened freedom, liberty, and democracy if allowed to take root in Vietnam. American military technology was brought to bear against the smaller nation, just as the reegs suffer from Lilistar's military aggression.

Dick shrewdly depicts Earth as an outpost of Lilistar whose obedience, rather than counsel, is sought. This plotline echoes America's colonial treatment of the South Vietnamese government, which became a distant voice in the conflict raging on its own land. Dick therefore attacks his own nation's aggression against foreign peoples to demonstrate the moral depravity of militaristic imperialism masquerading as democratic liberation. Freneksy's amiable assurances about the war's short but necessary duration cannot deny the disheartening truth of Eric's realization that Earth and its ally are losing a conflict whose noble intent is a lie.

This development demonstrates how Dick's 1965 revision of *Now Wait for Last Year*'s manuscript incorporates the facts of American involvement in Vietnam that, according to H. Bruce Franklin, had recently come to light:

> In April 1965, just a few weeks after the first overt dispatch of U.S. combat troops to Vietnam, the first large anti-war demonstration took place in Washington. In the same period, an intense campaign began to educate the American people about the history of the war, a campaign featuring the teach-in movement on college campuses and the publication of an avalanche of historical books, journals, and pamphlets. Millions of Americans were beginning to learn that the government had been deceiving them about how and when the United States had intervened in Vietnam, as well as about the conduct and current state of the war. They discovered that the war had begun not as the defense of a nation called "South Vietnam" from an invasion by the Communist nation of "North Vietnam," but as a war of independence by Vietnam first against France and then against a dictatorship installed in the south in 1954 by the United States in violation of the Geneva Accords. They read and heard about how the Eisenhower, Kennedy, and Johnson Administrations had gradually escalated a covert war into what could already be considered America's longest overseas military conflict.[25]

Earth, in Dick's novel, fights for independence from a foreign aggressor (Lilistar) just as Vietnam fought for independence from France and the United States. The novel's solution—Earth's alliance with the reegs—parallels Ho Chi Minh's solution of allying Vietnam with Communism in its struggle for political liberation.

Dick then deepens Earth's fictional symbolism by combining the American and Vietnamese positions. Jonas Ackerman, the great-grandnephew of Eric Sweetscent's employer Virgil Ackerman, voices this situation's upsetting reality while conversing with Eric:

> "Our best bet," Jonas said, "is simply to lose. Slowly, inevitably, as we're doing."
> He lowered his voice to a rasping whisper. "I hate to talk defeatist talk—"
> "Feel free."
> Jonas said, "Eric, it's the only way out, even if we have to look forward to a century of occupation by the reegs as our punishment for picking the wrong

ally in the wrong war at the wrong time. Our very virtuous first venture into interplanetary militarism, and *how* we picked it—how the Mole picked it." He grimaced.

"And we picked the Mole," Eric reminded him. So the responsibility, ultimately, came back to them.[26]

If, in Jonas's formulation, the reegs symbolize Communists, then Earth becomes Dick's metaphorical fusion of the United States and Vietnam. The planet, by attempting to liberate itself from Lilistar's duplicitous involvement in its civic affairs,[27] functions both as aggressor and victim. The necessity of accepting reeg occupation (or, in the novel's symbolic economy, Communist rule), while far from ideal, becomes the unhappy historical consequence of colonial occupation's militant imperialism.

Earth, particularly when Eric blames its occupation on Molinari's ostensibly free election to office, fictionally reproduces the democratic ambiguities that surrounded American involvement in Vietnam. Neither North nor South Vietnam elected its leader after the nation's 1954 partition. The Vietnamese people never consented to Ho Chi Minh's or to Ngo Dinh Diem's ascent to power (in, respectively, the nation's northern and the southern halves). Minh, a military leader of Indochina's nationalist army, began governing the north after delegates to a 1954 Geneva peace conference divided Indochina into North and South Vietnam. The United States, meanwhile, installed Diem as the south's democratic ruler, although Diem was widely regarded as America's puppet dictator. *Now Wait for Last Year* fictionalizes these historical events when Eric blames Molinari's election as Earth's leader for Lilistar's conquest of the planet. This development metaphorically holds America responsible for prosecuting the Vietnam War by electing Lyndon Johnson as president in 1964. Johnson, after John F. Kennedy's 1963 assassination, sent combat troops to supplement the military advisers Kennedy had assigned to South Vietnam.

Molinari shares other similarities with Johnson. The Mole's frequent physical ailments, which Eric diagnoses as psychosomatic manifestations of "twin, opposing drives"[28] that trap the Mole between suicide and life, function as physical metaphors for Johnson's emotional distress, voiced during public appearances, about being torn between terminating American intervention in Vietnam and ensuring the survival of democracy.

Other Vietnam-era parallels are notable. Molinari, the beleaguered leader who resists foreign occupation, also represents Ho Chi Minh; Eric Sweetscent, a man whose political lethargy transforms into passionate commitment to prevent colonial aggression, reflects the American public's changing attitudes toward the war; and Lilistar's Minister Freneksy, who leads the war effort against Earth while serving as chief of Lilistar's secret police, combines the personality traits of Johnson and J. Edgar Hoover, the FBI chief who authorized his agents to monitor (and to intimidate) antiwar activists.

Now Wait for Last Year, as this list makes clear, engages rich political discourse about Vietnam-era America. The novel, like much of Dick's fiction, mercilessly satirizes America's imperialistic aggression against foreign peoples by staging Earth as a colonized, conquered planet. This satire, as unmistakable as it is melancholy, exaggerates the Vietnam War's grim realities, just as Dick's characters, according to Mary Kay Bray, "are extremes: as well as being individualized, each is a type designed to comment on human strengths and shortcomings."[29]

So, too, are Dick's depictions of the novel's fictional economic powerhouses, the Hazeltine and Tijuana Fur & Dye corporations. Dick's damning commentaries about the collusion of corporate capitalism, advanced technology, and military aggression in promoting colonialism, however, are not unusual for a 1960s American novelist, as Scott Durham notes: "Dick emerges as particularly symptomatic of the transformations that American culture has undergone with the emergence of late capitalism."[30] The corporate malfeasance involved in JJ-180's distribution diminishes the republican values of freedom, liberty, and democracy, as even Jonas Ackerman acknowledges when recounting the drug's origin: "Frohedadrine, or JJ-180, was developed in Detroit, last year, by a firm which [Tijuana Fur & Dye] controls called Hazeltine Corporation. It's a major weapon in the war—or will be when it's in production, which will be later this year."[31] Tijuana Fur & Dye's contribution to the war effort may not be unusual, but the size of Earth's military-industrial complex is: "As soon as hostilities with the reegs had begun, Tijuana Fur & Dye had converted from the luxury trade of ersatz fur production to war work, as, of course, had all other industrial enterprises."[32] Earth's whole economy pursues the goal of supporting Lilistar's military campaign against the reegs, meaning that humanity contributes to its own subjugation by providing material goods to an ally that employs this technology to oppress its human producers. Human beings, therefore, become beggars to their own demise and willing accomplices to their own political enslavement.

Kathy Sweetscent's plight poignantly realizes this cynical political development. Bert Hazeltine, president of JJ-180's manufacturer, and Hilda Bachis, agent of the United Nations Narcotics Control Bureau, reveal this disquieting truth to Eric:

> "Doctor," Hazeltine said, "don't you understand? JJ-180 was not designed as a medicine; *it's a weapon of war*. It was *intended* to be capable of creating an

absolute addiction by a single dose; it was *intended* to bring about extensive nerve and brain damage. It's odorless and tasteless; you can't tell when it's being administered to you in, say, food or drink. From the start we faced the problem of our own people becoming accidentally addicted; we were waiting until we had the cure and then we would use JJ-180 against the enemy. But—" He eyed Eric. "Your wife was not accidentally addicted, doctor. It was done with deliberate intent. We know where she got it." He glanced at Miss Bachis.

"Your wife couldn't have obtained it from Tijuana Fur & Dye," Miss Bachis said, "because no quantity of the drug whatsoever has been released by Hazeltine to its parent company."

"Our ally," Bert Hazeltine said. "It was a protocol of the Pact of Peace; we had to deliver to them a sample of every new weapon of war produced on Terra. The UN compelled me to ship a quantity of JJ-180 to Lilistar." His face had become slack with what for him was now a stale, flat resentment.[33]

This dialogue does not mitigate Bert Hazeltine's (or his corporation's) complicity in helping Lilistar poison the human populace with a toxin ostensibly developed to protect Earth from the reegs. Such aggressive capitalism embodies the dangers of the military-industrial complex that President Dwight D. Eisenhower warned against in his 1961 Farewell Address to the Nation. JJ-180, moreover, symbolizes toxic chemicals like Agent Orange and napalm that American military forces deployed during the Vietnam War. The drug also evokes the use of LSD, marijuana, and heroin by U.S. troops and civilians during the 1960s. Drug subcultures frequently appear in Dick's novels, but *Now Wait for Last Year* illustrates the perils of drug abuse as starkly and as compassionately as Dick's two other masterpieces about this theme, *The Three Stigmata of Palmer Eldritch* (1964) and *A Scanner Darkly* (1977).

Kathy Sweetscent, therefore, is victimized by industrial capitalism and aggressive militarism. This conspiracy becomes, in Durham's words, "a vast and more or less respectable capitalistic monopoly"[34] with colonial ambitions. Kathy's mental deterioration echoes, in fictional form, the cultural deterioration of conquered peoples. Her forced JJ-180 addiction (Lilistar's secret police, the reader learns, have tricked Kathy into ingesting the drug) represents the immoral, imperial, and undemocratic actions inflicted upon the Vietnamese people by France's colonial authority, South Vietnam's unelected government, and America's military might.

Kathy, however, privately experiments with drugs, making it simpler for Freneksy's agents to funnel JJ-180 to her. Dick refuses to moralize about this tragedy or about the dangers of drug experimentation. He instead dramatizes the wonder and terror that JJ-180 produces:

Under the influence of JJ-180, [Kathy] had experienced the world as consisting of airy, penetrable, and benign entities, like so many bubbles; she had found herself able—at least in hallucination—to pass through them at will. Now, in the familiar environment of her office, she experienced a transformation of reality along the lines of an ominous progression: ordinary things, whichever way she looked, seemed to be gaining density. They were no longer susceptible to being moved or changed, affected in any way, by her. . . .

And, even as the objects in her office settled massively against her, they became, on another level, remote; they receded in a meaningful, terrifying fashion. They were losing, she realized, their animation, their—so to speak—working souls. The animae which inhabited them were departing as her powers of psychological projection deteriorated. The objects had lost their heritage of the familiar; by degrees they became cold, remote, and—hostile.[35]

JJ-180 invigorates Kathy, freeing her from the constraints of physical sensation. This liberating experience soon wears off, causing the physical density of objects to disappear. This strange amalgam of substance and spirit, of perception and reality, and of subject and object demonstrates that JJ-180, by making external reality indistinguishable from internal perception, destroys the drug's victim from the inside. The moral sickness of distributing this narcotic illustrates how far Lilistar will go to repress humanist values.

This assault on freedom, democracy, and self-determination rejects the "dominant popular conception of history as a steadily progressive record in which increased knowledge, technological development, and political liberty moved hand in hand"[36] that Kasson sees in late nineteenth- and early twentieth-century America. The Vietnam War, in *Now Wait for Last Year*'s metaphorical rendering, is a *regressive* example of technology's ability to diminish political liberty into outright tyranny.

Molinari's solution to Earth's subjugation is also technological: He uses JJ-180's temporal dislocations to recruit his parallel selves to continue the fight against Lilistar if he dies. Eric, however, realizes how staggeringly antirepublican Molinari's plan has become: "We're going to have to face a fact, he realized, that perhaps none of us wants to face because it means we're in for a kind of government—have had a kind of government already—hardly in accord with our theoretical ideas. Molinari had founded a dynasty consisting of himself."[37] The Molinari the doctor has treated throughout the novel, Eric eventually discovers, comes from a parallel universe. Molinari's dynastic plan functions perfectly despite its logical inconsistencies (how, for instance, could the original Molinari be certain that his counterparts would agree to guide Earth toward liberation?), raising the specter of perpetual rule by a man who does not seek the consent of the people he governs. The inherent paradox of the Mole's administration—Molinari, after all, both *is* and *is not* the man the public believes him to be—suggests that democracy is uncomfortably tenuous. Earth's citizens have been completely deceived, while no guarantee exists that Molinari will renounce his authority even if he liberates the planet from Lilistar's control.

Eric, by supporting Molinari and by caring for Kathy, still manages to redeem a potentially nihilistic novel. He travels to an alternate future hoping to overthrow Lilistar's occupation, but stays with Kathy to counteract the nightmarish consequences of colonial occupation. These compassionate decisions, in the end, offer little hope for a happy resolution because *Now Wait for Last Year*, by fracturing its narration, raises two important questions about human identity: (1) Who exactly is Eric Sweetscent? and (2) Whom does Eric save when he agrees to care for his wife? Eric's and Kathy's multiple selves (meaning the many versions of each person that inhabit the novel's different time periods) not only disrupt conventional formulations of unitary identity and individual consciousness, but also imperil the survival of freedom, self-determination, and independence in *Now Wait for Last Year*'s colonial world.

Sex(ism) and the Married Man

The Sweetscents' divisive marriage is *Now Wait for Last Year*'s most potent symbol of political, economic, and ethical exhaustion. This private relationship speaks to the public difficulties of maintaining humanist values when confronted by postmodern life's overwhelming problems. The couple argues in the novel's early pages about Kathy's purchase of the Lucky Strike package as a gift for their employer, Virgil Ackerman. This dispute only ends when Ackerman's great-grandnephew Jonas interrupts them, but aptly illustrates Eric's sexist attitude:

> "Company business takes priority," Eric said, "over the creature pleasures." He was glad of the intervention by even this junior member of the organization's convoluted blood hierarchy. "Please scram out of here, Kathy," he said to his wife, and did not trouble himself to make his tone jovial. "We'll talk at dinner. I've got too much to do to spend my time haggling over whether a robant bill collector is mechanically capable of telling lies or not." He escorted his wife to the office door; she moved passively, without resistance. . . .
>
> Presently Jonas Ackerman shrugged and said, "Well, that's marriage these days. Legalized hate."

"Why do you say that?"

"Oh, the overtones came through in that exchange; you could feel it in the air like the chill of death. There ought to be an ordinance that a man can't work for the same outfit as his wife; hell, even in the same city." He smiled, his thin, youthful face all at once free of seriousness. "But she really is good, you know; Virgil gradually let go all his other antique collectors after Kathy started here . . . but of course she's mentioned that to you."

"Many times." Almost every day, he reflected caustically.[38]

Eric's patriarchal behavior toward Kathy—particularly his dismissive manner in ordering her from the room—is full of masculine hubris. Kathy's passive obedience is equally disturbing. Eric and Jonas then infantilize Kathy even more by discussing her much as two parents discuss the tiresome habits of an absent child. *Now Wait for Last Year*, as this passage demonstrates, is not a feminist manifesto, although feminism is one of the novel's chief concerns. Jonas's definition of marriage as legalized hate, however, reveals such deep cynicism about Eric and Kathy's relationship that the reader may mistake the novel for little more than an antifeminist tirade.

Eric, for instance, feels threatened by Kathy's successful career at Tijuana Fur & Dye. Her status as a star employee and her professional competence rankle Eric, while Kathy's personal confidence compounds a problem that even Jonas acknowledges: Kathy gets the best of Eric by reminding him of her greater achievements, as well as the social status they confer. Eric's dissatisfaction with his career indicates that spousal jealousy has become a persistent feature of the Sweetscent marriage. Eric, the reader recalls, "managed to park in the tiny stall allocated him"[39] in the novel's opening sentence. His petty disregard for the corporate hierarchy that privileges his wife grows more intense when Eric "passed on into the inner office which was his alone; Virgil Ackerman had insisted on it as a suitable mark of prestige—in lieu of a raise in salary."[40] Had it been granted, this raise, the reader infers, would have awarded Eric a higher income than Kathy.

Eric's humiliation, however, goes much deeper. Gino Molinari telepathically reads Eric's mind after wondering why Eric understands suicidal tendencies so well. Eric then shamefully recalls how he came to work at Tijuana Fur & Dye:

Through Kathy's intercession, he had been hired by Virgil Ackerman. His wife had made it possible for him to take a notable leap in the hierarchy of econ and sose—economic and social—life. And of course he felt gratitude toward her; how could he not? His basic ambition had been fulfilled.

> The means by which it had been accomplished had not struck him as over-poweringly important: many wives helped their husbands up the long steps in their careers. And vice versa. And yet—
>
> It bothered Kathy. Even though it had been her idea.
>
> "*She* got you your job here?" the Mole demanded, scowling. "And then after that she held it against you? I seem to get the picture, very clear." He plucked at a front tooth, still scowling, his face dark.[41]

The gratitude Eric feels, in his account of the story, does not satisfy Kathy, tempting the reader to agree with Molinari's negative impression of her. Both Molinari and Eric, however, rationalize Eric's masculine inadequacy by accentuating Kathy's emotional irrationality in a bid to affirm Eric's economic potency. Molinari's scowling countenance not only certifies Eric's perspective, but also endorses the sexist notion that ambitious women inevitably diminish the men in their lives.

Now Wait for Last Year's suspicion of successful women, moreover, resonates with Dick's autobiography. The author's third marriage, to Anne Williams Rubenstein, was stormy, but Dick's reaction to Anne's success at managing her own jewelry-making business mirrors Eric's response to Kathy's financial acumen. Lawrence Sutin states the matter simply: "The threat Phil saw in the jewelry business—the possible economic eclipse of his writing career—brought about Phil's self-termed third 'nervous breakdown,' at age thirty-three, in 1962."[42] Dick's solution to this crisis was to rent a small shack (just up the road from the house that he, Anne, and their four daughters shared) where he wrote in private. Dick, however, perceived the daily separation from Anne as one of painful necessity. He not only called this hut "the Hovel," but also wrote his Hugo Award–winning novel *The Man in the High Castle* there. This accolade, as Sutin recounts, did not improve Dick's view of himself or his marriage: "The jewelry experience had left him humiliated both as a writer and as practical breadwinner. Phil would bemoan the double bind of facing complaints both about how little money he made and about the long writing stints that kept him away from his family."[43] Many of these financial complaints, it should be noted, came from Dick, not Anne. The family's large size and Dick's small income from fiction writing (he averaged $1,500 per SF novel from Ace Books)[44] prompted Anne to pursue her jewelry business as a way to supplement the family's income.[45]

Dick's distrust of his wife's talent finds fictional expression in the masculine distress that Kathy Sweetscent's accomplishments elicit in Eric, who chooses to blame his wife for her competence and ambition rather than appreciating the material wealth and social status they make possible. Eric's problems result from his insecurity about Kathy's professional success, especially after she directly intervenes in his career, but he cannot admit these truths to himself. Her crimes against Eric's masculinity do not end here, either, as Molinari soon discovers:

> "One night in bed—" [Eric] stopped, feeling the difficulty of going on. It had been too private. And too awfully unpleasant.
>
> "I want to know," the Mole said, "the rest of it."
>
> He shrugged. "Anyhow—she said something about being 'tired of the sham we're living.' The 'sham,' of course, being my job."
>
> Lying in bed, naked, her soft hair curling about her shoulders—in those days she had worn it longer—Kathy had said, "You married me to get your job. And you're not striving on your own; a man should make his own way." Tears filled her eyes, and she flopped over on her face to cry—or appear, anyhow—to cry.
>
> "'Strive'?" he had said, baffled.
>
> The Mole interrupted, "Rise higher. Get a better job. That's what they mean when they say that."
>
> "But I like my job," he answered.
>
> "So you're content," Kathy said, in a muffled, bitter voice, "to *appear* to be successful. When you really aren't." And then, sniffling and snuffling, she added, "And you're terrible in bed."[46]

Kathy reproaches Eric for his stagnant ambition and his sexual inadequacy. This passage sympathizes with Eric despite Kathy's legitimate dissatisfaction with his idle career and his ungrateful attitude (she has, after all, helped secure Eric the job he enjoys). Kathy does not want Eric to take care of her, yet she feels that a man should contribute to his household's finances rather than relying on his wife—or any woman—to nurture him. Kathy rejects the maternal role Eric would have her play by refusing to baby him or to affirm his fragile masculinity. She also reverses traditional gender stereotypes by accusing Eric of marrying her as a way to rise higher in their corporate workplace. Kathy thereby assigns the negative traits associated with femininity—passivity, gold-digging, and implicit sexual frigidity—to her husband.

Eric's feminization, however, is hardly a strike against patriarchy, because his self-serving account of their marriage portrays Kathy's behavior as unduly petty. Kathy's petulance, in fact, provokes murderous rage in Eric after she confesses to destroying "one of his treasured Johnny Winters tapes."[47] These recorded performances of the twentieth-century comedian provide

Eric respite from his unhappy home life, leading Kathy to make the worst accusation of all:

> "I knew," Kathy said, in a harsh, bleak voice as she watched him with withering contempt, "that your—tapes meant more to you than I do or ever did. . . . You know what I'm going to do? I'm going to ruin all of them. . . . You deserve it . . . for holding back and not giving me all your love. . . . You know something, Eric? Do you know, really know, why you like watching men on tape?"
>
> The Mole grunted; his heavy, fleshy, middle-aged face flinched as he listened.
>
> "Because," Kathy said, "you're a fairy."
>
> "Ouch," the Mole murmured, and blinked.
>
> "You're a repressed homosexual. I sincerely doubt if you're aware of it on a conscious level, but it's there." . . . She turned away from the door then. "Good night. And have fun playing with yourself." Her voice—actually and unbelievably—had become controlled, even placid.
>
> From a crouched position he bolted toward her. Reached for her as she retreated smooth and white and naked down the hall, her back to him. He grabbed her, grabbed firm hold, sank his fingers into her soft arm. Spun her around. Blinking, startled, she faced him.
>
> "I'm going to—" He broke off. *I'm going to kill you*, he had started to say. But already in the unstirred depths of his mind, slumbering beneath the frenzy of his hysterical antics, a cold and rational fraction of him whispered its ice-God voice: Don't say it. Because if you do, then she's got you. She'll never forget. As long as you live she'll make you suffer. This is a woman that one must not hurt because she knows techniques; she knows how to hurt back. A thousandfold. Yes, this is her wisdom, this knowing how to do this. Above all other things.[48]

This passage scorns Kathy's shrewdness rather than Eric's violent response to her accusations of homosexuality. Eric, to demonstrate his virility, lashes out at Kathy, but the novel sides with Eric by blaming Kathy's emotional intelligence rather than condemning his moral cowardice. Kathy's actions, however, result from the love she feels for Eric (but that he has failed to reciprocate), not from her delight in making him suffer. Eric's violent chauvinism, in this excerpt, resembles outright misogyny.

Dick's critics and admirers have frequently accused him of treating his female characters insensitively. Istvan Csicsery-Ronay Jr., reviewing the history of Dickian criticism, claims that "[f]eminist criticism had nothing good to say about Dick (what *could* it say, when Dick seemed incapable of depicting women as other than terminally weird vamps and bitchy wives?); it preferred to say nothing."[49] Darko Suvin divides Dick's female characters into a trinity: "Dick has three basic female roles . . . . The first role is that of castrating bitch, a female *macho*, striving to rise in the corporative power-world (see Kathy in *Now Wait for Last Year* . . .); the second that of weak but stabilizing influence . . . ; and the third, crowning one, that of a strong but warm sustaining force."[50] Mary Kay Bray, discussing the satirical nature of Dick's characters, notes that "as well as being individualized, each is a type designed to comment on human strengths and shortcomings. Hence bitch-goddesses, earth mothers, boy-men, and other stock figures pervade Dick's writing."[51]

The bitch image, as these comments make clear, is prevalent in Dick's fiction. The author himself admits to difficulty in crafting female characters in a 1960 letter to Harcourt, Brace and Company editor Eleanor Dimoff:

> I do have the suspicion that I'm writing the same woman into one book after another. . . . I tend to take it for granted in a novel that a man's wife is not going to help him; she's going to be giving him a bad time, working against him. And the smarter she is, the more likely she's up to something. A woman schemes. And one of her techniques is *culture*. . . . It may be that one of the genuinely weak elements in my books is the female co-lead. I either romanticize them or paint them as harpies. . . . I may see all women as Becky Sharps or Amelias.[52]

Becky Sharp and Amelia are the central female characters of William Makepeace Thackeray's *Vanity Fair*, one of Dick's favorite novels. Kim Stanley Robinson picks up this theme in his assessment of Dick's fictional women:

> The Becky Sharps are ambitious, manipulative, attractive, and dangerous to the men who are attracted to them. The Amelias are passive, weak, clinging; they tend to be wives who complain to, but never help, their husbands. We will meet these types again and again, to the point where any individual example has little interest for us, for she is merely the representative of a type. One of the distinguishing features of Dick's strongest novels is the ability to rise above this Becky-Amelia duality, and to show female characters who embody some of the humane and heroic qualities that mark the male protagonists.[53]

On this score, *Now Wait for Last Year* fails because Kathy, rather than transcending the Becky-Amelia duality, enacts a transition from one to the other. Kathy, the fiercely intelligent and independent career woman, so damages her mind by ingesting JJ-180 that she comes to rely upon Eric for care and compassion. Kathy fulfills all the female roles that Ursula K. Le Guin, an otherwise enthusiastic admirer of Dick's writing, believes mar his novels of the 1960s and 1970s: "The women were symbols—whether goddess, bitch, hag, witch—but there weren't any women left, and there used to be women in his books."[54]

Le Guin's comment is especially true of Kathy Sweetscent, who hardly seems human, much less female, in *Now Wait For Last Year*'s most melodramatic moments. Sutin's description of Kathy as "a brilliant, driven harridan"[55] perfectly suits her most morally objectionable act: deliberately addicting Eric to JJ-180 after he threatens to have her arrested. Eric's initial reaction to learning this fact is uncharitable:

> Her voice was flat and drab. "I did it because I thought you were going to have me arrested; you said you were and I believed you. So it's your own fault. I'm sorry . . . I wish I hadn't, but anyhow now you have a motive for curing me; you've *got* to find a solution. I just couldn't depend on your sheer goodwill; we've had too much trouble between us. Isn't that so?"
>
> He managed to say, "I've heard that about addicts in general; they like to hook other people."
>
> "Do you forgive me?" Kathy said, also rising.
>
> "No," he said. He felt wrathful and dizzy. Not only do I not forgive you, he thought, but I'll do everything I can to deny you a cure; nothing means anything to me now except getting back at you. Even my own cure. He felt pure, absolute hate for her. Yes, this was what she would do; this was his wife. This was precisely why he had tried to get away.
>
> "We're in this together," Kathy said.[56]

Kathy's final comment is accurate. Eric learns, after traveling ten years into the future, that he will continue to monitor her declining condition. This knowledge changes his opinion of Kathy: Rather than seeing her as a harpy, Eric realizes that she is a victim of Lilistar's immoral policy of addicting human beings to JJ-180. Kathy, a direct conduit to the inner workings of Gino Molinari's senior staff once Eric becomes the Mole's personal physician, is targeted because of her husband. Kathy, Eric comes to believe, does not deserve the terrible consequences of JJ-180 addiction. The neurological damage Kathy suffers, in other words, is an unreasonable punishment for a woman who emotionally manipulates him. Eric's angry reaction to Kathy's decision to addict him does not persist, although it perfectly illustrates the emotional distress that characterizes their relationship.

The fact that Eric must care for his debilitated wife is also no stunning success for feminism. Kathy, like all of *Now Wait for Last Year*'s female characters, is victimized by patriarchal representations of women as sexualized ciphers. Eric, for instance, perceives his secretary, Miss Perth, in strictly physical terms: "This time she had sprayed herself a shiny blue, inlaid with sparkling fragments that reflected the outer office's overhead lighting";[57] "Miss Perth smiled at him engagingly, showing spotless synthetic ebony teeth, a chilling affectation which had migrated with her from Amarillo, Texas, a year ago";[58] and, most tellingly, "her long-lashed blue eyes showed sympathy and her large breasts seemed to swell a trifle in a motherly, mobile, nourishing way."[59] Mary Reineke, Gino Molinari's wise-beyond-her-years teenage mistress, is an "astonishingly small, dark, pretty girl wearing a man's red silk shirt with the tails out and tapered, tight slacks . . . . She held a pair of cutical [sic] scissors; evidently she had been trimming and improving her nails, which Eric saw were long and luminous."[60] Patricia Garry, Mary's cousin, has "a sharp face, tapered to a flawless chin, and lips so dark as to appear black. Every feature had been cut cleanly and with such delicate precision as to suggest a new order of perfection in human symmetry and balance."[61] These sensual, almost voyeuristic descriptions depict *Now Wait for Last Year*'s female characters as little more than erotic objects, unlike the men, who never endure such coarse visual appraisals.

Kathy fares no better in the novel's libidinal economy, which persistently stresses the male gaze. Bruce Himmel, a fellow TF&D employee, ogles Kathy's amazing appearance at a gathering where the participants try JJ-180 for the first time (this meeting, significantly, begins Kathy's addiction):

> Kathy had arrived naked from the waist up, except, of course, for her nipples. They had been—not gilded in the strict sense—but rather treated with a coating of living matter, sentient, a Martian life form, so that each possessed a consciousness. Hence each nipple responded in an alert fashion to everything going on.
> The effect on Himmel was immense.[62]

This absurd parody of the American fixation with women's breasts sexualizes Kathy in a particularly crude way by stressing a single anatomical feature, her nipples, over all other qualities. *Now Wait for Last Year*, indeed, so frequently describes Kathy as sexy, lithe, and attractive that the reader may believe her physical beauty to be all that matters.

Eric, however, demystifies her sexual appeal with remarkable cruelty:

> God, how physically appealing his wife was; she wore nothing, of course, under the black dress and each curved line of her confronted him with its savory familiarity. But where was the smooth, unyielding, familiar mentality to go with this tactile form? The furies had seen to it that the curse—the curse in the house of Sweetscent, as he occasionally thought of it—had arrived full-force; he faced a creature which on a physiological level was sexual perfection itself and on the mental level—

Someday the hardness, the inflexibility, would pervade her; the anatomical bounty would calcify. And then what? Already her voice contained it, different now from what he remembered of a few years back, even a few months. Poor Kathy, he thought. Because when the death-dealing powers of ice and cold reach your loins, your breasts and hips and buttocks as well as your heart—it was already deep in her heart, surely—then there will be no more woman. And you won't survive that. No matter what I or any man chooses to do.[63]

Brusquely portraying Kathy as a sexual object reveals Eric's deep ambivalence about female sexuality, while reducing her to a sexual stereotype (she becomes the alluring prima donna whose beauty forgives her bitchy personality) emphasizes Eric's massive insecurity. Kathy, therefore, symbolizes the failures of masculinity in *Now Wait for Last Year*'s colonized world. This patriarchal development reveals how individualism, when equated with chauvinism, cannot preserve freedom, democracy, or self-determination. Reclaiming these humanist values becomes Eric Sweetscent's (and *Now Wait for Last Year*'s) primary goal.

Reflected and Reflexive Selves

Eric's reaction to Kathy's illness exemplifies the dilemma that Earth's colonization by Lilistar poses for human agency because she is the living symbol of Eric's (and humanity's) imperial subjugation. Eric, after learning about Kathy's forcible addiction to JJ-180, recognizes an important truth:

It still dazed him that his wife had, just like that, addicted him. What hatred that showed. What enormous contempt for the value of life. But didn't he feel the same way? He remembered his initial discussion with Gino Molinari [the discussion in which Molinari, reading Eric's mind, learns that Eric hates married life]; his sentiments had emerged then and he had faced them. In the final analysis he felt as Kathy did. This was one great effect of war; the survival of one individual seemed trivial. So perhaps he could blame it on the war. That would make it easier.

But he knew better.[64]

Eric, by diagnosing himself, realizes that he is as much to blame as Kathy for his addiction. Acknowledging his cruelly sexist sentiments about Kathy may be commendable, but it does not absolve Eric of his responsibility for contributing to her mental and physical degeneration. Eric's compassion for Kathy expands only when he realizes that his own mental acuity, if left untreated, will decline as badly as hers. Kathy remains a victim in Eric's eyes, demonstrating that he does not fully renounce the sexist attitudes that characterize his thinking.

Now Wait for Last Year, however, offers a more postmodern view of patriarchy when the novel moves toward its conclusion. No equality, or even parity, exists between Eric and Kathy, especially considering that he initially defines his masculinity against the qualities he finds detestable in women. The mental instability, the willingness to destroy another person's happiness, and the need for protection that Eric sees in Kathy's behavior disgust and depress him. After realizing how susceptible he is to these same behaviors, however, Eric begins to accept what Dick's narrative makes clear: that Kathy is a symbol of Eric's own weakness.

This metaphor becomes literal when Eric travels forward in time by one year, to 2056. The haggard, overweight appearance of Eric's future self not only shocks the Eric of 2055 into realizing his complicity in Kathy's illness, but also indicates how ambivalently *Now Wait for Last Year* constructs human identity. Eric's future counterpart explains that caring for Kathy has changed his attitude toward the concept of subjectivity:

> "It's rough," his 2056 self said finally, "to be married to a woman with psychotic traits. As well as showing her physical deterioration. She's still my wife. Our wife. Under phenothiazine sedation she's quiet, anyhow. You know, it's interesting that I—we—didn't pick it up, weren't able to diagnose a case we're living with day in, day out. A commentary on the blinding aspects of subjectivity and over-familiarity."[65]

Kathy, in this passage, may be a passive victim, but Eric, the active caretaker, finally discerns his own inadequacies as a husband and as a doctor. His reference to the "blinding aspects of subjectivity" is notable because Eric, for much of the novel, cannot see his role in Kathy's deterioration. The individual autonomy that patriarchy reserves for men alone cannot sustain Eric, while the male agency that traditional masculinity offers him begins to disappear.

This self-recognition, which forces Eric to face himself, disrupts his identity. Eric's unified personality splinters in the face of his ability to converse with a version of Eric Sweetscent that exists one year in the future. Eric's subjectivity, therefore, bifurcates, leading the reader to pose fundamental questions: Which man (the 2055 or 2056 self) is Eric? Do they share the same identity, or are they two separate individuals? What, more importantly, are the implications of this fractured identity for *Now Wait for Last Year*'s discourse about humanist values within the novel's imperialistic political system?

These questions suggest a profound philosophical debate about human identity. Partha Chatterjee assesses the complexity of this topic, which can become so contentious that it threatens to overwhelm even discriminating thinkers, with honesty and humor:

> What constitutes the identity of a person? This is the sort of question that philosophers ponder. Indeed, this specific question has produced a large philosophical literature in the Western world at least since the seventeenth century, following the landmark effort by René Descartes to posit a duality between mind and body and to locate the self in consciousness, that is, in the faculty of knowing that is independent of the knower's bodily organs, including the brain. Western philosophers have since puzzled over numerous intricacies concerning the precise role of physical and mental properties in the constitution of the identity of a person. Most of these debates, especially in recent Anglo-American academic philosophy, completely bewilder us ordinary mortals.[66]

Chatterjee acknowledges the overwhelming intellectual richness of studies into human identity by emphasizing Descartes's significance to this field of scholarship. Cartesian mind-body duality, in fact, is important to understanding *Now Wait for Last Year*. Differences between the bodies and the minds of Eric Sweetscent's 2055 and 2056 selves (to say nothing of Gino Molinari's plan to indefinitely substitute parallel versions of himself) imply that human identity may be a complex tangle of fragments that rarely coalesce into unitary selves.

The possibility of multiple selves firmly locates Dick's novel within the tradition of postmodern fiction, even if the idea that a human being might comprise more than one distinct personality predates postmodernism. Sigmund Freud's and Carl Jung's psychoanalytic writings, James Joyce's *Ulysses*, Virginia Woolf's *Mrs. Dalloway*, Mary Shelley's *Frankenstein*, and Goethe's *Faust* all posit the notion that human identity transcends singular consciousness, placing *Now Wait for Last Year* in a literary lineage that stretches from German Romanticism and Gothic fiction through the twentieth century's modernist and postmodernist periods.

Now Wait for Last Year is also an exemplary SF text. Science fiction provocatively deals with questions of identity by allowing human consciousness to adopt many different forms. Tales of mind-body switches and of one person transferring his or her consciousness into a separate body (or, in cybernetic science fiction, into a computer) are common, with authors as diverse as A. E. Van Vogt, Arthur C. Clarke, and Octavia E. Butler writing such stories. Dick holds a special place in this subgenre by creating fiction that consistently questions the differences between human and machine identities, with his 1968 book *Do Androids Dream of Electric Sheep?* being one of this tradition's landmark novels.

Now Wait for Last Year employs SF tropes such as time travel and parallel realities to explore the intricacies of human identity by engaging what Anthony Giddens calls "the reflexive project of the self."[67] Giddens, in *Modernity and Self-Identity: Self and Society in the Late Modern Age*, uses the term "modernity" not only to encompass the literary periods of modernism and postmodernism, but also to elucidate three major intellectual dimensions (or, in Giddens's term, axes) of the twentieth century:

> I use the term "modernity" in a very general sense, to refer to the institutions and modes of behaviour established first of all in post-feudal Europe, but which in the twentieth century increasingly have become world-historical in their impact. "Modernity" can be understood as roughly equivalent to "the industrialised world," so long as it be recognised that industrialism is not its only institutional dimension. I take industrialism to refer to the social relations implied in the widespread use of material power and machinery in production processes. As such, it is one institutional axis of modernity. A second dimension is capitalism, where this term means a system of commodity production involving both competitive product markets and the commodification of labour power. Each of these can be distinguished analytically from the institutions of surveillance, the basis of the massive increase in organisational power associated with the emergence of modern social life.[68]

All three axes are visible in *Now Wait for Last Year*. Lilistar's colonization of Earth depends upon industrialism, commodification, and surveillance, while its effects on human identity are most clearly seen in Eric and Kathy Sweetscent's multiple selves. Eric comes face to face with his older self in a reflexive process that compels him to confront uncomfortable truths about his character. Eric's flaws, embodied in his older self, stare back at him.

This ability to literalize metaphors is, as F. Scott Walters notes, "a strength of fantasy and SF"[69] that sets *Now Wait for Last Year* apart from other postmodern novels that represent self-reflexive identity more figuratively (such as Robert Coover's *The Origin of the Brunists* and Thomas Pynchon's *The Crying of Lot 49*). Dick's novel, indeed, evocatively realizes Giddens's ideas about reflexive identity in the modern age:

> In the post-traditional order of modernity, and against the backdrop of new forms of mediated experience, self-identity becomes a reflexively organized endeavour. The reflexive project of the self, which consists in the sustaining of coherent, yet continuously revised, biographical narratives, takes place in

the context of multiple choice as filtered through abstract systems. In modern social life, the notion of lifestyle takes on a particular significance. The more tradition loses its hold, and the more daily life is reconstituted in terms of the dialectical interplay of the local and the global, the more individuals are forced to negotiate lifestyle choices among a diversity of options. Of course, there are standardizing influences too—most notably, in the form of commodification, since capitalistic production and distribution form core components of modernity's institutions.[70]

Eric's ability to converse with himself, as well as Molinari's ability to replace his ailing body with parallel selves, extends the notion of continuously revised biographical narratives to preposterous limits. Both men do so in response to a technological innovation (JJ-180) driven by the dictates of an overwhelming colonizing force (Lilistar's war effort). These developments not only reconstitute Eric's and Molinari's daily lives as the dialectical interplay of local and global (even cosmic) forces, but also force them to construct their identities through several parallel realities and temporal dislocations. Lilistar's colonization may limit Eric's choices in his primary 2055 reality, but Dick uses parallel worlds and time travel to demonstrate how Eric personifies an insoluble paradox: He is both selves (2055 and 2056), despite this situation's logical impossibility (and the dispersed identity that it implies). Eric's subjectivity, therefore, becomes ambiguous, leaving the reader to ponder the personal, political, and institutional perplexities of *Now Wait for Last Year*'s exploration of identity, love, and humanism.

Identity, Politics, and Time

These perplexities find direct expression in the Sweetscent marriage. Eric's failures as a husband (he cannot adequately meet the emotional or institutional demands of matrimony) indirectly cause his JJ-180 addiction, which, in one of *Now Wait for Last Year*'s primary ironies, allows Eric to visit the future to meet an older version of himself. This reflexive encounter revises Eric's biographical narrative to provide a coherent (if disturbing) picture of how his life as Kathy's caretaker will unfold. Giddens's definition of reflexivity nicely summarizes Eric's complex identity in *Now Wait for Last Year*:

Modernity's reflexivity refers to the susceptibility of most aspects of social activity, and material relations with nature, to chronic revision in the light of new information or knowledge. Such information or knowledge is not incidental to modern institutions, but constitutive of them—a complicated phenomenon, because many possibilities of reflection about reflexivity exist in modern social conditions.[71]

Eric experiences diachronic revisions of personality after meeting his 2056 self. The knowledge that 2055 Eric receives from his future self not only revises his attitude toward Kathy and his melancholic acceptance of Lilistar's colonization, but also constitutes a more complicated institutional identity. Eric's newfound compassion for Kathy offers tenuous hope, as well as fragile faith, that Earth can liberate itself from Lilistar's political tyranny.

Eric's time jumps provoke extraordinary doubt about the effectiveness of humanist values such as individual choice, personal agency, and self-determination. Eric, for instance, frequently doubts his effectiveness as a citizen and as a man. As Giddens writes, "Doubt, a pervasive feature of modern critical reason, permeates into everyday life as well as philosophical consciousness, and forms a general existential dimension of the contemporary social world."[72] This description elegantly summarizes *Now Wait for Last Year*'s narrative.

The novel's ambivalent conclusion may permit moments of freedom from Lilistar's authoritarian regime, but *Now Wait for Last Year* finally endorses a pessimistic attitude toward human agency. The novel's corrupt world, in perhaps its most mature development, prevents human beings from making their own choices even as they struggle to reclaim the self-restraint and moral decency that characterize democratic republicanism. Eric's visit to Kathy after returning from 2056 with the antidote to JJ-180 illustrates this point. Eric can cure Kathy's addiction, but not repair her brain damage. Their conversation bleakly demonstrates how unresolved their relationship is:

> He made an attempt to smile encouragingly; it failed. "How do you feel?"
> "Fine now. Since you brought me the news." She was surprisingly matter-of-fact, even for her with her schizoid ways. The sedation no doubt accounted for it. "You did it, didn't you? Found it for me." Then, at last remembering, she added, "Oh yes. And for yourself, too. But you could have kept it, not told me. Thanks, dear."
> "'Dear.'" It hurt to hear her use such a word to him.
> "I can see," Kathy said carefully, "that underneath you really are fond of me still, despite what I've done to you. Otherwise you wouldn't—"
> "Sure I would; you think I'm a moral monster?"[73]

Eric has not become a perfectly solicitous or sensitive husband, even though he will care for, and care about, his sick wife (whose "schizoid ways" still bother him). Dick's talent for realism grounds Eric and Kathy's fantastic experience in believable human emotions, for Eric, rather than forgiving Kathy, asks for a divorce. Kathy agrees to separate if Eric assures her that he is not having romantic affairs with other women. Her response demonstrates that they are far from rapprochement:

> "If I find out there is," she stated, "I'll fight a divorce; I won't co-operate. You'll never get free from me; that's a promise, too."
> "Then it's agreed." He felt a great weight slide into the abyss of infinity, leaving him with a merely earthly load, one which an ordinary human being could bear. "Thanks," he said.[74]

Eric rejects Kathy's invocation of spousal love by claiming that acquiring JJ-180's antidote was the correct moral decision, not an act of personal compassion. Pressing Kathy for a divorce is an escape from, not a true acknowledgement of, Eric's responsibility for her condition. Eric may reclaim agency by traveling forward in time to change the future, but he cannot cure his wife or repair their marriage.

This depressing reality illustrates the complicated masculinity that *Now Wait for Last Year* manifests. Individual choice, personal agency, self-determination, and self-identity become illusory phenomena that disappear in the face of political oppression and personal inadequacy. Even so, the novel offers its readers an emotionally moving conclusion. Eric travels forward in time by a full decade, to 2065. He learns that Earth mounts a resistance to Lilistar's occupation, but cannot discover whether this resistance will succeed. Eric then contacts his older self to see how new treatments for JJ-180 addiction have affected Kathy. The prognosis is not optimistic:

> "To be truthful with you, it [the newest medical treatment for Kathy's condition] should have worked right away."
> "So you don't think it's going to."
> "No," the older Eric Sweetscent said.
> "Do you think if we hadn't divorced her—"
> "It would have made no difference. Tests we give now—believe me."
> Then even that wouldn't help, Eric realized. Staying with her, even for the rest of my life. "I appreciate your help," he said. "And I find it interesting—I guess that's the word—that you're still keeping tabs on her."
> "Conscience is conscience. In some respects the divorce put more of a responsibility on us to see about her welfare. Because she got so much worse immediately after."
> "Is there *any* way out?" Eric asked.

The older Eric Sweetscent of the year 2065, shook his head.

"Okay," Eric said. "Thanks for being honest with me."[75]

The decency of Eric's older self reveals the man's latent humanity. Nothing can alter the gloomy truth that Eric and Kathy will be trapped in an unhappy relationship for the rest of their lives. Eric's realization that he will never separate from Kathy makes it impossible for the Sweetscents to live free from the consequences of Lilistar's occupation. Eric's moral recovery, in other words, cannot alter the terrible fate to which Kathy or Earth has been condemned.

Eric's final decision to stay with Kathy, therefore, complicates the novel's attitude toward individual choice. After returning to 2055, Eric boards an autonomic taxi to travel to Tijuana Fur & Dye, which will not only become the first site of Molinari's colonial resistance to Lilistar, but also the first stage of Eric's new relationship with his wife:

> At Tijuana Fur & Dye, he realized, I'll undoubtedly run into Kathy.
>
> To the cab he said suddenly, "If your wife were sick—"
>
> "I have no wife, sir," the cab said. "Automatic Mechanisms never marry; everyone knows that."
>
> "All right," Eric agreed. "If you were me, and your wife were sick, desperately so, with no hope of recovery, would you leave her? Or would you stay with her, even if you had traveled ten years into the future and knew for an absolute certainty that the damage to her brain could never be reversed? And staying with her would mean—"
>
> "I can see what you mean, sir," the cab broke in. "It would mean no other life for you beyond caring for her."
>
> "That's right," Eric said.
>
> "I'd stay with her," the cab decided.
>
> "Why?"
>
> "Because," the cab said, "life is composed of reality configurations so constituted. To abandon her would be to say, I can't endure reality as such. I have to have uniquely special easier conditions."
>
> "I think I agree," Eric said after a time. "I think I will stay with her."
>
> "God bless you, sir," the cab said. "I can see that you're a good man."
>
> "Thank you," Eric said.
>
> The cab soared on toward Tijuana Fur & Dye Corporation.[76]

The cab's advice is couched in unusual philosophical terms ("reality configurations so constituted"), while the fact that Eric seeks the mechanism's counsel is equally unexpected. Eric's decision not to abandon Kathy, moreover, results from accepting the depressing reality that confronts him, not from empathizing with her sickness. The cab's analysis goads Eric into staying with his wife to affirm his fractured masculinity (Eric, after all, chooses to endure circumstances that lesser men might flee). Eric, indeed, seems curiously emotionless compared to the cab, which renders moral judgments about his choices and his character.

Dick, in one of *Now Wait for Last Year*'s narrative triumphs, refuses a melodramatic conclusion in which Eric professes his love for Kathy by resolving to stay with her no matter the cost. The novel instead ends quietly as Eric makes an ambiguous moral choice that may condemn him to political and personal ruin. Earth's resistance to Lilistar may not overthrow the extraterrestrial colonizer to restore human agency and liberty, while Eric cannot escape Kathy's tragic condition. This fate, the cab recognizes, means unending emotional torment for Eric.

Now Wait for Last Year, therefore, does not endorse utopian platitudes about the triumph of individualism over state power or the significance of human agency in a corrupt world. Dick instead creates a protagonist riddled with weaknesses who tries to preserve the humanist values that he and his culture have lost. Since Eric Sweetscent cannot be certain that his mission will succeed or that life will improve, *Now Wait for Last Year* becomes one of Dick's most sophisticated novels.

Conclusion

Now Wait for Last Year fruitfully examines human identity's survival within an imperial bureaucracy. The novel is not only a mature evocation of postmodern humanism, but also an intriguing fictional reflection of 1960s America's most pressing concerns. The changing roles of men and women; America's military intervention in Vietnam; and colonialism's suppression of free, authentic, and autonomous individuals are crucial to *Now Wait for Last Year*'s narrative success. The novel's most revealing aspect, however, is the bitter marriage it documents. Eric and Kathy Sweetscent, after all, destroy one another's happiness and freedom. Eric's unhappy decision to care for his sick wife does not represent the victory of decency over imperialism so much as the moral impoverishment of his colonial world.

Redemption, therefore, is neither untroubled nor assured in *Now Wait for Last Year*. Lilistar's political power and Eric Sweetscent's emotional confusion make it nearly impossible for the man to honor his commitments. He struggles to make moral choices, but time travel, parallel realities, technology, and colonialism disrupt his subjectivity and personal freedom. Dick, in the end, cannot ensure the triumph of democracy over authoritarianism because such assurance would naively affirm the humanist and republican values that the author so consistently questions. These personal and political ambiguities, however, create a meaningful and resonant novel. *Now Wait for Last Year*, thanks to Dick's artistry, transcends the status of forgettable SF potboiler to become a politically astute, socially mature, and emotionally devastating account of postmodern American life.

Notes

1. Lawrence Sutin, *Divine Invasions: A Life of Philip K. Dick* (New York: Citadel-Carol, 1989), 128.

2. The novel's full title, *Dr. Bloodmoney, or How We Got Along After the Bomb*, clearly alludes to Stanley Kubrick's landmark 1964 film *Dr. Strangelove, or: How I Learned to Stop Worrying and Love the Bomb*. Ace Books editor Don Wollheim altered both of Dick's proposed titles, *A Terran Odyssey* and *In Earth's Diurnal Course*, before the novel's publication.

3. Dick once admitted that "[t]he words come out of my hands not my brain, [*sic*] I write with my hands" (Sutin, 107). John Gildersleeve, a University of California Press copyeditor who read some of Dick's 1950s' mainstream manuscripts, told Sutin that Dick could type eighty to one hundred words per minute (87), although other sources—Dick's wives, his agent, his fellow SF writers, and the author himself—attest to his phenomenal typing speed.

Gildersleeve also provides insight into Dick's actual writing process by commenting that Dick "[made] up his story as he typed it out, and he typed so fast he had to keep one jump ahead of himself on one side or the other" (Sutin, 87). This ability allowed Dick to maintain a punishing compositional schedule that saw him "keep to a pace of two novels per year—each novel taking six weeks for the first draft and another six weeks for the second (retyping and minor copy editing). Between each novel would be six months devoted to thinking out the next plot" (107).

Dick, therefore, did not rush into writing a novel without planning, consideration, or forethought. He sometimes took extensive notes, although he did not slavishly adhere to them (Sutin, 163–64). Sutin quotes a 1969 letter in which Dick emphasizes both "the slow gestation of a novel idea within him" (163) and his organic writing process: "Thus I frequently find myself arriving at a point in the novel where, for example, the notes (and if there is an outline, then the outline) calls for the protagonist to say 'Yes,' where in fact he, being what he is, would say 'No,' so 'No' he says, and I must go on from there" (164). Dick did not enjoy the encumbrance of notes or outlines, using them as compositional aids rather than writing necessities.

The contrast between Dick's lengthy conceptualization of his novels and their speedy, almost frantic composition, moreover, offers insight into the workings of his authorial mind: Ideas were worthy of extended reflection, while the task of writing was a feverish attempt to transcribe these ideas into physical form. This organic method of writing, which Dick once acknowledged "depend[s] on the inspiration of the moment" (Sutin, 164), not only accounts for his novels' narrative urgency, authorial energy, and amazing power, but also explains his stylistic excesses, lapses, and defects.

4. Jonathan Culler, *Structuralist Poetics: Structuralism, Linguistics and the Study of Literature* (Ithaca, NY: Cornell University Press, 1975), 118. "Literary Competence" is also the title of the sixth chapter of Culler's study.

5. Philip K. Dick, *Now Wait for Last Year* (1966; New York: Vintage-Random, 1993), 3.

6. Dick, *Now Wait for Last Year*, 3.

7. Dick, *Now Wait for Last Year*, 30.

8. Dick, *Now Wait for Last Year*, 64.

9. Dick, *Now Wait for Last Year*, 11.

10. Dick, *Now Wait for Last Year*, 11.

11. Dick, *Now Wait for Last Year*, 111.

12. Dick, *Now Wait for Last Year*, 225. The emphasis is Dick's.

13. Fredric Jameson, *Postmodernism, or, the Cultural Logic of Late Capitalism* (1991; Durham, NC: Duke University Press, 1992), 284.

14. Dick, *Now Wait for Last Year*, 166.

15. Dick, *Now Wait for Last Year*, 170.

16. Dick, *Now Wait for Last Year*, 170.

17. Dick, *Now Wait for Last Year*, 170.

18. Dick, *Now Wait for Last Year*, 203.

19. Ursula K. Le Guin, "Science Fiction as Prophesy," *New Republic*, October 30, 1976, 33.

20. John F. Kasson, *Civilizing the Machine: Technology and Republican Values in America 1776–1900* (1976; New York: Hill and Wang, 1999), 4. Kasson's full definition of republicanism is notable:

> The notion of republicanism began with a conception of the relationships among power, liberty, and virtue. The balance among these elements, Americans' reading and experience taught them, remained delicate and uneasy at best. Power, as they conceived it, whether wielded by an executive or by the people, was essentially aggressive, forever in danger of menacing its natural prey, liberty or right. To safeguard the boundaries between the two stood the fundamental principles and protections, the "constitution," of government. Yet this entire equilibrium depended upon the strict rectitude both within government and among the people at large. To the eighteenth-century mind republicanism denoted a political and moral condition of rare purity, one that had never been successfully sustained by any major nation. It demanded extraordinary social restraint, what the age called "public virtue," by which each individual would repress his personal desires for the greater good of the whole. Public virtue, in turn, flowed from men's private virtues, so that each individual vice represented a potential threat to the republican order. Republicanism, like Puritanism before it, preached the importance of social service, industry, frugality, and restraint. Their opposing vices—selfishness, idleness, luxury, and

licentiousness—were inimical to the public good, and if left unchecked, would lead to disorder, corruption, and, ultimately, tyranny. The foundation of a just republic consisted of a virtuous and harmonious society, whose members were bound together by mutual responsibility. (4)

Kasson's book, by examining these ideas in sophisticated detail, remains a significant scholarly contribution to the study of American republicanism more than thirty years after its initial publication.

21. Kasson, *Civilizing the Machine*, 110.

22. Sutin, *Divine Invasions*, 160.

23. Sutin, *Divine Invasions*, 160.

24. Dick, *Now Wait for Last Year*, 11.

25. H. Bruce Franklin, "*Star Trek* in the Vietnam Era," *Film and History* 24, no. 1–2 (1994): 37–38. For more information about the history of the Vietnam War, see Weldon A. Brown's *Prelude to Disaster: The American Role in Vietnam, 1940–1963* (Port Washington, NY: Kennikat, 1975); J. Justin Gustainis's *American Rhetoric and the Vietnam War* (Westport, CT: Praeger, 1993); Marvin Kalb and Elie Abel's *Roots of Involvement: The U.S. in Asia, 1784–1971* (New York: Norton, 1971); Kevin Ruane's *War and Revolution in Vietnam: 1930–75* (London: UCL, 1998); and Melvin Small's *Covering Dissent: The Media and the Anti-Vietnam War Movement* (New Brunswick, NJ: Rutgers University Press, 1994).

26. Dick, *Now Wait for Last Year*, 15. The emphasis is Dick's.

27. The duplicity of American involvement in Vietnam is now unquestionable. David Halberstam, in chapter 27 of *The Fifties* (New York: Fawcett, 1994), notes that Harry Truman helped France finance its war in Indochina as early as 1951 to contain Asian Communism. Fearing that a French withdrawal from Indochina would bring Vietnamese nationalists like Ho Chi Minh (who were nearly all Communists) to power, the United States had contributed, by the end of 1953, as much as $1 billion to the French effort.

The Vietminh, Indochina's army, seized Dien Bien Phu, a French garrison along the Laotian border, in March 1954, increasing the likelihood of American military intervention. The post fell, however, on May 7, 1954, after a two-month battle. The resulting Geneva peace conference renamed the country Vietnam and partitioned it into two separate nations. The south became an anti-Communist nation under the rule of Ngo Dinh Diem, a puppet dictator backed (and eventually installed) by the United States, while Ho Chi Minh governed the north.

Diem was assassinated in a 1963 coup by some of his own generals, "whose efforts," H. Bruce Franklin notes, "were coordinated by U.S. Ambassador Henry Cabot Lodge" and approved by President John F. Kennedy ("*Star Trek* in the Vietnam Era" 36). Kennedy's assassination three weeks later allowed Lyndon Johnson to sign National Security Action Memorandum 273, which authorized covert attacks against North Vietnam in an effort to provoke Communist retaliation that would legitimize an American invasion.

28. Dick, *Now Wait for Last Year*, 84.

29. Mary Kay Bray, "Mandalic Activism: An Approach to Structure, Theme, and Tone in Four Novels by Philip K. Dick," *Extrapolation* 21, no. 2 (1980): 155.

30. Scott Durham, "P.K. Dick: From the Death of the Subject to a Theology of Late Capitalism," *Science Fiction Studies* 15, no. 2 (1988): 173.

31. Dick, *Now Wait for Last Year*, 80.

32. Dick, *Now Wait for Last Year*, 11–12.

33. Dick, *Now Wait for Last Year*, 151. The emphasis is Dick's.

34. Durham, "P.K. Dick," 177.

35. Dick, *Now Wait for Last Year*, 72–73.

36. Kasson, *Civilizing the Machine*, 185.

37. Dick, *Now Wait for Last Year*, 202.

38. Dick, *Now Wait for Last Year*, 7–8.

39. Dick, *Now Wait for Last Year*, 3

40. Dick, *Now Wait for Last Year*, 5

41. Dick, *Now Wait for Last Year*, 49. The emphasis is Dick's.

42. Sutin, *Divine Invasions*, 111.

43. Sutin, *Divine Invasions*, 120–21.

44. Sutin, *Divine Invasions*, 121.

45. Sutin, *Divine Invasions*, 121. Dick also felt threatened by the mainstream literary success and wealth of Anne's first husband, the deceased poet Richard Rubenstein. Dick lived in the large, ornate house that the Rubensteins owned. This home became an almost constant reminder of Dick's limited financial earnings, while Richard's renown in the California literary scene further exacerbated Dick's feelings of artistic inadequacy.

46. Dick, *Now Wait for Last Year*, 49–50. The emphasis is Dick's.

47. Dick, *Now Wait for Last Year*, 50.

48. Dick, *Now Wait for Last Year*, 50–52. The emphasis is Dick's.

49. Istvan Csicsery-Ronay Jr., "Pilgrims in Pandemonium: Philip K. Dick and the Critics," in *On Philip K. Dick: 40 Articles from Science-Fiction Studies*, ed. R. D. Mullen et al. (Terre Haute, IN: SF-TH, 1992), xii. The emphasis is Csicsery-Ronay's.

50. Darko Suvin, "P.K. Dick's Opus: Artifice as Refuge and World View," *Science Fiction Studies* 2, no. 1 (1975): 18. The emphasis is Suvin's.

51. Bray, "Mandalic Activism," 155.

52. Gregg Rickman, *To the High Castle: Philip K. Dick: A Life 1928–1962* (Long Beach, CA: Fragments West/Valentine, 1989), 356. The emphasis is Dick's. The letter also appears under the title "A Letter from Philip K. Dick February 1, 1960" in the Philip K. Dick Society's *Pamphlet 1* (Glen Ellen, CA: Philip K. Dick Society, 1963). Sutin also quotes part of it on page 109 of *Divine Invasions*.

53. Kim Stanley Robinson, *The Novels of Philip K. Dick*, Studies in Speculative Fiction, no. 9 (Ann Arbor: UMI Research, 1984), 5–6.

54. Sutin, *Divine Invasions*, 276. Le Guin made these comments during an interview Sutin conducted for his book.

55. Sutin, *Divine Invasions*, 125.

56. Dick, *Now Wait for Last Year*, 142–43. The emphasis is Dick's.

57. Dick, *Now Wait for Last Year*, 5.

58. Dick, *Now Wait for Last Year*, 5.

59. Dick, *Now Wait for Last Year*, 193.

60. Dick, *Now Wait for Last Year*, 90–91.

61. Dick, *Now Wait for Last Year*, 209.

62. Dick, *Now Wait for Last Year*, 38.

63. Dick, *Now Wait for Last Year*, 56.

64. Dick, *Now Wait for Last Year*, 156.

65. Dick, *Now Wait for Last Year*, 184.

66. Partha Chatterjee, *A Princely Impostor? The Strange and Universal History of the Kumar of Bhawal* (Princeton, NJ: Princeton University Press, 2002), 115.

67. Anthony Giddens, *Modernity and Self-Identity: Self and Society in the Late Modern Age* (Stanford, CA: Stanford University Press, 1991), 5.

68. Giddens, *Modernity and Self-Identity*, 14–15.

69. F. Scott Walters, "The Final Trilogy of Philip K. Dick," *Extrapolation* 38, no. 3 (1997): 228.

70. Giddens, *Modernity and Self-Identity*, 5.

71. Giddens, *Modernity and Self-Identity*, 20.

72. Giddens, *Modernity and Self-Identity*, 3.

73. Dick, *Now Wait for Last Year*, 194–95.

74. Dick, *Now Wait for Last Year*, 196.

75. Dick, *Now Wait for Last Year*, 221.

76. Dick, *Now Wait for Last Year*, 229–30.

CONCLUSION

~

The Postmodern Humanist: Philip K. Dick in the Twenty-First Century

Istvan Csicsery-Ronay Jr., in an articulate survey of Philip K. Dick's critical reputation titled "Pilgrims in Pandemonium," locates the writer squarely within the tradition of postmodern literature by noting that Dick, in many quarters, is no longer regarded as a hack science-fiction author:

> Dick has ceased to be a marginal writer. He has become so interesting, so often written about and interpreted, that readers can hardly come to his fiction without going through the thickets—indeed by now, the forests—of criticism, simulation, and cultural propaganda. The margin has moved to the center. And even though that center is the shattered bullet hole of postmodernism, it is, like all centers, under the custodial care of cultural bodyguards.[1]

These cultural bodyguards, particularly literary scholars who promote authors they consider worthy of preservation, constitute, in Csicsery-Ronay's telling, a historical force all their own. Dick, without their intervention, might have been lost on the scrap heap of an unimportant and intellectually suspect genre.

Dick's oeuvre, however, cannot be confined to the ambivalent generic boundaries of science fiction or of postmodernism. He is, in many ways, an old-fashioned writer who privileges narrative clarity over ambiguity, narrative coherence over fragmentation, and narrative continuity over disruption. Since Dick's extensive reading of eighteenth- and nineteenth-century novelists influenced him at least as much as his enthusiasm for modernist innovators such as James Joyce, William Faulkner, and Ernest Hemingway, lucid formulations of Dick's place within the modernist and postmodernist literary traditions are difficult to crystallize. Dick's life (1928–1982), in fact, spans American modernism and postmodernism insofar as postmodernism's slippery origins, conventions, and boundaries make it notoriously difficult to define. Few clear distinctions between modernism's end and postmodernism's beginning are possible because one era blurs into the other. "Postmodernism," indeed, is an indistinct critical label that reflects literary scholarship's inability to precisely define, analyze, and categorize the era that succeeded modernism. The best critics can do, it seems, is add the prefix "post" to the word "modernism" to indicate that the latter period succeeds the former.

Dick's fiction reproduces this ambiguity by containing as many characteristics of modernist fiction as it does of postmodern narrative. Dick is willing to disrupt the conventions of nineteenth-century fiction as much as any modernist author by employing stream-of-consciousness narration, multiple viewpoints, and nonlinear chronology. He also includes the psychological breakdowns, unstable subjectivities, and narrative fragmentation associated with (but that cannot be confined to) postmodern fiction. Although Dick's authorial career (1952–1982) may seem to place him almost entirely within American postmodernism (broadly defined as a post–World War II cultural phenomenon), his allegiance to older forms of storytelling makes his fiction a fascinating hybrid of modernist and postmodernist thought.

Dick's writing frequently seems old-fashioned not only because it hearkens back to nineteenth-century narrative, but also because it examines, explores, and encourages humanist values. Individual agency, personal autonomy, political liberty, and social justice are important to Dick. Postmodernism may contest the reality, or even the possibility, of these values in a world rife with technological paranoia, political oppression, and social instability, but Dick's humanism cannot be undone simply because it may be the relic of a bygone era. His fiction demonstrates that, no matter how impractical humanism may appear to readers accustomed to the diminishing liberties, massive bureaucracies, and capitalist exploitations of twentieth-century history, humanist values are crucial to maintaining the sense of authenticity individuals must experience in order to endure their complicated lives.

Dick, as much as any twentieth-century American author, acknowledges the contradictions and complications of preserving freedom, authenticity, and agency within the postmodern period's political, economic, and social mayhem. Dick's fiction acknowledges how imperfectly humanism responds to the convoluted complexities of postmodern life, but his writing also validates humanism's merit in an era that, per Csicsery-Ronay's evocative metaphor, shatters all certainties. Personal agency, autonomy, and liberty may seem outdated (even desiccated) to postmodern eyes, but Dick's fiction laments the loss of these humanist values by furiously demanding their conservation.

This ambivalent attitude toward humanism's survival within the hostile territory of twentieth-century politics connects Dick with Franz Kafka, Jorge Luis Borges, and Italo Calvino. Dick may be a quintessentially American author, but he also participates in an international tradition of visionary fiction that, by imagining alternate worlds and alternative lives, perceptively examines the limitations, possibilities, and intricacies of quotidian reality. Kafka is perhaps this tradition's foremost writer, while Borges and Calvino are significant participants. So, too, is Philip K. Dick. His literature skillfully combines postmodern anxieties with humanist principles to produce fiction that, although unique in voice, tone, and content, resonates with Kafka's, Borges's, and Calvino's writing.

All four authors honestly face the profound anxieties, doubts, and fears that the twentieth century's massive institutional bureaucracies provoke within their citizens. These uncertainties fragment human identity and historical memory to produce the narrative incoherency and unstable subjectivities strongly associated with postmodern literature. Dick's fiction is a laboratory of these effects that employs the tropes, conventions, and symbols of science fiction to demonstrate how postwar culture eviscerates humanist values so deeply that they become unrecognizable. Dick consistently questions human freedom, agency, and identity by submerging his characters in nightmarish dystopias that break down at a moment's notice. He rarely depicts the categorical triumph of good over evil, but instead emphasizes the need for people to recognize that their terrible living conditions are as much the product of their own inadequacies as the fault of political, economic, social, and bureaucratic repression. Dick portrays lonely and fractured people whose salvation is uncertain, who struggle against (even if they cannot defeat) the institutions that circumscribe them, and who embody humanist principles even if these principles lose their potency.

Dick's fiction is not, however, a pitiless rendering of postmodern blight. The most striking aspect of his writing is its tremendous compassion. Dick's empathy for his characters not only prevents his fiction from descending into unbearable bleakness, but also connects it with Kafka's, Borges's, and Calvino's writing. All four authors destabilize scientific rationality, cultural progress, and personal agency to portray how ambiguously human consciousness reacts to the historical events, mammoth bureaucracies, industrial exploitations, technological advances, and political consolidations (of small powers into large states) that characterize the twentieth century.

Dick uses science fiction to reflect these complexities in ways similar to Kafka's, Borges's, and Calvino's fabulist fiction. With Kafka, Dick shares an interest in employing animal metaphors to portray the contradictions and compromises forced upon human beings by authoritarian governments. With Borges, Dick shares an interest in creating alternative or parallel worlds to illustrate how history (and human memory) can be manipulated to force entire populations to participate in their own subjugation by adopting the fearsome ideologies of the political forces that repress history and memory in the first place. With Calvino, Dick shares a fascination with cosmic and transcendental subject matter to probe the nature of enlightenment and sacredness in a secular world whose human inhabitants desire spiritual, or at least metaphysical, succor from a hostile and unfeeling universe.

These comparisons, however, do not capture the uniqueness of Dick's fiction or his insistently recognizable literary voice. Dick, this study argues, now enjoys the company of canonical writers like Kafka, Borges, and Calvino because his science fiction consistently probes the ambiguities and deficiencies of postwar American culture. Dick's writing, in fact, is a crucial addition to postmodern American literature because it refuses to dismiss humanist concerns, no matter how dated they may seem.

Dick's fiction, therefore, is a significant contribution to postwar American literature, to international literary postmodernism, and to literary humanism. The popularity and critical acclaim Dick's writing has received in France, Germany, Italy, Poland, and Japan testifies not only to his international appeal, but also to the importance of science fiction's literary explorations of pressing political, economic, social, and cultural questions. Dick is not only one of science fiction's foremost American practitioners, but also a figure of notable accomplishment and influence.

Dick may be as gifted a postwar American novelist as Thomas Pynchon, Kurt Vonnegut Jr., and Vladimir Nabokov, but he is also a kindred spirit to Franz Kafka, Jorge Luis Borges, and Italo Calvino. Locating Dick as part of this complicated lineage acknowledges how well his concerns about the survival of American democracy, freedom, and liberty correspond to international apprehensions about the survival of humanism in the postmodern world.

Dick's fiction, moreover, expands the traditional boundaries of science fiction to make the SF label one that literary scholars may accurately assign to Dick even if this label does not fully describe him. Like Kafka, Borges, and Calvino, Dick is a writer of thematically open-ended fiction. His stories and novels, like theirs, conclude ambiguously, causing the reader to question the endurance of liberty, freedom, autonomy, and agency. Dick's unresolved resolutions and ambivalent narratives repeatedly demonstrate that his characters cannot successfully embrace or enact the humanist values of individuality, self-determination, and personal freedom for which they strive. Outrageous humor, merciless satire, and forlorn hope typify Dick's fiction, even if they cannot dispel the sobering realities about which he writes. Dick's complicated storylines unseat the reader's ability to articulate, much less resolve, the difficult challenges of twentieth-century life, making his fiction, particularly *Now Wait for Last Year*, a mature assessment of postmodern doubt.

Dick's fiction refuses firm answers while creating a bizarre milieu whose SF trappings explore the intricacies, anxieties, and paradoxes of postmodernism. Dick is therefore not only a worthy heir to Kafka, Borges, and Calvino, but also a fascinating author in his own right. Dick's science fiction, for much of his authorial career, may not have received respect from the cultural bodyguards Csicsery-Ronay mentions in "Pilgrims in Pandemonium," but Dick's writing is now an essential component of postmodern literature. Dick, indeed, is an author whose fiction demands that the reader return to it again and again to discover its intellectual, symbolic, and emotional richness.

Philip K. Dick, as a result, is a beguiling author whose work unseats conventional notions about the nature of science fiction, American literature, and humanism's survival in the postmodern era. These projects are all unfinished, much like the critical dialogue about Dick's literary significance. His fiction may not always succeed, but it always probes the philosophical, political, and personal perplexities of human identity, agency, and freedom. Dick, like Kafka, Borges, and Calvino, initiates a spellbinding conversation about the ambiguities and ambivalences of postmodern life that he cannot complete. Dick's harrowing visions of the future, however, finally reflect his faith in humanism's ability to navigate the uncertainties of twentieth-century American life.

Dick, therefore, is a postmodern humanist. His fiction is expansive, cynical, paradoxical, and witty. He has become a necessary author for twenty-first century readers who wish to understand their fractured and fragmented lives. Dick's power, artistry, and relevance can no longer be ignored, diluted, or denied. He is one of the most talented American authors of the second half of the twentieth century. Newcomers to his fiction will discover what his admirers have known for so long: that, as the recipients of Dick's literary vision, we are better for having encountered him.

Note

1. Istvan Csicsery-Ronay Jr., "Pilgrims in Pandemonium: Philip K. Dick and the Critics," in *On Philip K. Dick: 40 Articles from Science-Fiction Studies*, ed. R. D. Mullen et al. (Terre Haute, IN: SF-TH, 1992), vi.

Bibliography

Amis, Kingsley. *New Maps of Hell: A Survey of Science Fiction*. New York: Harcourt, Brace, 1960.

Asimov, Isaac. *The Complete Robot*. Garden City, NY: Doubleday, 1982.

Babylon 5. Created by J. Michael Straczynski. Perf. Michael O'Hare, Bruce Boxleitner, Claudia Christian, Jerry Doyle, Mira Furlan, Richard Biggs, Andreas Katsulas, Stephen Furst, Tracey Scoggins, and Peter Jurasik. Los Angeles: Babylonian Productions, 1994–1998.

Barnatán, Marcos-Ricardo. *Borges: Biografía Total*. Madrid: Temas de Hoy, 1995.

Bell-Villada, Gene H. *Borges and His Fiction: A Guide to His Mind and Art*. Austin: University of Texas Press, 1999.

Belton, John. *American Cinema/American Culture*. New York: McGraw-Hill, 1994.

Benjamin, Walter. *Illuminations*. Edited by Hannah Arendt. Translated by Harry Zohn. 1955. New York: Schocken, 1968.

Bernstein, Barton J., and Allen J. Matusow, eds. *The Truman Administration: A Documentary History*. New York: Harper Colophon, 1966.

Bertrand, Frank C. "How Jeet Heer Betrayed Philip K. Dick Admirers to Marxist Literary Critics." May 14, 2002. http://www.philipkdickfans.com/frank/jeetheer.htm.

Blade Runner. Dir. Ridley Scott. Screenplay by Hampton Fancher and David Peoples. Based on the novel *Do Androids Dream of Electric Sheep?* by Philip K. Dick. Perf. Harrison Ford, Sean Young, Rutger Hauer, Daryl Hannah, and Edward James Olmos. Los Angeles: Warner Bros., 1982.

Blish, James. *A Case of Conscience*. New York: Ballantine, 1958.

Booker, M. Keith. *Monsters, Mushroom Clouds, and the Cold War: American Science Fiction and the Roots of Postmodernism, 1946–1964*. Contributions to the Study of Science Fiction and Fantasy, no. 95. Westport, CT: Greenwood, 2001.

Borges, Jorge Luis. *Labyrinths: Selected Stories and Other Writings.* Edited by Donald A. Yates and James E. Irby. New York: New Directions, 1964.

Bouson, J. Brooks. "The Repressed Grandiosity of Gregor Samsa: A Kohutian Reading of Kafka's *Metamorphosis.*" In *Narcissism and the Text: Studies in Literature and the Psychology of Self,* edited by Lynne Layton and Barbara Ann Schapiro, 192–212. New York: New York University Press, 1986.

Bray, Mary Kay. "Mandalic Activism: An Approach to Structure, Theme, and Tone in Four Novels by Philip K. Dick." *Extrapolation* 21, no. 2 (1980): 146–57.

Brittain, Vera. *Testament of Experience: An Autobiographical Story of the Years 1925–1950.* New York: Macmillan, 1957.

———. *Testament of Youth: An Autobiographical Study of the Years 1900–1925.* New York: Macmillan, 1933.

Brod, Max. *Franz Kafka: A Biography.* Translated by G. Humphreys Roberts and Richard Winston. 2nd ed. New York: Schocken, 1960.

Broderick, Damien. *Reading by Starlight: Postmodern Science Fiction.* London: Routledge, 1995.

Brown, J. Andrew. "Edmundo Paz Soldán and His Precursors: Borges, Dick, and the SF Canon." *Science Fiction Studies* 34, no. 3 (2007): 473–83.

Brown, Weldon A. *Prelude to Disaster: The American Role in Vietnam, 1940–1963.* Port Washington, NY: Kennikat, 1975.

Butler, Andrew M. "Science Fiction as Postmodernism: The Case of Philip K. Dick." In *Impossibility Fiction: Alternativity—Extrapolation—Speculation,* edited by Derek Littlewood and Peter Stockwell, 45–56. Amsterdam: Rodopi, 1996.

Calinescu, Matei. *Five Faces of Modernity: Modernism, Avant-Garde, Decadence, Kitsch, Postmodernism.* Durham, NC: Duke University Press, 1987.

Calvino, Italo. *The Baron in the Trees.* Translated by Archibald Colquhoun. 1959. New York: Harcourt Brace, 1977.

———. *Cosmicomics.* Translated by William Weaver. 1965. New York: Harvest–Harcourt Brace, 1968.

———. *If on a winter's night a traveler.* Translated by William Weaver. 1979. New York: Harvest–Harcourt Brace, 1981.

———. *Invisible Cities.* Translated by William Weaver. 1972. New York: Harvest–Harcourt Brace, 1974.

———. *t zero.* Translated by William Weaver. 1967. New York: Harvest–Harcourt Brace, 1969.

Campbell, Joseph. *The Inner Reaches of Outer Space: Metaphor as Myth and as Religion.* New York: A. van der Marck Editions, 1986.

Caute, David. *The Great Fear.* New York: Simon and Schuster, 1978.

Ceplair, Larry, and Steven Englund. *The Inquisition in Hollywood: Politics in the Film Community, 1930–1960.* Berkeley and Los Angeles: University of California Press, 1983.

Chandos, Oliver Lyttelton. *From Peace to War: A Study in Contrast, 1857–1918*. London: Bodley Head, 1968.

Chase, Richard. *The American Novel and Its Tradition*. Garden City, NY: Doubleday Anchor, 1957.

Chatterjee, Partha. *A Princely Impostor? The Strange and Universal History of the Kumar of Bhawal*. Princeton, NJ: Princeton University Press, 2002.

Coover, Robert. *The Origin of the Brunists*. 1966. New York: W.W. Norton, 1989.

Corngold, Stanley. "Allotria and Execreta in 'In the Penal Colony.'" *Modernism/Modernity* 8, no. 2 (2001): 281–93.

———. "Kafka's Other Metamorphosis." In *Kafka and the Contemporary Critical Performance: Centenary Readings*, edited by Alan Udoff, 41–57. Bloomington: Indiana University Press, 1987.

Csicsery-Ronay Jr., Istvan. "Kafka and Science Fiction." *Newsletter of the Kafka Society of America* 7, no. 1 (1983): 5–14.

———. "Pilgrims in Pandemonium: Philip K. Dick and the Critics." In *On Philip K. Dick: 40 Articles from Science-Fiction Studies*, ed. R. D. Mullen et al., v–xviii. Terre Haute, IN: SF-TH, 1992.

Culler, Jonathan. *Structuralist Poetics: Structuralism, Linguistics and the Study of Literature*. Ithaca, NY: Cornell University Press, 1975.

de Lauretis, Teresa. "Reading the (Post)Modern Text: *If on a winter's night a traveler*." In *Calvino Revisited*, edited by Franco Ricci, 131–45. University of Toronto's Italian Studies 2. Ottawa: Dovehouse Editions, 1989.

Derrida, Jacques. *Of Grammatology*. Translated by Gayatri Chakravorty Spivak. 1967. Baltimore: Johns Hopkins University Press, 1976.

———. *Writing and Difference*. Translated by Alan Bass. 1967. Chicago: University of Chicago Press, 1978.

Dick, Anne R. *Search for Philip K. Dick, 1928–1982: A Memoir and Biography of the Science Fiction Writer*. Lewiston, NY: Edward Mellen, 1995.

Dick, Philip K. *The Broken Bubble*. 1988. New York: HarperCollins, 1991.

———. *Clans of the Alphane Moon*. 1964. New York: Vintage-Random, 2002.

———. *The Collected Stories of Philip K. Dick, Volume One: The Short, Happy Life of the Brown Oxford*. New York: Citadel-Kensington, 1987.

———. *The Collected Stories of Philip K. Dick, Volume Two: We Can Remember It for You Wholesale*. 1987. New York: Citadel-Kensington, 1995.

———. *The Collected Stories of Philip K. Dick, Volume Three: Second Variety*. 1987. New York: Citadel-Kensington, 1991.

———. *The Collected Stories of Philip K. Dick, Volume Four: The Minority Report*. 1987. New York: Citadel-Kensington, 1991.

———. *The Collected Stories of Philip K. Dick, Volume Five: The Eye of the Sibyl*. 1987. New York: Citadel-Kensington, 1992.

———. *Confessions of a Crap Artist—Jack Isidore (of Seville, Calif.): A Chronicle of Verified Scientific Fact 1945–1959*. 1975. New York: Vintage-Random, 1992.

——. *Counter-Clock World.* 1967. New York: Vintage-Random, 2002.

——. *The Crack in Space.* New York: Ace Books, 1966.

——. *Dr. Bloodmoney, or How We Got Along After the Bomb.* New York: Ace Books, 1965.

——. *The Divine Invasion.* 1981. New York: Vintage-Random, 1991.

——. *Do Androids Dream of Electric Sheep?* 1968. New York: Del Rey-Ballantine, 1982.

——. *Eye in the Sky.* 1957. New York: A.A. Wyn, 1985.

——. *Flow My Tears, the Policeman Said.* 1974. New York: Vintage-Random, 1993.

——. *Gather Yourselves Together.* New York: eyeBALL Books, 1994.

——. *Humpty Dumpty in Oakland.* New York: Orion Publishing, 1986.

——. *In Milton Lumky Territory.* New York: Ultramarine, 1985.

——. *In Pursuit of VALIS: Selections from the Exegesis.* Edited by Lawrence Sutin. Novato: Underwood-Miller, 1991.

——. Interview with Mike Hodel. *Hour 25.* KPFK, North Hollywood. June 26, 1976. http://www.philipkdickfans.com/frank/hour25.htm.

——. "A Letter from Philip K. Dick February 1, 1960." *Pamphlet 1.* Glen Ellen, CA: Philip K. Dick Society, 1963.

——. *The Man in the High Castle.* 1962. New York: Vintage-Random, 1992.

——. *The Man Whose Teeth Were All Exactly Alike.* New York: Mark V. Ziesing, 1984.

——. *Martian Time-Slip.* 1964. New York: Vintage-Random, 1995.

——. *Mary and the Giant.* 1987. New York: St. Martin's, 1989.

——. *Now Wait for Last Year.* 1966. New York: Vintage-Random, 1993.

——. *The Penultimate Truth.* 1964. New York: Bluejay, 1984.

——. *Puttering About in a Small Land.* Chicago: Academy Chicago, 1985.

——. *Radio Free Albemuth.* 1985. New York: Vintage-Random, 1998.

——. *A Scanner Darkly.* 1977. New York: Vintage-Random, 1991.

——. *The Selected Letters of Philip K. Dick, Volume Two: 1972–1973.* Novato, CA: Underwood-Miller, 1993.

——. *The Selected Letters of Philip K. Dick, Volume Three: 1974.* Novato, CA: Underwood-Miller, 1991.

——. *The Selected Letters of Philip K. Dick, Volume Four: 1975–1976.* Edited by Don Herron. Novato, CA: Underwood-Miller, 1992.

——. *The Selected Letters of Philip K. Dick, Volume Five: 1977–1979.* Edited by Don Herron. Novato, CA: Underwood-Miller, 1993.

——. *The Shifting Realities of Philip K. Dick: Selected Literary and Philosophical Writings.* Edited by Lawrence Sutin. New York: Vintage-Random, 1995.

——. *The Simulacra.* 1964. New York: Vintage-Random, 2002.

——. *Solar Lottery.* 1955. New York: Vintage-Random, 2003.

——. *The Three Stigmata of Palmer Eldritch.* 1964. New York: Vintage-Random, 1991.

——. *Time Out of Joint.* 1959. New York: Vintage-Random, 2002.

———. *The Transmigration of Timothy Archer.* 1982. New York: Vintage-Random, 1991.

———. *Ubik.* 1969. New York: Vintage-Random, 1991.

———. *VALIS.* 1981. New York: Vintage-Random, 1991.

———. *We Can Build You.* 1972. New York: Vintage-Random, 1994.

———. *The Zap Gun.* 1966. New York: Vintage-Random, 2002.

———, and Ray Faraday Nelson. *The Ganymede Takeover.* 1967. London: Books Britain, 1990.

———, and Roger Zelazny. *Deus Irae.* New York: Collier-MacMillan, 1976.

Di Pace-Jordan, Rosetta. "Italo Calvino's Legacy: The Constant and Consistent Vision." *World Literature Today* 66, no. 3 (1992): 468–71.

DiTommaso, Lorenzo. "Gnosticism and Dualism in the Early Fiction of Philip K. Dick." *Science Fiction Studies* 28, no. 1 (2001): 49–65.

Durham, Scott. "P.K. Dick: From the Death of the Subject to a Theology of Late Capitalism." *Science Fiction Studies* 15, no. 2 (1988): 173–85.

Easterbrook, Neil. "Dianoia/Paranoia: Dick's Double 'Impostor.'" In *Philip K. Dick: Contemporary Critical Interpretations,* edited by Samuel J. Umland, 19–41. Contributions to the Study of Science Fiction and Fantasy, no. 63. Westport, CT: Greenwood, 1995.

Eco, Umberto, et al. *Interpretation and Overinterpretation.* Edited by Stefan Collini. Cambridge: Cambridge University Press, 1992.

Eliot, T. S. *The Waste Land: A Facsimile and Transcript of the Original Drafts Including the Annotations of Ezra Pound.* Edited by Valerie Eliot. San Diego: Harvest Books, 1971.

Fallada, Hans. *Little Man, What Now?* 1933. Translated by Eric Sutton. Chicago: Academy Chicago, 1992.

Feinstein, Wiley. "The Doctrinal Core of *If on a winter's night a traveler.*" In *Calvino Revisited,* edited by Franco Ricci, 147–55. University of Toronto Italian Studies 2. Ottawa: Dovehouse Editions, 1989.

Finney, Jack. *The Body Snatchers.* 1955. New York: Simon and Schuster, 1998.

Fitting, Peter. "Reality as Ideological Construct: A Reading of Five Novels by Philip K. Dick." *Science Fiction Studies* 10, no. 2 (1983): 219–36.

Franklin, H. Bruce. "*Star Trek* in the Vietnam Era." *Film and History* 24, no. 1–2 (1994): 36–46.

Freedman, Carl. "Editorial Introduction: Philip K. Dick and Criticism." *Science Fiction Studies* 15, no. 2 (1988): 121–29.

———. "Towards a Theory of Paranoia: The Science Fiction of Philip K. Dick." *Science Fiction Studies* 11 (1984): 15–24.

Freeland, Richard M. *The Truman Doctrine and the Origins of McCarthyism.* New York: Alfred A. Knopf, 1972.

Frisch, Adam J., and Joseph Martos. "Religious Imagination and Imagined Religion." In *The Transcendent Adventure: Studies in Science Fiction/Fantasy,* edited by Robert

Reilly, 11–26. Contributions to the Study of Science Fiction and Fantasy, no. 12. Westport, CT: Greenwood, 1985.

Fussell, Paul. *The Great War and Modern Memory*. Oxford: Oxford University Press, 1975.

Gaddis, John Lewis. *The United States and the Origins of the Cold War, 1941–1947*. Contemporary American History Series. New York: Columbia University Press, 1972.

Galbreath, Robert. "Salvation-Knowledge: Ironic Gnosticism in *VALIS* and *The Flight of Lucifer*." In *Science Fiction Dialogues*, edited by Gary Wolfe, 115–32. Chicago: Academy Chicago, 1982.

Gibson, Andrew. *Towards a Postmodern Theory of Narrative*. Edinburgh: Edinburgh University Press, 1996.

Giddens, Anthony. *Modernity and Self-Identity: Self and Society in the Late Modern Age*. Stanford, CA: Stanford University Press, 1991.

Gillespie, Bruce. "Mad, Mad Worlds: Seven Novels of Philip K. Dick." In *Philip K. Dick: Electric Shepherd*, edited by Bruce Gillespie, 9–21. Melbourne: Norstrilia Press, 1975.

———, ed. *Philip K. Dick: Electric Shepherd*. Melbourne: Norstrilia Press, 1975.

Goethe, Johann Wolfgang von. *Faust: Part I*. Translated by Peter Salm. Rev. ed. New York: Bantam, 1988.

Golumbia, David. "Resisting 'the World': Philip K. Dick, Cultural Studies, and Metaphysical Realism." *Science Fiction Studies* 23 (1996): 83–100.

Graves, Robert. *Goodbye to All That*. 1929. London: Folio Society, 1981.

Green, Geoffrey. "Ghosts and Shadows: Reading and Writing in Italo Calvino's *If on a winter's night a traveler*." *Review of Contemporary Fiction* 6, no. 2 (1986): 101–105.

Guardiani, Francesco. "Optimism without Illusions." *Review of Contemporary Fiction* 6, no. 2 (1986): 54–61.

Gustainis, J. Justin. *American Rhetoric and the Vietnam War*. Westport, CT: Praeger, 1993.

Halberstam, David. *The Fifties*. New York: Fawcett, 1994.

Hamby, Alonzo L. *Man of the People: A Life of Harry S. Truman*. New York: Oxford University Press, 1995.

Hart, Liddell. *A History of the World War, 1914–1918*. Boston: Little, Brown, 1935.

Hartwell, David G. "The Religious Visions of Philip K. Dick." *New York Review of Science Fiction* 7, no. 5 (January 1995): 12–16.

Heer, Jeet. "Marxist Literary Critics Are Following Me!" *Lingua Franca* 11, no. 4 (2001): 26–31.

Heinlein, Robert A. *The Puppet Masters*. New York: Del Rey, 1984.

Hinds, Lynn Boyd, and Theodore Otto Windt Jr. *The Cold War as Rhetoric: The Beginnings, 1945–1950*. Praeger Series in Political Communication. New York: Praeger, 1991.

Hoberek, Andrew P. "The 'Work' of Science Fiction: Philip K. Dick and Occupational Masculinity in the Post–World War II United States." *Modern Fiction Studies* 43, no. 2 (1997): 374–404.

Holquist, Michael. "Jorge Luis Borges and the Metaphysical Mystery." In *Mystery and Suspense Writers: The Literature of Crime, Detection, and Espionage*, edited by Robin W. Weeks, 83–96. New York: Charles Scribner's Sons/Macmillan, 1998.

Hume, Kathryn. "Calvino's Framed Narratives: Writers, Readers, and Reality." *Review of Contemporary Fiction* 6, no. 2 (1986): 71–80.

———. "Science and Imagination in Calvino's *Cosmicomics*." *Mosaic* 15, no. 4 (December 1982): 47–58.

Hunt, Robert. "Visionary States and the Search for Transcendence in Science Fiction." In *Bridges to Science Fiction*, edited by George E. Slusser, George R. Guffey, and Mark Rose, 64–77. Carbondale: Southern Illinois University Press, 1980.

Hutcheon, Linda. *The Politics of Postmodernism*. London: Routledge, 1989.

Invasion of the Body Snatchers. Screenplay by Daniel Mainwaring. Based on the novel *The Body Snatchers* by Jack Finney. Dir. Don Siegel. Perf. Kevin McCarthy, Dana Wynter, Larry Gates, and King Donovan. Los Angeles: Walter Wanger Productions, 1956.

Irby, James E. "Borges and the Idea of Utopia." In *Modern Critical Views: Jorge Luis Borges*, edited by Harold Bloom, 91–101. New York: Chelsea House, 1986.

Jakaitis, Jake. "Two Cases of Conscience: Loyalty and Race in *The Crack in Space* and *Counter-Clock World*." In *Philip K. Dick: Contemporary Critical Interpretations*, edited by Samuel J. Umland, 169–95. Contributions to the Study of Science Fiction and Fantasy, no. 63. Westport, CT: Greenwood, 1995.

Jameson, Fredric. *Postmodernism, or, the Cultural Logic of Late Capitalism*. Durham, NC: Duke University Press, 1992.

Joseph, John Earl. "Man, History, Subject, Object: Calvino in Crisis." *Review of Contemporary Literature* 6, no. 2 (1986): 24–30.

Joyce, James. *Finnegan's Wake*. 1939. New York: Penguin Books, 1999.

———. *Ulysses*. 1934. New York: Vintage-Random, 1990.

Junger, Ernst. *On the Marble Cliffs*. 1939. New York: Viking, 1984.

Kafka, Franz. *The Complete Stories*. Edited by Nahum N. Glatzer. New York: Schocken, 1971.

———. *The Trial: The Definitive Edition*. Translated by Willa and Edwin Muir with E. M. Butler. 1925. New York: Schocken Books, 1984.

Kalb, Marvin, and Elie Abel. *Roots of Involvement: The U.S. in Asia, 1784–1971*. New York: Norton, 1971.

Kaldor, Mary. *The Imaginary War: Understanding the East-West Conflict*. Oxford: Basil Blackwell, 1990.

Kasson, John F. *Civilizing the Machine: Technology and Republican Values in America 1776–1900*. 1976. New York: Hill and Wang, 1999.

Kerman, Judith B., ed. *Retrofitting "Blade Runner": Issues in Ridley Scott's "Blade Runner" and Philip K. Dick's "Do Androids Dream of Electric Sheep?"* 2nd ed. Bowling Green, KY: Bowling Green State University Press, 1997.

Ketterer, David. *New Worlds for Old: The Apocalyptic Imagination, Science Fiction, and American Literature.* Bloomington: Indiana University Press, 1974.

Kinney, Jay. "The Mysterious Revelations of Philip K. Dick." *Gnosis* 1 (1985): 6–11.

Knight, Damon. *In Search of Wonder: Essays on Modern Science Fiction.* 2nd ed. Chicago: Advent, 1967.

Lee, Gwen, and Doris Elaine Sauter, eds. *What If Our World Is Their Heaven? The Final Conversations of Philip K. Dick.* Woodstock, NY: Overlook, 2000.

Le Guin, Ursula K. "Science Fiction as Prophesy." *New Republic,* October 30, 1976: 33–34.

Levack, Daniel J. H., comp. *PKD: A Philip K. Dick Bibliography.* San Francisco: Underwood/Miller, 1981.

Littlewood, Derek, and Peter Stockwell, eds. *Impossibility Fiction: Alternativity—Extrapolation—Speculation.* Amsterdam: Rodopi, 1996.

Lupoff, Richard. "A Conversation with Philip K. Dick." *Science Fiction Eye* 1, no. 2 (August 1987). http://www.philipkdick.com/frank/lupoff.htm.

———. "The Realities of Philip K. Dick." *Starship* 16, no. 3 (1979) 29–33.

Lyotard, Jean-François. *The Postmodern Condition: A Report on Knowledge.* Translated by Geoff Bennington and Brian Massumi. Theory and History of Literature, vol. 10. 1979. Minneapolis: University of Minnesota Press, 1984.

Mackey, Douglas A. "Science Fiction and Gnosticism." *Missouri Review* 7, no. 2 (1984): 112–20.

Malmgren, Carl. "Philip Dick's *Man in the High Castle* and the Nature of Science-Fictional Worlds." In *Bridges to Science Fiction,* edited by George E. Slusser, George R. Guffey, and Mark Rose, 120–30. Carbondale: Southern Illinois University Press, 1980.

———. "Romancing the Reader: Calvino's *If on a winter's night a traveler.*" *Review of Contemporary Fiction* 6, no. 2 (1986): 106–15.

McHale, Brian. *Postmodernist Fiction.* New York: Methuen, 1987.

McNelly, Willis E., and Sharon K. Perry. "The Manuscripts and Papers at Fullerton." In *On Philip K. Dick: 40 Articles from "Science-Fiction Studies,"* edited by R. D. Mullen et al., xviii–xxx. Terre Haute, IN: SF-TH, 1992.

Minority Report. Screenplay by Scott Frank and Jon Cohen. Based on the short story "The Minority Report" by Philip K. Dick. Dir. Steven Spielberg. Perf. Tom Cruise, Max von Sydow, Colin Farrell, Samantha Morton, and Kathryn Harris. Los Angeles: Dreamworks, 2002.

Motte, Warren F., Jr. "Calvino's Combinatorics." *Review of Contemporary Fiction* 6, no. 2 (1986): 81–87.

Mullen, R. D., et al., eds. *On Philip K. Dick: 40 Articles from "Science-Fiction Studies."* Terre Haute, IN: SF-TH, 1992.

The Munsters. Developed by Allan Burns, Ed Haas, Chris Hayward, and Norm Liebman. Perf. Fred Gwynne, Yvonne De Carlo, Al Lewis, Butch Patrick, Beverly Owen, and Pat Priest. Los Angeles: Kayro-Vue Productions, 1964–1966.

Olds, Marshall C. "Another Book, Another Author: Calvino, Flaubert, Mallarmé." *Review of Contemporary Fiction* 6, no. 2 (1986): 117–23.

Olsham, Matthew. "Franz Kafka: The Unsinging Singer." In *Modern Jewish Mythologies*, edited by Glenda Abramson, 174–90. Cincinnati: Hebrew Union College Press, 2000.

Palmer, Christopher. "Postmodernism and the Birth of the Author in Philip K. Dick's *Valis.*" *Science Fiction Studies* 18 (1991): 330–42.

Pascal, Roy. *Kafka's Narrators: A Study of His Stories and Sketches.* Anglica Germanica Series, no. 2. Cambridge: Cambridge University Press, 1982.

Philmus, Robert M. "The Two Faces of Philip K. Dick." *Science Fiction Studies* 18, no. 1 (1991): 91-103.

Potin, Yves. "Four Levels of Reality in Philip K. Dick's *Time Out of Joint.*" Translated by Heather McLean. *Extrapolation* 39, no. 2 (1998): 148–65.

Pound, Ezra. *Cantos.* London: Faber and Faber, 1954.

Pynchon, Thomas. *The Crying of Lot 49.* 1965. New York: Perennial-HarperCollins, 1999.

Quinn, William A. "Science Fiction's Harrowing of the Heavens." In *The Transcendent Adventure: Studies in Science Fiction/Fantasy*, edited by Robert Reilly, 37–54. Contributions to the Study of Science Fiction and Fantasy, no. 12. Westport, CT: Greenwood, 1985.

Rankin, Ian. "The Role of the Reader in Italo Calvino's *If on a winter's night a traveler.*" *Review of Contemporary Fiction* 6, no. 2 (1986): 124–29.

Rees, David. *The Age of Containment: The Cold War 1945–1965.* London: Macmillan, 1967.

Reilly, Robert, ed. *The Transcendent Adventure: Studies in Science Fiction/Fantasy.* Contributions to the Study of Science Fiction and Fantasy, no. 12. Westport, CT: Greenwood, 1985.

Remarque, Erich Maria. *All Quiet on the Western Front.* 1922. Translated by A. W. Wheen. New York: Fawcett, 1995.

Rickman, Gregg. "Dick, Deception, and Dissociation: A Comment on 'The Two Faces of Philip K. Dick.'" In *On Philip K. Dick: 40 Articles from "Science-Fiction Studies,"* edited by R. D. Mullen et al., 262–64. Terre Haute, IN: SF-TH, 1992.

———. *Philip K. Dick: In His Own Words.* 2nd ed. Long Beach, CA: Fragments West/ Valentine, 1988.

———. *Philip K. Dick: The Last Testament.* Long Beach, CA: Fragments West/Valentine, 1985.

———. *To the High Castle: Philip K. Dick: A Life 1928–1962.* Long Beach, CA: Fragments West/Valentine, 1989.

Ricoeur, Paul. "The Task of Hermeneutics." In *Heidegger and Modern Philosophy: Critical Essays*, edited by Michael Murray, 141–60. New Haven, CT: Yale University Press, 1978.

Rieder, John. "The Metafictive World of *The Man in the High Castle*: Hermeneutics, Ethics, and Political Ideology." *Science Fiction Studies* 15, no. 2 (1988): 214–25.

Robertson, Ritchie. *Kafka: Judaism, Politics and Literature*. Oxford: Clarendon, 1985.

Robinson, Kim Stanley. *The Novels of Philip K. Dick*. Studies in Speculative Fiction, no. 9. Ann Arbor: UMI Research, 1984.

Ruane, Kevin. *War and Revolution in Vietnam: 1930–75*. London: UCL, 1998.

Ryan, Michael P. "Samsa and *Samsara*: Suffering, Death, and Rebirth in 'The Metamorphosis.'" *German Quarterly* 72, no. 2 (1999): 133–52.

Salvatori, Mariolina. "Italo Calvino's *If on a winter's night a traveler*: Writer's Authority, Reader's Autonomy." *Contemporary Literature* 27, no. 2 (1986): 182–212.

Sammon, Paul M. *Future Noir: The Making of Blade Runner*. New York: HarperPrism-HarperCollins, 1996.

Schmid, Georg. "The Apocryphal Judaic Traditions as Historical Repertoire: An Analysis of *The Divine Invasion* by Philip K. Dick." *Degrés* 51 (1987): f/1–f/11.

Seed, David. *American Science Fiction and the Cold War: Literature and Film*. Edinburgh: Edinburgh University Press, 1999.

———. "Mediated Realities in the Works of Philip K. Dick." In *Narrative Turns and Minor Genres in Postmodernism*, edited by Theo D'haen and Hans Bartens, 203–205. Postmodernism Studies 11. Amsterdam: Rodopi, 1995.

Shelley, Mary. *Frankenstein, or the Modern Prometheus*. 1831. Oxford: Oxford University Press, 1998.

Slusser, George E., George R. Guffey, and Mark Rose, eds. *Bridges to Science Fiction*. Carbondale: Southern Illinois University Press, 1980.

Small, Melvin. *Covering Dissent: The Media and the Anti-Vietnam War Movement*. New Brunswick, NJ: Rutgers University Press, 1994.

Sokel, Walter H. "From Marx to Myth: The Structure and Function of Self-Alienation in Kafka's *Metamorphosis*." *Literary Review* 26, no. 4 (1983): 485–95.

Spengler, Oswald. *The Decline of the West*. Edited by Helmut Werner. Translated by Charles F. Atkinson. 1918–1923. Oxford: Oxford University Press, 1991.

Star Trek. Created by Gene Roddenberry. Perf. William Shatner, Leonard Nimoy, DeForest Kelley, James Doohan, Walter Koenig, Nichelle Nichols, and George Takei. Los Angeles: National Broadcasting Company, 1966–1969.

Star Trek: Deep Space Nine. Created by Rick Berman and Michael Piller. Perf. Avery Brooks, René Auberjonois, Nicole deBoer, Michael Dorn, Terry Farrell, Cirroc Lofton, Colm Meaney, Armin Shimmerman, Alexander Siddig, and Nana Visitor. Los Angeles: Paramount Television, 1993–1999.

Steiner, George. Introduction. *The Trial: The Definitive Edition*. By Franz Kafka. Translated by Willa and Edwin Muir with E. M. Butler. 1925. New York: Schocken, 1984. vii–xxi.

Stiehm, Bruce. "Borges: Cultural Iconoclast, Dissident Creator of Semantic Traps." *West Virginia University Philological Papers* 44 (1998–1999): 104–11.

Stilling, Roger J. "Mystical Healing: Reading Philip K. Dick's *VALIS* and *The Divine Invasion* as Metapsychoanalytic Novels." *South Atlantic Review* 56, no. 2 (1991): 91–106.

Sutin, Lawrence. *Divine Invasions: A Life of Philip K. Dick.* New York: Citadel-Carol, 1989.

Suvin, Darko. *Metamorphoses of Science Fiction: On the Poetics and History of a Literary Genre.* New Haven, CT: Yale University Press, 1979.

———. "P.K. Dick's Opus: Artifice as Refuge and World View." *Science Fiction Studies* 2, no. 1 (1975): 8–22.

———. "The Science Fiction of Philip K. Dick." *Science Fiction Studies* 2.1 (1975): 3–4.

Taylor, Angus. "Can God Fly? Can He Hold Out His Arms and Fly?: The Fiction of Philip K. Dick." *Foundation* 4 (1973): 32–47.

Total Recall. Screenplay by Ronald Shusett, Dan O'Bannon, and Gary Goldman. Based on the short story "We Can Remember It for You Wholesale" by Philip K. Dick. Dir. Paul Verhoeven. Perf. Arnold Schwarzenegger, Sharon Stone, Michael Ironside, Rachel Ticotin, and Ronny Cox. Los Angeles: Carolco, 1990.

Umland, Samuel J., ed. *Philip K. Dick: Contemporary Critical Interpretations.* Contributions to the Study of Science Fiction and Fantasy, no. 63. Westport, CT: Greenwood, 1995.

———. "To Flee from Dionysus: *Enthousiasmos* from 'Upon a Dull Earth' to *VALIS.*" In *Philip K. Dick: Contemporary Critical Interpretations,* edited by Samuel J. Umland, 81–99. Contributions to the Study of Science Fiction and Fantasy, no. 63. Westport, CT: Greenwood, 1995.

Walters, F. Scott. "The Final Trilogy of Philip K. Dick." *Extrapolation* 38, no. 3 (1997): 222–35.

Warren, Eugene. "The Search for Absolutes." In *Philip K. Dick,* edited by Martin Harry Greenberg and Joseph D. Olander, 161–87. Writers of the 21st Century Series. New York: Taplinger, 1983.

Warrick, Patricia S. *Mind in Motion: The Fiction of Philip K. Dick.* Cardondale: Southern Illinois University Press, 1987.

———. "Philip K. Dick's Answers to Eternal Riddles." In *The Transcendent Adventure: Studies in Science Fiction/Fantasy,* edited by Robert Reilly, 107–26. Contributions to the Study of Science Fiction and Fantasy, no. 12. Westport, CT: Greenwood, 1985.

Wessel, Karl. "Worlds of Chance and Counterfeit: Dick, Lem, and the Preestablished Cacophony." In *Philip K. Dick: Contemporary Critical Interpretations,* edited by Samuel J. Umland, 43–59. Contributions to the Study of Science Fiction and Fantasy, no. 63. Westport, CT: Greenwood, 1995.

White, Hayden. "Historical Emplotment and the Problem of Truth." In *Probing the Limits of Representation: Nazism and the "Final Solution,"* edited by Saul Friedlander, 37–53. Cambridge: Harvard University Press, 1992.

Williams, Paul. *Only Apparently Real*. New York: Arbor House, 1986.

———. "The True Stories of Philip K. Dick." *Rolling Stone*, November 6, 1975, 45+.

Woodall, James. *The Man in the Mirror of the Book: A Life of Jorge Luis Borges*. London: Hodder and Stoughton, 1996.

Woolf, Virginia. *Mrs. Dalloway*. 1925. San Diego: Harvest-Harcourt, 1953.

Zizek, Slavoj. *The Sublime Object of Ideology*. London: Verso, 1989.

Index

~

About the Author

Jason P. Vest is assistant professor of English in the University of Guam's Division of English and Applied Linguistics. He specializes in modernist and postmodernist literature; twentieth- and twenty-first-century American literature; crime fiction; science fiction; and film, television, and media studies. Vest is the author of *Future Imperfect: Philip K. Dick at the Movies*. He lives and works in Mangilao, Guam.